MW00353537

MISSISSIPPI PRAYING

Mississippi Praying

Southern White Evangelicals and the
Civil Rights Movement, 1945–1975

Carolyn Renée Dupont

NEW YORK UNIVERSITY PRESS
New York and London

LIBRARY
NORTHERN VIRGINIA COMMUNITY COLLEGE

NEW YORK UNIVERSITY PRESS
New York and London
www.nyupress.org
© 2013 by New York University
All rights reserved

References to Internet Websites (URLs) were accurate at the time of writing.
Neither the author nor New York University Press is responsible for URLs that
may have expired or changed since the manuscript was prepared.

LIBRARY OF CONGRESS CATALOGING-IN-PUBLICATION DATA
Dupont, Carolyn Renée.
Mississippi praying : southern white evangelicals and the Civil Rights movement, 1945–1975 /
Carolyn Renée Dupont.
pages cm
Includes bibliographical references and index.
ISBN 978–0–8147–0841–5 (alk. paper)
1. Mississippi—Church history—20th century. 2. Evangelicalism—Mississippi—History—
20th century. 3. Civil rights movements—Mississippi—History—20th century. I. Title.
BR555.M7D87 2013
277.62′0285—dc23   2013009417

New York University Press books are printed on acid-free paper, and their binding materials
are chosen for strength and durability. We strive to use environmentally responsible
suppliers and materials to the greatest extent possible in publishing our books.

Manufactured in the United States of America

10 9 8 7 6 5 4 3 2 1

To Greg, Julianne, Daniel, and Elise

CONTENTS

ILLUSTRATIONS

ACKNOWLEDGMENTS

Mississippi Praying has taken a long time to write, and I have acquired many debts along the way. I owe gratitude that extends back to my years as a graduate student at the University of Kentucky, where I benefited from the encouragement and wisdom of mentors like Kathi Kern, Joanne Pope Melish, Jeremy Popkin, Patricia Cooper, Ron Eller, Phil Harling, James Albisetti, William H. Freehling, and Dwight Billings.

Good librarians and archivists have been crucial to this project. At Eastern Kentucky University, I have so appreciated the graciousness of Pat New, whose great skill in tracking down sources is exceeded only by her patience with my inability to return materials on time. Bill Sumners at the Southern Baptist Historical Library and Archives possesses indispensable knowledge of his collections, an energetic spirit, and a capable staff. Debra McIntosh and Jamie Bounds at the J. B. Cain Archive of Mississippi Methodism, Heather Weeden at the Mississippi Baptist Historical Commission, and Wayne Sparkman at Covenant Theological Seminary have been quick to respond to my queries and to go the extra mile to help. I also appreciate the expertise of Frances Lyons-Bristol and Dale Patterson of the Methodist General Commission on Archives and History, and Grace Yoder and Eugene Quek at the Bosworth Memorial Library at Asbury Theological Seminary.

I pursued some of the research for this project with grant funding from the Louisville Institute. The piece has benefited from the able research assistance of Kris Kirkpatrick, Sarah Simmers, Glen Cox, Aaron Clark, Eric Lewis, Deb Boggs, Laura Cost, Amanda Pippitt, and Beverly Hackney. I also owe a debt of gratitude to people who helped me secure permissions or access to records: Frances Mack; Christie House of the General Board of Global Ministries of the United

Methodist Church; Ken Lundquist of First Baptist Church, Jackson; and Roger Dermody, Rebecca Snipp, and Rhashell Hunter, all of the Presbyterian Mission Agency.

Several colleagues read portions of the manuscript along the way and offered comments, suggested improvements, or called my attention to issues that merited consideration. At Eastern Kentucky University, those who gave of their time and talents in this way include Tom Appleton, John Bowes, Rob Weise, Brad Wood, David Blaylock, Jenn Spock, Jackie Jay, Cat Stern, and the late Bob Topmiller. Cate Fosl, Tracey K'meyer, David Hamilton, Tom Kiffmeyer, James Klotter, Darrell Meadows, Tammy Van Dyken, Jeff Freyman, Paul Jones, Paul Harvey, Ed Blum, Rusty Hawkins, and Curtis Freeman all read and commented on portions or chapters. The anonymous readers for New York University Press engaged in the manuscript deeply and made specific suggestions that dramatically improved its quality. No colleague, however, has been more generous than Joe Reiff. A deep wellspring of insights about Mississippi and Methodists, Joe read two complete and vastly different drafts and offered the benefit of his prodigious knowledge.

Many people who lived lives of faith in Mississippi during this period shared their stories or those of their loved ones with me, and I am grateful for the windows into this world that they have provided. Richard T. Harbison, Jim Lacy, Earl Kelly, Virginia Quarles, Chester Quarles, Jr., Sarah Odle Maddox, James Porch, Dick Brogan, Bradley Pope, Clarke Hensley, Ralph Noonkester, Maxie Dunnam, Gerald Trigg, Jerry Furr, Keith Tonkel, and the late Emmett Barfield all offered insights and information that informed this project, though only a few of their names made it into the text and the notes.

Such are my professional debts, but my personal ones extend much deeper. Some folks who had little direct input on this project nonetheless deserve credit for contributing to whatever balance, joy, and sanity I possess. Among them, a cadre of delightful colleagues and students make Eastern Kentucky University a rewarding place to work. Good friends, especially my "book club women" Kelli Carmean, Dee Fizdale, Melanie Beals Goan, Melissa McEuen, Dixie Moore, and Sharon Brown, as well as Mary Nan Dupont are gifts of regenerating water to my soul.

And finally, family. For the most part, we don't get to choose these people, but I have had extraordinarily good luck. I am grateful for my parents, Lynnell Carter Dupont and the late Jean-René Dupont, who both loved the life of the mind. They blessed me with four impressive and inspiring siblings. My brother Vincent and his wife, Ceci Scott, have been especially enthusiastic cheerleaders, warm supporters, and great friends. My three children, Julianne, Daniel, and Elise, have grown into generous, loving, and thoughtful human beings, in spite of my best efforts. In their presence, I have learned more about what really matters than I ever found in an archive. Finally, my husband Greg Partain is my partner in life, mind, and love. He has read more drafts, offered more suggestions, and endured more discussions of Mississippi, religion, and race than could be expected of any human being. Generous soul that he is, he loves me still.

History, White Religion, and the Civil Rights Movement

Most Sunday mornings from June 1963 through April 1964, as white Christians flocked to church in Jackson, Mississippi, they met chaos. Amidst the buzz of a police force with dogs, billy clubs, and walkie talkies, small groups of curiosity seekers and angry layfolk loitered under church porticos; sometimes a complement of local and national press representatives stood by, too. All awaited the arrival of interracial groups of civil rights activists who sought entry to these sanctuaries but endured repeated rejection from the majority of them. Sometimes members of a "color guard" formed physical barricades, and police often arrested the would-be worshippers. Special gall issued from this spectacle on Easter Sunday 1964, when Galloway Memorial Methodist Church rebuffed Bishop Charles Golden, a black leader of its own denomination. Almost simultaneously with this theater in Jackson, ninety miles to the southeast in Hattiesburg, scores of white ministers in clerical collars picketed on behalf of black citizens seeking the right to vote. Police arrested a few of the clerics, who later celebrated communion in their jail cells using coffee and county-issued biscuits as the elements. Local white religious leaders offered neither physical nor moral support to their northern coreligionists who came to challenge Mississippi's racial hierarchy; instead they publicly castigated them for "prostitut[ing] the church to political purposes." Meanwhile, in Canton, white congregations almost unanimously pledged to spurn civil rights workers—white or black—who flooded the town. While three white activists worshipped at the local Presbyterian church, someone poured sugar in the oil reservoir of their car. Two others who tried to visit First Methodist encountered a more brutal unwelcome. After ushers turned them away, thugs pursued and beat them.

The above vignettes suggest religion's significance in the struggle against black equality, the central theme of this book. This story follows Mississippi's three most numerically and historically significant white Protestant faith communities at ground-zero of the social revolution that rocked America. As a religious history of white Southern Baptists, Methodists, and Presbyterians in the civil rights era, it examines these evangelicals' two great enthusiasms—ardent devotion to the Christian gospel and equal zeal for what can only be described as white supremacy—and explains how these commitments interacted with one another.

The black freedom struggle deeply engaged white evangelicals, and profound concern about the prospect of racial equality saturated their religious lives. Religious literature, deacons' meetings, Bible classes, Sunday school conversations, and even worship services pulsed with fear about integration and its consequences. No other issue so occupied the religious attention of white Mississippians nor so worried church leaders, and nothing elicited greater religious energy or creativity. Turmoil often rode into Mississippi's faith communities on the waves of civil rights events, but sometimes whites' own deep fears of integration manufactured civil rights crises without an activist in sight.

Fixated on the potential advent of black equality, white Christians joined the fight to preserve white power and privilege in all its forms. Having accepted both evangelicalism and white supremacy as unassailable truths for years, these Mississippians generally regarded as patently absurd the notion that God frowned on their racial arrangements; the sudden appearance of segregation in some syllabus of sins jolted their sensibilities. In their religious world, racial integration represented a heinous moral evil—and they fought it as if against the devil himself. White Mississippians' fierce and tenacious defense of their segregated society relied heavily on religious ideas and frames of reference. Their segregationist polemics employed biblical apologetics, but religion figured in the defense of the racial hierarchy in other far more significant ways, including the overt sanctification of a political philosophy that underpinned segregation. And evangelicals went well beyond rhetoric. They marshaled the power of the state, warred against their own denominations, caucused and organized, and ejected black worshippers from their sanctuaries.

Yet, for all white Mississippi evangelicals' devotion to segregation, faith motivated some moderates to reevaluate do-or-die commitments to the racial hierarchy. These outliers seldom championed integration outright, but they contributed important support for free speech and basic decency as both became endangered. While moderates, their denominational leaders, and black activists competed against segregationists, Mississippi's once-placid religious communities transmogrified into civil rights battlegrounds. Many believers passed the civil rights years conflicted and confused, and debates over the meanings of spiritual commitments wracked local congregations. As local leaders feared that the centrifuge of racial turmoil would hurl their parishioners in a thousand directions, Mississippi religious life devolved into a tortured, splintered, and ravaged affair. Certainly, the moral clarity about human equality that seems so compelling in retrospect often eluded the white Christians who filled Mississippi sanctuaries.

At the time and since, many Americans have wondered how a society so vociferously Christian could also fight so tenaciously to preserve an oppressive racial system. But few of the evangelicals who people this story believed that the Gospel required them to dismantle segregation; thus they did not generally believe that they embodied some great paradox. The events described here unfolded in an intellectual universe whose inhabitants understood the Christian faith and its implications quite differently from the meanings today's believers give it. This book depicts that foreign landscape and re-creates white Americans' dialogue about the implications of faith for racial justice. Focused on a time when the outcome of that debate remained undecided, this study examines almost exclusively the side of the conversation that lost.

Mississippi Praying and the Historians

Though white religion played an important role in the fight against racial equality, many volumes in the recent rich outpouring on massive resistance include religion only incidentally in the narrative, if at all, and only a few essays comprise the periodical treatments on the topic.[1] Important exceptions to this trend include some literature that appreciates religion's centrality to politics, but few such works aim to tell an essentially religious story or to grapple with the relationship between white supremacy and white religion.[2] In this book, on the other hand, questions of religion drive the analysis. Drawing significantly on insights from American religious history, the book takes the experiences of religious individuals, leaders, congregations, and faith communities as the basis of the narrative.

Some historians have examined white religion's encounter with black equality through the activities of the major denominations.[3] While such studies remain exceedingly useful, institutional histories often tell us little about the people who fill the pews—their experiences, ideas, and activities. A story centered in local religious communities offers quite a different perspective. At the local level, denominational identity commonly melted into a more general, popular southern Protestantism, and local culture, the pastor, and the Bible class teacher wielded great influence. Even more central to this story, religious folk often famously contravene their leaders and institutional bodies. Early on in Mississippi and eventually in many other places as well, this very tension rose to nearly intolerable levels over issues of black equality, and constant haranguing against denominational leaders constituted a central feature of religious life during the civil rights years. Intense conflict between layfolk and national religious leaders revealed the strength of religious commitments to segregation and white supremacy—commitments that often appear weak and muted in denominational histories.

As frequently happens, misconceptions and inaccuracies have moved in to fill the gaps in our knowledge. These misapprehensions have generally leaned in two directions. On the one hand, since local white congregations and people of faith fail to appear in many civil rights narratives, the assumption thrives that white religion passed the civil rights years as a silent, passive, or unimportant player. The language of white evangelicals, who often belied their own ardor for white supremacy by describing the question of segregation as political and therefore outside the sphere of appropriate Christian concerns, indeed bolsters this impression. By their criticisms of politically outspoken ministers and church leaders, by the silence about black suffering that billowed from their most prestigious sanctuaries, and by their emphasis on the non-political mission of evangelism, Southern Baptists, Methodists, and Presbyterians often pretended simply to have neither time nor concern for the cause of racial equality. Contemporary onlookers noted, and sometimes critiqued, this apparent insouciance. Among them, Martin Luther King, Jr., in his *Letter from Birmingham Jail,* famously expressed his deep disillusionment with southern white Christians and their failure to join the struggle for black equality: "In the midst of blatant injustices inflicted upon the Negro, I have watched white churches stand on the sideline and merely mouth pious irrelevancies and sanctimonious trivialities. In the midst of a mighty struggle to rid our nation of racial and economic injustice, I have heard so many ministers say, 'Those are social issues with which the gospel has no real concern.'"[4] Scholars—at the time and since—have often actively contended for or worked with the same notion that local white congregations, ministers, and people of faith fairly yawned with disinterest as black Americans waged a death-defying struggle for their full humanity. In his well-known 1966 social critique, *Southern Churches in Crisis*, the historian Samuel S. Hill, Jr., argued that southern Christianity had stuck its head in the other-worldly sands of personal salvation and evangelism, ignoring the swelling tide of social change.[5] More recently, David L. Chappell's *A Stone of Hope: Prophetic Religion and the Death of Jim Crow* characterizes white religious support for segregation as "weak," as if white Mississippi Baptists, Methodists, and Presbyterians really cared little about preserving the institution.[6]

Frustrated that their common faith did not compel white Protestant solidarity with the cause of racial justice, King and Hill chided southern Christians for *indifference to* the civil rights movement. But white evangelicals in Mississippi and many other locales could no more ignore the challenge to white supremacy than those at the epicenter of an earthquake can ignore the pitching and roiling of the ground around them. These Christians did not pass the civil rights years floating beatifically on clouds of cool detachment; such a response, as the segregated structures of southern life came crashing down around them, hardly seems plausible. Ever so disappointed in their evangelical brethren, King and Hill generously read their silence as apathy or preoccupation. But the façade of silence cloaked a truth far more revealing: not only did white Christians fail to fight *for* black equality, they often labored mightily *against* it.

A second and related distortion in the literature focuses on the biblical defense of segregation and too flatly equates southern religious resistance to integration with these race-based exegetics.[7] Mississippians did indeed offer scriptural defenses for preserving their racial hierarchy, citing the story of Noah's curse on the descendants of his son, Ham, as a favorite proof text. Mississippians composed such polemics and delivered them in print, from pulpits, and on the radio; they also circulated a wide variety of similar texts by other southerners. However, though their influence and the assumptions that underpinned them appear everywhere, only a relatively small number of these texts remain extant. Scholars who look for religious commitments to segregation only in these biblical defenses underestimate the strength of evangelicals' commitment to the institution. Christians fought for white supremacy in ways that extended beyond simply preaching the biblical case for it. Furthermore, overemphasizing the role of these exegetics pins the defense of segregation on a few unsophisticated extremists, rather than demonstrating the racial hierarchy's powerful but often subtle articulation by more polished religious leaders and prominent laymen. Some of the state's most prestigious ministers and many devoutly segregationist laymen never deployed such arguments, though these individuals played important roles in resisting black equality.

The first generation of scholars to examine white religion's response to the civil rights challenge wrote in the midst of the revolution itself, hoping to prod their coreligionists to confront blacks' demands more proactively.[8] Believing that a mandate for human equality inhered in the Christian Gospel, this cohort framed southern evangelicalism's failure in the arena of race relations as a problem of "cultural captivity." In this formulation, something foreign had trapped the church; southern Christianity needed but to wrest its soul from enslavement to southern racial mores and recover its true redemptive essence. Though this group of scholars contributed significantly to studies in the field of southern religion, this book challenges the framework of cultural captivity on several grounds and offers an essentially different conception of southern religion's role in creating and sustaining racial oppression.[9]

Perhaps most problematically, the idea of cultural captivity erects a false distinction between religion and culture by supposing that religion somehow stands apart from culture as either adversary or accomplice. Far more than the cultural captivity framework suggests, religion develops with, aids, and bolsters the political, economic, and social conditions around it. Southern religion did not just guiltily "come along" with segregation in a bad and ugly business; rather, it served actively in the phalanx of institutions by which white domination perpetuated itself.

Not only does the notion of cultural captivity propose a false distinction between people's religious and ostensibly non-religious worlds; it also perhaps unintentionally endows churchfolk with an entirely implausible passivity. No southern cultural terrorists drugged the church with a stupefying elixir to co-opt its acquiescence in racial domination. Such a depiction ignores the active role the church played in creating and sustaining the system of oppression. As this volume shows, the proactive defenders of segregation who defied the Supreme Court, voted for segregationist candidates, drafted and promoted anti–civil rights legislation, herded black activists into jail, and formed citizens' groups to keep the dream of white supremacy alive did not morph into weak, mealy, other-worldly idealists upon entering their houses of worship. To the contrary, they employed the same pragmatic calculation and worked with the same enthusiasm for white supremacy inside the sanctuary as out. They cared no less about keeping their churches segregated than their schools, and they worked as diligently to control religious discourses as political ones.

Finally, the cultural captivity interpretation inappropriately excuses religion from historical contingency, treating matters of faith as constant and unchanging. Rather than receiving the commands of God as fixed tablets of stone, people *make* and remake their religion, and white southerners crafted a faith divinely suited for white supremacy. The historically determined and continually transforming nature of religion and religious belief illustrate themselves nowhere better than in white Americans' changing conceptions of the demands of Christianity with regard to race relations. In twenty-first century America, evangelicals have widely come to accept that their Gospel includes a mandate for racial equality. Yet this thoroughgoing embrace causes them to forget that their rather immediate forbearers served as serious obstacles to the aspirations of black Americans because they regarded this very principle as profoundly *un*christian.

White Supremacy, Religion, and Politics

This book probes the links between theology and white supremacy. The term "white supremacy" may jar a bit; the phrase conjures up militant devotion to a racist ideology, and may seem ill applied to ordinary people who go about their lives and work, never dressing up in sheets, wielding a lynch rope, or spewing racial epithets. In fact, however, this phrase describes the American racial hierarchy more accurately and honestly than the milder "segregation," which technically identifies only a policy of keeping whites and blacks apart. Segregation never aimed only for separation, the assertion of many of its defenders to the contrary. Instead, it calculated to advantage whites in every facet of their lives and to saddle blacks with corresponding and unyielding disadvantages.

In an important sense, a struggle for the soul of American Christianity lies at the heart of this story. The racial hierarchy required a certain theological approach—the specific understandings of salvation, morality, and biblical interpretation that dominated in the Magnolia State. Thus white evangelicals' efforts to retain segregation included intense battles to preserve the orthodoxy of their kind of evangelical belief. Simultaneous with their efforts to thwart black equality, Mississippi's evangelicals argued vigorously with other whites about the meaning and implications of Christianity. Disagreements over the proper response to the black freedom struggle fell along fault lines remarkably consistent with theological divides, whether among white Mississippians themselves or between them and their coreligionists outside the state. Conservative evangelicals recognized that white religious champions of black equality generally embraced an essentially different Gospel. They did not always emphasize the centrality of individual salvation or the primacy of evangelism, and they tended to construe the mission of the church far more broadly and to accept a wide range of scriptural readings—trends Mississippians despised as dangerously apostate. The fight to preserve the racial hierarchy thus included an earnest contest for the faith that had bolstered and sanctified it.

As a work of religious history, *Mississippi Praying* places these matters of faith at the center of the narrative and the analysis. Yet because religion helps a society decide and justify who shall have access to its resources, power, and privilege, this study ultimately concerns matters of politics. Mississippi evangelicals ostensibly claimed an apolitical mission; they wanted only to bring the message of salvation to all, changing society "one heart at a time." In spite of this confessed avoidance of politics, a specific political orientation lay embedded in evangelical doctrine. The oft-repeated notions that social problems merely reflected individual problems and that social change would come only as each individual embraced the Gospel obscured the reality that the system itself needed a good deal of saving. Contrary to evangelicals' assertions, the conversion of every Mississippian in the state would never correct the sufferings caused by an exclusionary political system, a deficient educational system, a discriminatory economic system, and an unfair judicial system. Yet this individualistic notion of social change allowed Mississippians to decry government initiatives as ineffective and unwarranted intrusions.

A political philosophy thus inhered within evangelical theology, as it does to an extent in all theologies. Furthermore, these white Christians *never* avoided politics, though they professed to. Long before the religious right burst on the national scene, Mississippians mobilized against forces that undermined their values through grassroots campaigns in the churches. In the immediate post–World War II years, they formed Christian Citizens' Leagues that worked to promote "civic righteousness." They used their resources to promote issues important to them and to elect candidates whose values reflected their own. This activity continued seamlessly through evangelicals' resistance to black equality, another struggle they undertook in order to preserve their wholesome Christian society. Religious leaders who claimed to be apolitical nonetheless preached philosophies of limited government that denied blacks any means for addressing grievances. The campaigns that brought evangelicals out in large numbers in the 1970s—opposition to abortion, concerns over the sexual content of television and movies, a rising divorce rate—represented still another phase in a long, unbroken stream of activity, not a new departure.[10]

Mississippians worked diligently in the political arena to create and maintain a Christian society, but the national religious backdrop against which they pursued this activity changed dramatically over the course of the civil rights years. Scholars interested in the rise of the religious right have recently emphasized the contested political climate of the cold war years, but this book demonstrates that evangelicals resisted black equality in a similarly fluid national *religious* environment. During most of the years covered by this study, no political party claimed the exclusive allegiance of religion. And though quite religiously homogenous themselves, Mississippians belonged to larger national bodies rich with theological diversity. Fundamentalists, social gospelers, ecumenists, and Christian socialists all shared membership in the same communion. Rather than basking in consensual post-war harmony, the denominations suffered severe convulsions over the meanings of real Christianity, biblical interpretation, and their political implications. Mississippians played important roles in these contests, the most important of which concerned the movement for racial justice.

Though political activity always characterized Mississippians' religious life, their enemies changed over time, and in the civil rights era their own national bodies joined the ranks of their worst foes. As racial turmoil in America reached a climactic moment in 1968, white Mississippians' larger denominational worlds of the Southern Baptist Convention, the United Methodist Church, and the Presbyterian Church, U.S., seemed irredeemable threats to their faith. To one degree or another, in Mississippians' minds these denominations advanced an apostate theology, an activist social ethic, a lax biblical interpretation, and a misguided politics. Conservatives led battles to reclaim their traditions from heresies and to capture these bodies as unalloyed champions of their theological—and consequently political—perspective. Having failed to deprive the movement for black equality of its legitimacy, Mississippi evangelicals employed their well-honed organizational skills and contributed significant leadership to this struggle to save the souls of their religious traditions. Conservatives initiated a takeover of the Southern Baptist Convention (SBC), eviscerating the voices that had most eagerly pressed for systemic change. Presbyterians organized a new communion, the Presbyterian Church in America, based on pristine commitments to the exclusively spiritual mission of the church. For its part, the United Methodist Church lost its most conservative members in droves. Participants in these struggles insisted— and today continue to maintain—that these massive transformations revolved exclusively around theology and had no connection to the civil rights struggle. In fact, however, the theological diversity these belligerents sought to eliminate had characterized these denominations for years; only in the midst of racial revolution did tensions reach a point of intolerability. This book, then, links the late-twentieth-century shifts in American religion directly to the civil rights revolution, and it emphasizes an important step—the expunging from power of moderate evangelicals—in evangelicals' larger political mobilization. Only as well-honed and homogenously conservative instruments could formerly diverse bodies like the SBC wield their weight in national politics.

This volume addresses an important question about the relationship between conservative faith and conservative politics. Today's evangelical Christians embrace the politics of the right with a consistency that masquerades as organic affinity. So predictable has the relationship between the two become that participants and observers alike assume that faith in Jesus also demands a belief in small government, untrammeled markets, and a strong national defense. Not only do many viable readings of the Bible dismantle such assumptions, but history upends them as well. The past brims with the records of sincere believers who took the Bible at face value and arrived at different conclusions about the demands of faith for politics; many earnest Christians have devoted themselves to extraordinarily radical, rather than conservative, causes. Contemporary America's small but vital evangelical left also affirms that no congenital ties bind heartfelt and conservative faith to the politics of the right. At the same time, however, this book argues that the conservative faith of its subjects—conservative because it claims to read the Bible closely, seriously, and even literally—did, in fact, lead adherents inevitably to conservative politics. Thus, while all conservative biblical interpretations do not necessarily dictate right-of-center politics, the *specific kind* of conservative religion that arose in the racially stratified society of the Jim Crow era did demand these affinities.

Mississippi Praying and Memory of the Civil Rights Movement

Finally, the story of white religion in the civil rights years suggests much for the larger narrative about the quest for black equality. In particular, it speaks to the persistent popular tendency to view this struggle primarily as a morality play. Clear-cut notions of good and evil, right and wrong, pervade our narratives of the racial revolution as perhaps few others in American history, and this rendering often depends on a depiction of Mississippians as exceptionally backward, violent, and resistant. Many of the episodes chronicled in this book endowed those images with extraordinary credibility. Consider the movement's "high holy days" between 1963 and 1965, when large numbers of northern white ministers forayed into southern communities to confer a Christian endorsement on the struggle. Race-based violence surged dramatically in response to their visits, but the Civil Rights Act of 1964 and the

Voting Rights Act of 1965 passed triumphantly, and there you have it—a tale replete with uncomplicated heroes and villains: true white Christians ascendant over ignorant thugs; the forces of good come to slay the demons of racism; America versus Mississippi.[11]

This book aims to locate the moral dimensions of this story where they properly belong. Several essential and counterproductive misconceptions about the civil rights struggle ensue from framing it primarily as a tale about progressive egalitarians versus unenlightened racists. In the first place, understanding this quest as a matter of people's personal morality furthers an important error about the sources and causes of blacks' suffering. It locates the problem of racial injustice almost exclusively in the racist attitudes of mean-spirited individuals. Indeed, some of the problem lay exactly there, but the emphasis on individual racism and the readiness to identify it as such obscures the fact that *systems* constituted the main instrument of racial subordination. More effectively than psychotic individuals with an inexplicable hatred of black folks, whites cooperated together to create insidious, opaque, and intractable obstacles to black advancement. These pervasive and unyielding barriers, which were both embedded in institutions and self-perpetuating, created corporate economic, social, and political advantages for whites, and many people who displayed little personal racial hatred cherished these systems, participated in them, and benefited from them. And even while they did so, they condemned the personal racism of others and prayed that the thugs in their midst would stop behaving so badly. Good people can and do participate in larger corporate evils, and this paradox renders these systems all the more unyielding, for individual responsibility cannot be easily identified where everyone colludes.

Second, identifying civil rights victories by the conversion of individual racial attitudes significantly distorts movement goals and methods, suggesting that black Americans sought mainly to change white hearts through moral suasion. Indeed, many civil rights activists understood their quest as a moral one; they worked to make America a more just place—one that reflected a new organization of society on essentially different theological foundations. But they also understood that this moral quest required more than changing individuals' minds. It demanded a radical transformation in the raw distribution of resources, power, and privilege, all of which relate to matters of right and wrong in complicated and often easily obscured ways. In the pursuit of this goal, moral suasion proved one of the *least* effective and most readily circumvented strategies, especially where whites' heavy investments in the racial hierarchy benefited them so stupendously. Movement activists understood that power would concede nothing without a demand, and they effectively deployed their own power in the form of economic coercion, social disruption, government intervention, and public opinion. The movement won victories when it achieved these kinds of essential social, economic, and political alterations, rather than changes in whites' attitudes.

In fact, blacks happily voted, integrated schools, ran for office, and availed themselves of new economic opportunities in Mississippi, all *before* white hearts there endured a transformation. Indeed, to the extent that the racial structure changed, these transformations owed little to adjustments in white Mississippians' moral or religious convictions. Economic coercion and political necessity, not Christian morality, chipped away at the strength of white supremacy. Resistance to black equality from white communities of faith persisted long after the end of *de jure* segregation and well after high-profile civil rights activity ceased. While the shrillest voices of opposition grew quieter, subtler forms of resistance thrived with significant help from white evangelicals. Well into the 1970s, many Mississippians required convincing that, strange as it seemed, God really wanted them to embrace black folks on conditions of equality. And the continuing segregation of American life today—a reality nowhere more present than in churches—demonstrates that simple acceptance of the idea of racial equality has not necessarily destroyed racial divides.

Religion did little to effect change, but it did undergo its own important transformation as a result of the civil rights struggle. The ultimate arrival of greater equality changed Christian conceptions of morality, not vice versa. Today, Americans widely regard human equality as part and parcel of the Gospel. By 1995, even Southern Baptists, whose Mississippi constituency argued persistently for the racial status quo and on one occasion restrained the entire Southern Baptist Convention from endorsing black civil rights as a legitimate cause, felt compelled to approve a resolution that "affirm[ed] the Bible's teaching that every human life is sacred, and is of equal and immeasurable worth, made in God's image, regardless of race or ethnicity."[12] Yet this rather late pronouncement, with its specific application to race relations, articulated a truth newly elevated to status as an uncontested and important Christian tenet. A change in the culture found its way, after the fact, to expression in the churches. Because it too easily reverses itself in favorite tellings of the story, the actual sequence of this transformation merits underscoring: changes in Mississippi's racial structure came first, and the religious ideology to accompany it came afterward.

Though most evangelicals today believe that Christianity requires a commitment to racial equality, they continue to frame morality, and especially racial morality, in individual terms. "Thou shalt not be a racist" now ranks with proscriptions against sexual sin and taking the name of the Lord in vain. Thus white evangelicals, like many other Americans, celebrate racial egalitarianism and antiracism with little understanding of the movement's goals and methods and without grappling with the aspects related to power and privilege. Like the church of the civil rights years, they nourish a myth and a morality that render invisible the structural inequalities that continue to exist for black Americans and other groups as well as their own collusion in such systems. As Michael Emerson and Christian Smith have shown, though white Christians now enthusiastically support the idea of racial equality, they also nearly universally believe that all obstacles to black advancement have disappeared.[13] Not unlike the white Mississippi Christians of the mid-twentieth century, their descendants all over the country place sole blame for gaps in black and white achievement on black Americans themselves.

Writing in 1964, the historian and former Baptist preacher Richard Marius offered an analysis of the apparent paradox that Mississippi presented. Explaining that "the most abysmal failures of the church grow out of its most ringing triumphs," Marius laid a heavy responsibility for the South's racial system at the feet of evangelical religion. Yet Marius also contended that deep complicity in a great moral evil did not erase the great good that also ensued from this tradition: "we must be of two minds about the church in . . . the South or perhaps in the world. As moral beings and as Christians, we must judge it both theologically and ethically for what it has not done. But at the same time we cannot afford to wash our hands of a bad business and dismiss from serious consideration the potential contribution of this vast institution, so powerful and yet so weak."[14]

1

Segregation and the Religious Worlds of White Mississippians

In the two decades after World War II, Mississippians exuded religious zeal. Riding the crest of a national revival, the state ranked as one of only four where more than 80 percent of the population claimed a church affiliation.[1] Spiritual leaders celebrated as their institutions enjoyed heightened prosperity, their sanctuaries filled to capacity, and armies of young people chose vocations in Christian service. Yet to some outsiders, Mississippi reeked of contradictions. For even as religious observance soared to its zenith, whites' savage resistance to black equality turned the state into a metaphor for brutality and violence. The apparently untroubled coexistence of eager evangelicalism and crude white supremacy had long characterized life in Mississippi, but some attributed their simultaneous flowering at mid-century to simple hypocrisy. The award-winning Mississippi journalist Hodding Carter, Jr., seemed to offer just such an analysis when he called his native South "a land of churchgoers, who pay little attention to Christian concepts of the brotherhood of man."[2]

Scholars, on the other hand, have more often attributed the easy coexistence of faith and racial oppression to a failure of moral courage. In this "cultural captivity" interpretation, religion succumbed in the Jim Crow years to a dark force outside itself. In bondage to the racist impulses of its host culture, white evangelicalism played no active role in white supremacy, and segregation thrived almost by coincidence. Not surprisingly then, in the civil rights era, the faith of southerners continued to sit on the sidelines—too cowardly, too apathetic, or too weak to resist the powerful worldly evil of racism.[3]

Carter's cheeky assessment and the claims of previous scholarship notwithstanding, the evident and enduring compatibility of evangelicalism and black subordination suggests holy symbiosis, not hypocrisy or cultural captivity. Indeed, white supremacy flourished, in part, *because* of evangelical religion's strength and not in spite of it. Not that the state's white pulpits necessarily spewed racial hatred or that its Sunday schools offered instruction in racism; to the contrary, churches offered some of the few, if restrained, efforts at interracial goodwill, and white Christians often displayed kindness in their personal interactions with blacks. Nonetheless, Protestant evangelicalism played a defining role in the constellation of institutions that collectively consigned Mississippi's black citizenry to lives of limited opportunity, poverty, and fear. Religion's high regard in Mississippi culture—a prestige so great that more than one scholar has described evangelicalism as a *de facto* state religion—owed much to its effectiveness in assisting the enterprise of segregation.[4]

Incomplete conceptions of both religion and racial oppression obscure evangelicalism's relationship to white supremacy. Americans prefer to understand faith and racism as individual, rather than corporate, forces. Like their twenty-first century descendants, the Mississippi Christians who people the following pages regarded their spirituality as an interior matter of private belief, but this understanding fails to account for the public, performative, and grandly communal nature of their religious practices. They pursued their faith through collective activities in institutional settings; in the post–World War II era, few believers in Mississippi—as elsewhere in America—would have imagined a spiritual life independent of the organized church. Even that most pivotal and intimate experience of conversion, the new birth, often transpired in public gatherings and in the company of others immersed in the same profound transformation.

Many Americans also understand racial injustice as a problem of individual attitudes, not as a group effort. Yet contrary to notions that prevailed in the mid-twentieth century and remain lodged in the popular imagination, blacks suffered most from systemic arrangements that erected boulder-like obstacles in the path of their aspirations. White Mississippians collaborated to confine blacks to the lowest economic and social spaces. They created a two-tiered economic system that maintained black poverty, a segregated school system that perpetuated black ignorance, an exclusionary political system that rendered blacks powerless, a social system that required black deference, and a judicial system that assumed black criminality. Racists aplenty lived in Mississippi, and certainly their personal deeds inflicted incalculable harm on African Americans, but the system's core strength lay in its communal and self-perpetuating practices.[5]

Under segregation, paradoxes blossomed like Delta cotton. Though both religion and race drew their power from their collective and publicly enacted nature, Mississippians understood them as matters of the individual heart. Perhaps faith rendered its most important service to white supremacy by embodying, teaching, and perpetuating this individualistic ethos so expertly that collective actions seemed to disappear. And with the help of this same cosmology, white supremacy cultivated its central myth: that blacks' difficulties arose from their own failings, and whites bore neither guilt nor responsibility for them. White Mississippians thus believed thoroughly in their own innocence, even as they practiced an extravagantly wicked racial system.

A Land of Churchgoers

If measured by the preponderance of churches, religion indeed figured centrally in white Mississippians' lives. In Jackson, the state's only real city in the post-war era, the very centers of political and spiritual life commingled in symbolic physical proximity. With its gothic-style architecture and sprawling complex of educational buildings, First Baptist Church sat just across the street from the state Capitol building's eastern flank. Galloway Memorial Methodist, a stately brick building with a domed sanctuary and columned portico, lay immediately to the Capitol's south. Peppering the surrounding area between government offices and commercial concerns, other prestigious churches rivaled the best-known congregations. Calvary Baptist could boast weekly collection totals that competed well against First's; Parkway Baptist ran one of the largest Sunday schools in the city; and for ministerial cachet, an appointment to Capitol Street Methodist would do quite as well as Galloway. These large congregations served the city's upper-middle and professional classes and offered worship homes for the legislators who seasonally flooded the town on state business.

In mid-sized and smaller towns, churches also lay entangled in the physical and metaphorical core of political and commercial life. All over the state, town churches featured memberships disproportionately large for the communities they served, as grand sanctuaries rose imposingly around a central square. First Baptist Church of Grenada claimed 1,600 members in a county with a white population of less than 9,000. In Magee, a town of only about 1,800 whites, the First Baptist Church claimed 900 members. In the Delta, where Mississippi's twentieth-century planter class clung tenaciously to all forms of power, large congregations hired polished ministers worthy of their prominent parishioners. At the First Baptist Church in Cleveland, for example, affluent parishioners enjoyed the weekly preaching of Dr. Mackland Hubbell, a graduate of the Baptist Seminary in Basel, Switzerland.[6]

Yet most of Mississippi's churches lay outside urban areas, dotting the roads distant from centers of commerce and political power. Mirroring the population distribution almost exactly, three-quarters of all congregations lay in these rural areas. Most reflected the economic realities of their members in small, unadorned box-shaped buildings with clapboard exteriors. Periodically, folks from these churches repaired to a local pond or stream to watch exultantly as the preacher plunged new converts, twenty or thirty in turn, into the waters of baptism. Though these ill-credentialed pastors brought little prestige to their parishioners, the churches often served as the hub of their communities. As a Baptist seminary student in the 1950s, the historian Richard Marius preached a week-long revival in one such church on a 7,000-acre Delta plantation. None of the congregants shared Marius' concern over the dangerous tilt of the white frame building, as no one recalled it ever looking any different. Marius and the pastor worked daily in the fields alongside the members, mostly white tenant farmers who lived in "tumbledown shacks where we could look out through cracks in the walls." The experience gave him insight, he thought, into the church's special meaning for the rural poor. "Over . . . those who had so very little in life," he wrote, "the church threw its protective shadow, promising resurrection, golden streets, eternal song."[7]

Raw numbers confirm the impressionistic ubiquity of church buildings on Mississippi's landscape. In the mid-1950s, the state's eighty-two counties boasted 1,734 Southern Baptist Churches and 1,646 white Methodist congregations, with communicants of these two faiths totaling over 600,000, or slightly less than 60 percent of the white

Figure 1.1 First Baptist Church, Jackson, Mississippi. Courtesy of Southern Baptist Historical Library and Archives, Nashville, Tennessee.

population. Each county, then, averaged forty-one congregations of these two denominations alone. Even these numbers may not adequately convey Protestant evangelical pervasiveness, as most evangelical membership roles excluded children who had not yet experienced conversion. The religious historian and social critic Samuel S. Hill, Jr. placed actual evangelical adherence in the state—including Presbyterians and Disciples of Christ, "cousins of the 'big two,'"—at 93.9 percent. Hill's assessment may have been a bit high, since the Catholic Church constituted the state's third-largest denominational group, with a membership of 70,000. Smaller Christian denominations, members of the Nazarene, Pentecostal, or Church of Christ families, displayed an essential consonance with the large evangelical groups, while Lutherans and Episcopalians, also small in numbers, strove to retain a degree of their distinctiveness. Mississippi's religious landscape also included a few faiths not easily classified with any others: Jewish, Unitarian, and Mormon congregations that served small constituencies in Jackson and the larger towns. Rural areas harbored a smattering of independent or unaffiliated churches, usually Baptist or Pentecostal in style and name.[8]

The state's Baptists and Methodists displayed their dominance and nourished their vitality through two denominational newspapers, the

Baptist Record and the *Mississippi Methodist Advocate*. With a circulation of over 89,000 by 1956—by its own accounting "the largest circulation of any newspaper of any kind in Mississippi"—the *Baptist Record* claimed a larger readership than its counterpart in any other state, save Texas.[9] Many churches bought subscriptions for every family in the congregation. Looking much like secular weeklies in layout and coverage, the *Record* and the *Advocate* carried world and national news of religious interest, but they also cultivated their constituents' corporate identity by focusing on state and local religious issues. Baptists in Natchez celebrated the good revival at Tupelo's Friendship Baptist Church, and Methodists in Tunica admired the new parsonage in Pascagoula. Using the *Record*'s prayer calendar as a guide, Mississippi Baptists prayed daily by name for their coreligionists in leadership positions. As they followed the published attendance totals for Sunday school or weekly offerings, they could revel in their growing corporate strength.

Even more, the strength of evangelicals' religious commitments displayed itself in a robust financial generosity, all the more remarkable because Mississippians' personal incomes ranked nationally at rock bottom. Mississippi Baptists gave as much as their coreligionists in more populous and less impoverished states, and they repeatedly outstripped their own giving records. They took in $14.5 million in 1955 alone, and claimed property valued a bit shy of $60 million. Methodists gave with equal zeal. Just one of Mississippi's two Methodist Conferences raised nearly $5 million for building programs in 1960—more than twice the amount they had raised the year before—all while increasing ministerial salaries and enlarging their gifts to Methodist agencies.[10] Indeed, evangelicals prized financial support of the church as a religious practice nearly on par with conversion. Every fall, Baptists launched a statewide "stewardship revival" to solicit contribution pledges. This revival measured success by dollars rather than converts, and State Executive Secretary-Treasurer Chester Quarles promoted it as a spiritual enterprise, urging congregations to "do [their] best . . . so that we can go 'over the top.'"[11] Just as the *Record* and the *Advocate* reported the total conversion "decisions" in revivals around the state, so they listed the dollar figure collected or pledged in each congregation.[12]

For all the distinctions of class, environment, and heritage among the various expressions of Mississippi Christianity, the state's religious culture displayed a remarkable homogeneity. Hill described a tradition he called "popular southern Protestantism" that rendered the differences among the various communions relatively unimportant and created a "trans-denominational 'southern church.'" Thus, while Baptists and Methodists maintained the largest membership rolls by a significant margin, smaller denominations tended not to set themselves apart, emphasizing instead their doctrinal commonalities with the larger bodies and pursuing essentially the same practices. Richard Marius similarly suggested that a certain "catholicity" defined Mississippians' conception of religion: "The church through which [white] society expresses its religious concern is not one universal body but several churches—'churches' at least in name. . . Of the 'in' groups the Baptists and the Methodists are the most important, [with] smaller denominations holding to substantially the same principles. . . . Groups outside the 'true church'—Jews, Catholics, often Episcopalians—are regarded with a grudging and suspicious toleration."[13]

Indeed, Mississippians agreed widely about the kind of Christianity they practiced. Their evangelical faith differed little in its essentials from the one chosen by their forefathers in the antebellum era. Since then, America had offered an increasing variety of Christianities, but Mississippians continued to prefer conservative evangelicalism with only minor alterations. Whether among the professional classes in Jackson's elegant churches or among rural folk in simple sanctuaries, Mississippians embraced a faith that emphasized personal salvation and a strict individual morality; it highlighted an obligation to bring the Gospel to a lost world and rested on a very high regard for the Bible as the inspired Word of God. Mississippi's evangelicals practiced this faith almost entirely in public and institutional forms, though they regarded religious experience as essentially interior and personal.

Mississippians' emphasis on an experience of personal salvation defined them as evangelicals. "Getting saved" sat at the center of their Christianity, whether they broke through to salvation with great emotion after tears, prayer, and corporate encouragement, or came by it more dryly. Some felt their salvation with a strong "inner witness," and religious experience thus provided its own confirmation; others simply took it on faith. Baptists followed the new birth by full-bodied water immersion, and Methodists sprinkled their children in infancy to prepare them for salvation, but for all, the Christian life began in the new birth. Since all humanity desperately needed this salvation, evangelicals claimed a mandate to bring the Gospel to all peoples, and this obligation defined their labors. In their understanding, every human need remained secondary to this spiritual concern, and all earthly problems ensued from man's spiritually lost condition.

Protestant evangelicals regarded this central and defining religious experience as intensely interior and personal. Yet notably, this most intimate experience of salvation almost always happened in corporate settings that aimed specifically to catch up the individual in a collective experience. Evangelicals structured nearly every gathering—whether weekly worship or special revival—with the goal of bringing folks *en masse* to the moment of "decision," inviting them forward to be transformed in the presence of the community. Marius eloquently described the communal forces that worked as the service built to its peak: "the preacher is carried away by his own words and the people are washed along in a lump behind him. . . . At the end of the sermon the pianist and the song leader catch the seething stream and turn it through the gates of some sentimental hymn like 'Just As I Am' or 'Softly and Tenderly' and the people are carried irresistibly to the front—often in tears, often shouting. It is a grand feeling, a kind of religious orgasm." He conceded that "the emotional aspects are somewhat subdued" in the larger, more formal churches, but even there, collective religious release represented the acme of spiritual life as "people hunger[ed] for a 'great revival.'" Evangelicals publicly announced these personal transformations as aggregate totals—"additions" or "decisions"—and paraded them as the measure of corporate success: "The revival meeting closed at Longview Church July 31 . . . There were eight professions of faith, two by letter and five rededications. . . Fellowship Church, Lorman, had six additions, five for baptism during the recent revival meeting. There were two rededications. . . . There were 24 professions of faith during the recent revival meeting held at Enon Church in Panola County."[14]

Nor did the seething stream break into atomized parts after conversion. Evangelicals pursued their "walk of faith" as members of busy and animated communities rather than as cloistered and isolated contemplatives. White Mississippians talked a great deal about personal prayer and Bible study. No evidence can confirm how diligently they observed these practices, but clearly they went to church frequently and enthusi-astically. Congregations buzzed with a dizzying array of programs and activities. Sunday services, Training Union, and choir practice punctu-ated the week, and a host of age- and gender-specific gatherings pro-vided fellowship for men, women, boys, girls, and adolescents. Men could join the Baptist Brotherhood, a Methodist men's club, or a men's Bible class; adult women participated in the Women's Missionary Union, the Women's Society of Christian Service, or the Susannah Society. Bap-tists in Mississippi ran approximately 900 chapters of the boys' group, Royal Ambassadors, and a similar number of Girl's Auxiliary chapters. Though these groups met often locally, they also gathered annually for state- or conference-wide assemblies. In addition, Baptists, Methodists, and Presbyterians staged revivals in the spring and fall; they organized vacation Bible schools in the summer and Christmas pageants in the winter. Some layfolk served as deacons, on pulpit or pastoral relations committees, on the church's board, or as members of the Session (the governing body of a Presbyterian congregation). Locally defined bodies of each denomination met several times a year as county associations, district conferences, or presbyteries, and all sent lay messengers or del-egates annually to state-level meetings; the Mississippi Baptist Conven-tion and the Presbyterian Synod of Mississippi met every November, and white Methodists convened as two separate (Mississippi and North Mississippi) annual conferences in June. By the hundreds, Mississippi evangelicals streamed to the yearly or quadrennial national gatherings of their denominations. Even those confined to home or bed could par-take of community religious life through denominational newspapers and local television stations that broadcast worship services.

Moreover, Mississippi's profound religious unity rested on a wide-spread embrace of fundamentalist-type faith. Fundamentalism had arisen in the late nineteenth and early twentieth centuries to defend the literal truth of the Bible from threats like the theory of evolution and "modernistic" theology. As fundamentalists set themselves off from other forms of Christianity in the early twentieth century, they not only insisted on biblical literalism and infallibility, but also coalesced around a set of essential doctrines, or "fundamentals" of Christianity. Their fierce and uncompromising commitment to these positions led them to an often stridently defensive posture against other expressions of the

faith. Non-fundamentalist Christians often appeared as their worst enemies, for the believer who would compromise biblical truths posed a
far greater threat than the outright atheist or rank sinner. For their part,
non-fundamentalist evangelicals would sometimes admit to the possibility of errors of fact, history, or science in the Bible when pressed, but
they also held the Bible in very high esteem and regarded it as "the only
rule of faith and practice."[15]

As denominations, the Southern Baptist Convention, the Methodist Church, and the Southern Presbyterian Church (properly named
the Presbyterian Church, U.S.), harbored rich theological diversity and
did not embrace fundamentalism. Nonetheless, fundamentalists dominated the Mississippi expressions of these bodies. Outsiders driving
through the state noted the high density of prominent fundamentalist
preachers like Billy James Hargis, Bob Jones, and Carl McIntyre who
filled the radio waves.[16] The dogmatic and literalistic orientation displayed itself among educated Doctors of Ministry and the larger "first"
churches, as well as in the smaller, rural congregations. Pastor William
Potter of Carthage's First Baptist Church, for example, made classic fundamentalist arguments in 1946 when he railed against the writings of
Dr. Harry Emerson Fosdick. The well-known modernist, claimed Potter, did not believe "in the Virgin Birth, or . . . the substitutionary doctrine of the Atonement" and "Baptists do certainly not believe, preach,
talk or even think in the same vein as Dr. Fosdick." *Baptist Record* editor
A. L. Goodrich warned against "modernism . . . emphasis on the social
gospel and skepticism about the inspiration of the Holy Scriptures" as
forces that would undermine Baptists' evangelical effectiveness. Dr. P.
I. Lipsey cautioned Mississippians to stick with the King James Version
of the Bible and eschew the Revised Standard Version, because small
changes in the newly minted translation could undermine doctrinal
purity.[17] While many Southern Presbyterians had rejected biblical literalism and other fundamentalist tenets decades earlier, Mississippi
attracted an unusually high number of ministers from Westminster,
the Orthodox Presbyterian Seminary outside Philadelphia founded by
J. Gresham Machen, perhaps the country's best-known fundamentalist
of the 1920s and 1930s.[18] Candidates for ministry in Mississippi's Presbyterian pulpits often faced rigorous examinations designed to vet their
commitments to biblical literalism.[19]

The fundamentalist approach to the Bible relied on a thick consensus about its meanings. The literalist hermeneutic did not actually take the entire Bible literally, of course. It required a myriad of interpretive shifts—emphasizing some texts while downplaying others, relying on historical context in some instances while ignoring it in others, understanding certain biblical passages as spiritual, some as allegorical or figurative, and others as literary or didactic. Yet preachers, teachers, and their hearers denied making any interpretive choices and claimed that they simply took the Bible at face value. To preserve this consensus about the Bible's meanings, Mississippians studied the Bible corporately. They expounded the meaning of Scripture in worship services structured around the sermon, in large and well-attended Sunday schools, and through reading religious literature—practices that cut against their claim that each believer could ascertain the meaning for him- or herself in private.

Sheer bulk and homogeneity fostered evangelical cultural dominance. Hill judged that no other region in the country displayed such a "tight unity of general culture and the dominant religious body." Indeed, Marius thought that "Church and society have become almost indistinguishable." The pervasiveness of evangelicalism's outlook, frame of reference, and values profoundly, sometimes purposefully, blurred the boundaries between church and state. When disorder, vice, or sin menaced Mississippi communities, evangelicals organized against the threat through Christian Citizens Leagues that strove to maintain a Mississippi "governed . . . according to Christian principles." Whole congregations encouraged their coreligionists to "fill our public offices . . . with men who measure up to Christian standards." Owing to such evangelical exertions, Mississippi prohibited alcohol sales from the late nineteenth century, when the majority of the state's counties went dry, until 1966, when it reverted to a local option law, in a chronology that extends well past national prohibition on both ends. Indeed, the fundamentalist perspective enshrined its orthodoxy still further in Mississippi law. In the wake of the 1925 Scopes trial in Dayton, Tennessee, many southern states dismantled their prohibitions on teaching evolution. Mississippi, however, did quite the opposite, enacting a new law *against* teaching Darwin's theory. The bill breezed through both houses of the legislature with strong majorities, in spite of objections by the Senate and House educational committees. Continued popular support kept the law on the books until the Mississippi Supreme Court invalidated it in 1971. Even an academic leader so distinguished as Mississippi College President David Nelson dismissed evolution as merely a "fad" that had "little support in Scripture." Mississippians both accepted and expected that their public institutions would embody religious values. According to the Mississippi Baptist writer Will Campbell, "Religion simply flowed into school and school into family, and all of the social institutions which were not . . . sharply divided."[20]

No doubt, Mississippi evangelicals' collective activity created strong communal bonds and offered a deep sense of belonging. Importantly however, this imagined community appeared—quite artificially— all white. In keeping with the tenets of segregation, as these believers drank the cup of spiritual fellowship, they identified only with white coreligionists throughout the state. As they envisioned their religious communities while perusing the pages of the *Baptist Record* or the *Advocate*, only white folks appeared in their field of vision. And the community that bound itself together by sacrificial giving, so eager to "do their best," welcomed only other whites into their circle. Sometimes just a few blocks away, members of another racially homogenous body performed similar gathering, converting, and giving rituals in a rather parallel universe. Yet, these spirited black evangelicals remained all but invisible in whites' religious worlds.

Practicing Christianity: Segregated Faiths

This vibrant, thriving, bustling all-white religious domain represented only half of Mississippi's actual religious world, since black Baptists, Methodists, and Presbyterians also abounded there. But segregation placed all Mississippi blacks into a neatly distinct and self-contained imagined community. Segregated sabbaths did not passively reflect the culture. To the contrary, religion helped make and maintain this racially divided world.

Mississippi's racially homogenous evangelical communities belied the racially mixed reality around them. As many scholars have observed, for all Mississippi's insistence upon maintaining segregation, the races lived in close physical proximity. Concerned far more with maintaining superiority than with actual separation, whites brought blacks into close quarters for a variety of reasons, most often when they needed the benefit of their labor.[21] Black sweat built white agricultural and commercial enterprises, and black money often maintained white stores. Even whites of modest means hired African Americans to cook their food, wash and wipe their naked children, clean their toilets, and launder their underclothes. White Mississippians repeatedly, if inadvertently, acknowledged their abundant and intimate interracial contact when they argued that these quotidian interactions placed them in a position to know African Americans better than northerners did.

Segregation took Mississippi's messy and mixed racial reality and carefully arranged it into a neatly dichotomized imagined world. White supremacy worked as a "grand drama," in the words of Grace Elizabeth Hale, staged for whites' benefit, but acted out by everyone with careful coaching and plentiful intimidation. The fiction of white superiority required a meticulous arrangement of the sets and a studied performance of the roles. Many of Jim Crow's essential elements—the appropriate use of courtesy titles, requirements that blacks yield the sidewalk or use back entrances rather than front ones—served no function other than to guide black Mississippians in the proper execution of their parts in this theater. Yet, whites often mistook the play for reality and failed to see how the sets and costuming of Jim Crow carefully structured racial interactions so that whites always had the most favorable terms and primary control. White Mississippians regarded blacks' inferior education, poverty, low political participation, and high incarceration levels as the inevitable expressions of black inferiority, rather than as props for the parts whites forced them to play. Whites maintained their "natural" superiority only through great manipulation and, concomitantly, great expense and inconvenience—costs they foisted on blacks as often as possible.[22]

Segregated worship arose as the South assembled the other institutions, laws, and customs that collectively constituted the Jim Crow system. In the antebellum era, free blacks, slaves, and their masters had often attended the same churches, though black communicants usually worshipped in the back of the church or in the balcony and had no voice in church leadership. In the years immediately following the Civil War, many southern churches briefly retained their interracial characters. Though forced to accept black liberation, whites refused black equality, and they expected the freedpeople to continue the ecclesiastical submission they had displayed before the war. Furthermore, white church members cared little about helping former slaves find educational and leadership opportunities, financial independence, or community networks of support. Black believers, disgusted by white presumptions of power, found they preferred the autonomy of their own churches and gradually withdrew to form all-black congregations. Thus, even before the establishment of *de jure* segregation in the 1890s and early 1900s, the South's evangelical churches practiced segregation because whites refused to allow the freed people equality within the church.[23] Though African Americans, not whites, assumed the initiative in segregating southern Protestant churches, this arrangement fit neatly into the emerging system.

The withdrawal of black churches produced all-white administrative structures and racially homogenous faith communities well beyond the local congregation. Very occasionally, black congregations that separated from white ones remained within the structure of the white denominations, but more often they chose to separate administratively as well as physically. Some black congregations joined existing African American denominations like the African Methodist Episcopal (AME) Church, but freedpeople also organized entirely new communions in the decades after the Civil War. Both the Colored Methodist Episcopal (CME) Church, founded in 1871, and the National Baptist Convention, founded in 1880, exemplify black efforts to create spiritual and organizational autonomy and to resist the control of whites.

The withdrawal of black Baptists transformed the Southern Baptist Convention into an all-white body, rendering "Southern Baptist" a racial as well as a religious designation. Southern Methodists retained a small African American membership, but segregated this constituency physically and administratively to ensure that coreligionists of different races had virtually no contact with one another in matters ecclesiastical. Presbyterians tried two strategies. They created a separate black denomination, the Afro-American Presbyterian Church, in 1898. When this communion struggled because of its small size, Presbyterians received these black members back into the denomination, but placed them in a segregated unit, the Snedecor Memorial Synod, in 1915.[24]

Racial segregation remained a central feature of the Methodist Church when the northern and southern bodies healed their ninety-five year rift in 1939. Some northern Methodists had dreamt of reunion ever since

Appomattox, repeatedly offering olive branches to the southern church, but southern Methodists' lingering distaste for Yankees and the larger black constituency in the northern church mitigated the attractiveness of such offers. Even when reunion appeared inevitable, the issue of how to treat the black membership stalled negotiations and complicated ultimate approval of the merger. Since many of the southern church's blacks had long since fled to the CME church, southern Methodists worried about their future in a denominational body that would now contain a much expanded black constituency. To placate white southerners' fears, the reunited church wrote separation of the races into its administrative structure, creating five jurisdictions based on *geography* and a sixth, the all-black Central Jurisdiction, based on *race*. In spite of this provision for rigid physical and administrative segregation, the merger still encountered serious opposition in the South from those who considered the racial arrangements too porous. While the church adopted the Plan of Union in 1939, a single conference—North Mississippi—refused to endorse it, though ultimately even they had little choice but to go along.[25]

Administrative segregation guaranteed that no minister of one race could serve a church of another, since ministerial calls and appointments required conference or presbytery membership. Furthermore, this segregated structure precluded even ministerial fellowship between white and black ministers of the same denomination. Whites thus avoided both ecclesiastical contact with their black counterparts and the psychological identification that might arise by virtue of shared membership in an ecclesiastical body. The arrangement, like all aspects of segregation, placed the burden of its artificiality on black ministers. Since racially based jurisdictions and synods were not organized around geography like the white jurisdictions, they embraced immense areas. In an era when accommodations such as hotels, restaurants, and gas station restrooms excluded them, black ministers traveled long distances to provide spiritual oversight, find ministerial fellowship, and attend to church business. Needless to say, black Presbyterians and Methodists found these arrangements both trying and senseless. More African Americans preferred the autonomy of all-black denominations, and the white-dominated communions had little success attracting and retaining black members. Not surprisingly, by 1950 blacks constituted only 1 percent of Southern Presbyterians and 5 percent of Methodists.

In the ensuing decade in Mississippi, black Methodists streamed into the all-black communions at a rate that alarmed church leaders.[26]

In the mid-twentieth-century South, then, black Baptists, Methodists, and Presbyterians worshipped independently of their white coreligionists. White Methodists and Presbyterians often did not even know the names of local black leaders of their same denomination, for segregated faiths dictated that white and black coreligionists could not imagine themselves part of the same community. Here the racial hierarchy received a powerful corporate expression that did not require constant pulpit harangues on black inferiority. Like most aspects of segregation, separate religious communions taught the truth of a "natural" white superiority and black inferiority most powerfully by simply embodying it; too much commentary would undermine its appearance as transcendent and unassailable.

Most local white churches adopted no formal policy barring African Americans from worship services, as all so clearly grasped the requirements of racial separation that written statements seemed unnecessary. The "strangers welcome at all services" cheerily blazoned on Sunday bulletins and church marquees did not specify "white," yet no one misunderstood to whom "all" referred.[27] Certain exceptions to the rule of segregated worship—enacted within clearly established parameters—neither threatened nor disturbed white assumptions. African Americans could and did, in certain circumstances, enter white sanctuaries with the full knowledge and blessings of the church. Most notably, black employees of white families attended the families' weddings and funeral services, enjoying special seating with the white family. Yet the races mixed in the church in such instances exclusively within the patterns of paternalism established by whites. African Americans attended these events not as equal participants in a religious community, but rather as metaphoric children within an extended family—affectionate members, beholden both to the care and authority of the white parents. As long as the system of segregation itself appeared unthreatened, the occasional black presence in a white church—and vice versa—hardly warranted remark.[28]

Segregated worship thus assumed a place in the library of "texts" that tacitly and powerfully taught white supremacy as an immutable truth. In a white community with a vastly superior everything, segregation seemed to offer its own rationale. Whites easily found biblical evidence to prove that God himself had created this system, but absent an organized assault, southerners rarely wielded such defenses. Such expositions often seemed baldly strained and inappropriate in the more polished churches and, with the system securely in place and self perpetuating, an articulation of segregation's biblical underpinnings appeared almost superfluous.[29]

In spite of their invisibility in white religious imaginations, Mississippi's black evangelicals could claim a substantial list of achievements. Black Baptists had long run their own affairs, with leaders, government, and programs entirely separate from the white Southern Baptist Convention. Early in the twentieth century, National Baptists—the largest of Mississippi's seven black Baptist conventions—had claimed a state membership of 240,000, nearly two-and-a-half times that of white Baptists at the time. In spite of the obstacles imposed by inferior economic opportunities, bald discrimination, and increasing black out-migration, National Baptist membership in Mississippi continued to show substantial gains, climbing to about 350,000 by 1950—still an impressive showing against white Baptists' 400,000. Other black Baptist convention memberships numbered in the tens of thousands as well, placing total black Baptist membership significantly ahead of whites' tallies, in a state where the black population steadily declined from 900,000, while whites numbered just over a million and continued to grow.[30] Black Methodists had also achieved much against great odds. In 1940, black members of the Methodist Church in Mississippi totaled over 40,000, a figure that did not include those in larger independent black communions such as the CME, AME, and AMEZ churches. Including these uniquely black Methodist communions, among Deep South states, only South Carolina had a comparable number of black Methodists.[31]

When their black coreligionists entered whites' plane of vision at all, the lens of white supremacy contorted blacks' astounding religious accomplishments. Black Mississippians appeared in evangelical literature not as equal Gospel co-laborers, but as "mission fields" in need of white guidance, benevolence, and support. Mississippi Baptists believed that "half the Negroes [were] unchurched" and, despite the obvious independent initiative and religious zeal of black Mississippians, thought that this population "look[ed] hopefully to white Baptist churches for Christian action."[32] Presbyterians echoed the assumption that black

Mississippians "look[ed] up to [whites] for spiritual as well as economic guidance."[33] The *Baptist Record* and the *Mississippi Methodist Advocate* mentioned their robust black coreligionists mostly as the recipients of white aid, reinforcing notions of congenital black deficiencies.

Instead of seeing blacks' vigorous religious lives, whites saw only a presumably natural spiritual inferiority that, they believed, underpinned all other black weaknesses. Whites thought this inherent moral depravity displayed itself especially in black sexuality. A young parishioner from Madison thought "that the morals of the Negro are far below those of the average white . . . So far as sex is concerned, [the Negro] simply follows his natural instincts."[34] In a Sunday school lesson, the Disciples of Christ teacher Archibald Coody estimated that blacks were "25% bastards" with "strong sex passions."[35] The Presbyterian pastor Dr. Horace Villee found "a very infinitesimally small portion [of blacks] morally and spiritually on a higher plane than the masses of them."[36] This imagined black moral depravity served as a powerful argument for segregation. "We teach our children to keep good company," explained Coody.[37]

A research team that helped prepare Gunnar Myrdal's 1947 *An American Dilemma* found "astonishingly little interracial cooperation between the white and Negro churches of the same denomination," and the Methodist Church's own Committee on Jurisdictional Relations made essentially the same observation in 1956.[38] In the 1920s, the Federal Council of Churches began the tradition of observing a Sunday every February as "Race Relations Sunday," but a survey of southern Presbyterian pastors in 1954 revealed that none of the Mississippi respondents even observed the day, and none could provide a copy of a sermon he had preached on race relations.[39] Horace Villee said his church neglected the observance because southerners had "little consciousness of a real 'race problem'" and because he personally had never thought of black Mississippians as folk "with whom some proper relations must be achieved."[40] A Race Relations Sunday sermon in the *Mississippi Methodist Advocate* addressed the topic primarily by encouraging congregations to give generously in an offering designated for Methodism's twelve black colleges and universities. Yet, even here, the resourcefulness of black Methodists received little mention, as the sermon billed these colleges as a means for whites "to light the lamp of knowledge for a race coming up out of the darkness of ignorance."[41] Perhaps Reverend

J. C. Wasson of Itta Bena Methodist Church misunderstood the intent of Race Relations Sunday. His special sermon for "Segregation Sunday," as he dubbed it in 1953, explained why he believed "whole heartedly in the principle of white supremacy," a conclusion he had reached "from reading of the Bible." His explication assured his Delta audience that segregation would continue even in heaven, because "[a] niger [sic] has a soul, and if he is a Christian he will be saved in heaven."[42]

Before the years of high-profile civil rights activity, while Mississippi's white evangelical women did pursue limited interracial religious enterprises, they tended to conduct their work within the established lines of segregation. This was especially true of Baptist women, who led interracial work in their denomination until well into the 1950s, when the Mississippi Baptist Convention Association's Department of Negro Work, a segregationist stop-gap measure, gradually assumed much of this work (chapter 5 offers detailed treatment of this enterprise). Yet, considering what their remarkable numbers and extensive organizational connections might have enabled them to accomplish, white Baptist women's efforts appear as half-hearted tokens. The Methodist WMU conducted an annual four-day Institute for Negro Women, hosted four-day summer camps for black girls and boys, and ran vacation Bible schools in black communities. These projects did little to improve education, but they did raise awareness about mission opportunities and offer recreation for children. Special speakers and camp directors often included non-white missionaries who showed slides, spoke about their work, and solicited commitments to prepare for missionary service. In addition to these efforts, the WMU distributed Bibles as part of a "One Hundred Thousand Bible Project" that aimed to place a free Bible with every black family that lacked one.[43]

Clearly, Baptist women's interracial efforts flirted little with the boundaries of segregation. Other than to foster interracial contact— an already abundant enterprise in Mississippi—these projects failed to challenge the rules for black and white interactions and did little to improve the material or educational conditions of black Mississippians. Indeed, notwithstanding white Baptists' insistence on their goodwill toward Mississippi blacks, their record of such good works appeared remarkably thin. Perhaps most startlingly, in a tradition they honored until 1962, Mississippi's white Baptists did not speak collectively against the violence that enabled white supremacy to thrive. When the Association of Southern Women for the Prevention of Lynching (ASWPL) called for anti-lynching pledges at the 1933 Mississippi Baptist State Convention, their pleas fell on deaf ears.[44]

Methodist and Presbyterian women pushed against the boundaries of segregation a bit more forcefully. In the 1930s, Methodist women assumed leadership of an anti-lynching crusade in Mississippi. White Methodist and Presbyterian women also provided teacher training programs for black women and worked on other projects to improve the quality of black education in the state.[45] Efforts to stop lynching and to improve black education both struck at important foundations of segregation. Nonetheless, the real limits of faith-based interracial outreach revealed themselves in the 1950s, when viable challenges from black Mississippians and from whites' own national church leadership seriously threatened the racial hierarchy. In that changed context, some of the very same women's groups that had championed interracial cooperation in previous decades refused to support the dismantling of segregation. In 1955, women from the North Mississippi Conference of the Methodist Church, from which the most active and useful outreach to black women had arisen just decades earlier, explicitly rejected the racial charter of the Women's Society of Christian Concern, a document that committed Methodist women to the principle of racial equality.[46]

Religion erected walls between white and black life that remained as strong and impenetrable as political, economic, or educational barriers, and it thus helped bear the weight of white supremacy. In fact, white supremacy charged Mississippi's faith communities with an especially important task, the custody of the segregated society's foundational ethos. White Mississippians' religion embodied, transmitted, and protected white supremacy's central truth—that black Mississippians' inferior status ensued from their own failings and not from any doings of whites.

Individual Salvation and Collective Sin

While no one calculated nor schemed in back-rooms to design a faith with the deliberate intent of serving white supremacy, Jim Crow required a religion that would not mount a moral challenge. Thus, white Mississippians developed a Christianity tailor-made for racial subordination.

Their religious structures created racially specific faiths, and their religious lens distorted African American spirituality, but these would not quite suffice. Mississippi needed an ethos that reconciled segregation's fundamental ironies and contradictions while rendering its follies believable; it demanded a belief system that forestalled possibilities to envision an alternate racial structure. Mississippi's brand of evangelicalism, with its dogged emphasis on personal salvation, its individualistic understanding of sin, and its devotion to a literalist hermeneutic served these needs well. In Mississippi, these specific hallmarks of evangelical faith did not develop accidentally or thrive coincidentally.

White evangelicalism negotiated the tension between individuals' visions of their own goodness and the corporate evil of segregation. Mississippi's white Christians did not run from questions of morality; rather, they engaged them consciously, frontally, and eagerly, but their careful structuring of these concerns kept segregation from appearing in any catalogue of sins. Placing strong priority on individual morality and private action, their cosmology described a world in which personal choices determined all things in this life and the next and ignored to the point of absurdity the political, economic, educational, and social structures that shaped both blacks' and whites' realities. This ethos, so divinely suited to white supremacy, helped white consciences remain untroubled about segregation, because no one seemed responsible for that in which everyone colluded. Indeed, white religion completely confounded efforts to lay blame for the conditions of blacks on anyone except blacks themselves.[47]

The preference for an individualistic understanding of wrongdoing began in Mississippians' understanding of salvation. Here, the individual could determine his or her own eternal fate. Reverend Jack Southerland offered a typical sermon to his congregation at Fifteenth Avenue Baptist Church in Meridian in 1954: "Man is a free moral agent and God recognizes his choice. . . . All who believe and accept Christ will be saved." Even Bible lessons that expounded God's providence and guidance over the affairs of men ultimately ruled on the side of man as an unencumbered moral agent: "We choose and act freely, and are accountable for all we do."[48]

Evangelicalism shepherded the individualistic ethos beyond the moment of conversion. After salvation, Christians strove to overcome sin. As a Mississippi Baptist admonished, "Everything that impedes progress in the Christian life should be given up. These "weights" may not be wicked habits, but [rather] timidity, procrastination, preoccupation and neglect of spiritual resources . . . intemperance, impurity, dishonesty, jealousy, or covetousness." Yet, as this litany shows, evangelicals selected sins of an individual nature for excoriation. When the evangelist Billy Graham preached to segregated audiences averaging 16,000 per night in June 1952, he opened the crusade with a sermon on the sin of pride, which he called "deadlier than the poison of a rattle-snake." Focusing on such individual sins would eventually correct all larger problems because, as Graham explained, social problems "only reflect . . . individual problems." Religion gave white Mississippians few conceptual tools for understanding the reciprocal truth: that collective sins could create insurmountable individual problems.[49]

This conception of the autonomous individual, acting in a world unrestrained by social, political, or economic structures, shaped whites' vision of their own morality and that of their black coreligionists. Even as they ignored their own corporate behavior and its effects, white Mississippi Christians believed they showered goodness on their black fellows. A white woman from the Delta praised her church for teaching her "kindness toward the Negro," and a teen-aged Christian from Madison extolled her fellow white Mississippians who had "nurtured the Negro, taught him, provided for him, attempted to educate him and endeavored to make him a worthwhile citizen." She saw no obstacles to black advancement in Mississippi, for "The Negroes who have desired to do so have become well educated and wealthy. There is no field of economic endeavor which has been barred to them."[50] In their treatment of African Americans, Mississippians saw only their own individual moral virtue in full bloom. The corporate sin of segregation that they practiced fervently and ferociously against black communities failed to appear on any list of damnable deeds.

Indeed, looking through eyes trained to focus narrowly on individual accountability, white evangelicals could only place the blame for blacks' failings squarely on the shoulders of this oppressed people. The young Madison Christian described blacks as "irresponsible," with "little initiative, if [their] necessities are furnished."[51] Others concurred that "lack of initiative and desire" held blacks down.[52] Perhaps the prominent Methodist layman John Satterfield best revealed evangelical blindness to the way that segregation saddled black Mississippians with a host of burdens and then blamed them for their lack of achievement. Presenting a litany of African Americans' ostensibly inferior traits, Satterfield waxed incredulous at the suggestion that white Mississippians had any measure of responsibility for these difficulties: "When you tell your friends in other areas . . . you are then told, 'That's all your fault. You have kept them ground down. You did it.'"[53] Not coincidentally, white Mississippians' political philosophy also displayed the same overdrawn belief in unencumbered choices as the determinants of individual circumstances and the same apparent blindness to collective structures that limited individual options.

Yet the whole structure might have fallen apart without belief in the Bible as the inspired and infallible Word of God. In demanding a consensus about the meaning of the Bible, fundamentalism disqualified all other interpretations of Christianity, especially those versions of the faith that claimed a Gospel mandate for social change. Thus, segregation had a faith that would declare apostate and illegitimate any reading of the Scripture that did not reflect its own favored but narrow emphasis on individual salvation and personal evangelism. What often looked like bigotry was actually desperate message control.

* * *

As a corporate enterprise, then, segregation would encounter no challenge from Mississippi's evangelicals, who remained deeply committed to their kind of Christianity and highly scornful of other versions of the faith. And as a very secure institution, segregation could easily tolerate a wide variety of individual attitudes and actions toward African Americans. Individually, white Mississippians could and did display attitudes that ranged from the virulent racist hatred of Emmett Till's murderers, to the outwardly respectable and rational commitments to segregation articulated by countless defenders of the institution, to the paternalistic kindness of white families toward their black employees. Many whites felt genuine pangs of sympathy at the suffering of black Mississippians. Reverend W. J. Cunningham even openly questioned the notion of black inferiority in his 1943 sermon, "The Negro Question." Cunningham himself recollected that the sermon, though rare, was well received.[54] Even Methodist Bishop Marvin Franklin went so far in 1949 as to maintain that "Special privileges for the few, enslavement for the multitude is not fair or right . . . No race, or class, or people must be exploited."[55] As long as segregation appeared impervious to assault from a corporate standpoint, such statements and individual acts of kindness did not threaten white supremacy. A few whites—scattered, quiet, and unorganized—could even condemn segregation as wrong, but their isolated moralizing failed to trouble the corporate juggernaut. Tellingly, Bishop Franklin's boldness evaporated by the 1960s, when real threats challenged the survival of segregation.

In Mississippi, the church described, identified, and assigned matters of sin and redemption for the society that created it. Evangelical religion faithfully guarded white supremacy's central tenet and fundamental myth: blacks suffered, but whites bore no blame for these travails. Mississippi, however, could hardly claim distinction on this arrangement. Other than its detailing of features related more to degree than kind, much of the foregoing description could apply to almost any place in mid-twentieth century America. Everywhere, whites worshipped as part of racially exclusive communities, having little interaction with and little knowledge of their black coreligionists. Most American Christians thought of sin as an individual matter, and many believed an individual's effort mattered more than anything else in shaping his or her destiny. And even in parts of the country without legally mandated segregation, other factors like housing discrimination, inferior employment opportunities, and poor schools limited black opportunities for advancement. Though many American Christians claimed to believe in universal brotherhood and the equality of all before God, meaningful connections between these convictions and their lived racial realities proved elusive.

2

Conversations about Race in the Post-War World

Just after World War II, Mississippi's churches seemed to burst at the seams. Returning service personnel, new believers, and once-wayward backsliders all streamed to houses of worship. Scores of congregations rejoiced as they set new attendance records. Formerly small, struggling churches raised their status to "full time," finally able to support a pastor all their own. After fifteen lean years of depression and war, prosperity had surged again. As they poured forth from their new abundance, Mississippi evangelicals surpassed all previous giving records. Methodists pledged a "million for the Master" to refurbish and expand their facilities, while Baptists erected new sanctuaries and enlarged their Sunday schools to accommodate the swelling numbers.[1]

The new spiritual vitality included a sense of urgency to seize a unique spiritual moment, for it seemed the war had called forth a new openness to the Gospel. *Baptist Record* editor A. L. Goodrich thought evangelicals faced "one last chance in our generation to evangelize a world before a pagan world destroys itself and us."[2] Some answered this call by taking positions of national leadership in their denominations. Others displayed even more daring, relinquishing local opportunities for work in foreign mission fields. Convinced that "never were doors open wider to missionaries," Reverend Gerald Riddell forsook his pastorate in West Laurel to take a post in Colombia.[3] From the field, he wrote home to confirm that the great spiritual hunger there exceeded his resources: "Every city is open to us now."[4]

In their extraordinary spiritual energy, their increased connections to national faith communities, and their thick involvement in global religious affairs, Mississippians partook of important trends in American religious life. In the first post-war decade, a national revival and changing religious demography profoundly altered Mississippi evangelicals' world. Seemingly overnight, they found themselves joined to national—not merely regional—constituencies, and the institutions that had once marked their separateness as southerners now bound them to other Americans. Their newly expanded religious institutions fostered meaningful global ties as well. American evangelicals plunged into missionary work with unparalleled zeal, responding to catastrophic human need in Europe, Asia, and Africa. Mississippians who joined the swelling army of American religious workers around the globe pulled in their wake the prayers, interest, and dollars of folks back home.

These religious reconfigurations thrust Americans and Mississippians into potentially transformative conversations about faith and white supremacy. A religious elite advanced an understanding of Christianity that challenged America's racial arrangements, and they shared their concerns with a new national constituency that included the Deep South. And as missionaries labored in foreign fields where questions of race and empire impinged upon their work, they raised trenchant critiques of the United States and its complicity in racial exploitation. Few Americans of faith could fail to hear the insistent demand for a reexamination of their racial assumptions and practices.

In the post-war era, white American Christians everywhere practiced a faith deeply implicated in white supremacy. New and developing national communions embraced their southern constituencies and affirmed segregation. "Southern Baptist" designated a believer as white in California as surely as it did in Mississippi. Methodists accepted racial distinctions as an appropriate feature of the new national body they created in 1939. In all denominations with a black membership, African Americans suffered a second-class status that ran far up the ranks. Until internal and external pressures shamed these bodies into gradual, and often merely token, accommodations, segregation remained the rule even at those few gatherings where black and white coreligionists came together—every four years at the General Conference for Methodists and annually at the General Assembly for Presbyterians. Indeed, most white Americans remained uninterested in changing the racial status quo, as did most white Mississippians. Nonetheless, their religious connections plunged them into conversations about race that they could not avoid.

No North or South: White Mississippians and American Christianity

For much of the South's history since the Civil War, religious faith tied white evangelicals to their regional past as champions of slavery, the Confederacy, and white supremacy. Birthed in controversies over slave-holding, the Southern Baptist Convention (SBC), the Methodist Episcopal Church, South, and the Presbyterian Church, U.S., had fiercely defended the institution of slavery, the right of secession, and the esteemed place of white southerners in the divine plan. After the war, these bodies helped celebrate the "Lost Cause" as a civic and nationalistic faith rooted in the vaunted memory of the vanquished and vanished Confederacy. The South's major white religious traditions continued to foster its strong sense of distinctiveness well into the twentieth century, even as other forces strengthened southerners' national bonds. Southern Baptists, Methodists, and Presbyterians remained regionally separate bodies that regarded themselves as the custodians of true Christianity— the evangelical faith that emphasized personal salvation and holiness of life. Moreover, southern Protestants claimed a divine destiny to export their brand of faith to the rest of the nation. Northern Protestants, they believed, had corrupted the pure and simple Gospel of salvation by forsaking strict biblical interpretation, discarding their zeal to save lost souls, and striving to improve conditions in the present world.[5]

In the post–World War II era, however, Mississippians' imagined religious communities grew beyond their local congregations and their county, district, or presbytery affiliations. Their boundaries expanded past their statewide associations, conferences, and synods, and even transcended the "Southland." The connection between Mississippians' faith and their southern identities rapidly attenuated as they participated in vast religious networks that circulated ideas and people throughout the country. When Americans returned to church in droves and memberships soared to all-time highs, Southern Baptists gained prodigiously. The denomination exploded with growth in the first post-war decade, challenging Methodists for distinction as America's largest Protestant body. Southern Baptists who counted just over six million members in 1946 had reached 8,700,000 by 1956. Perhaps more significantly, membership blossomed in states outside the traditional South, as out-migrating southerners transplanted the faith to new areas. Whereas in 1940 Southern Baptists worked in only nineteen states, the denomination claimed a truly national constituency with work in forty-three states by 1957. Southern Baptists in Indiana, Illinois, and Michigan outnumbered American Baptists there, and even California, Oregon, and Washington State claimed large numbers of adherents to this once uniquely southern communion.[6] An important national religious force in size and scope, Southern Baptists now belonged to a nation and not just to a region.

While reveling in the opportunity to proselytize this rapidly opening home mission field, these changes moved Baptists with both pause and promise. As congregations multiplied in the Great Lakes region and the Pacific Northwest, the Convention debated the advisability of a name change. While some leaders insisted that "Southern Baptist" represented "more of a doctrinal idea than a locational one," others questioned the appropriateness of the regional appellation for their national constituency and wondered if such a name would hinder the faith's reception in new areas. Convention leaders also worried about encroaching on territory traditionally dominated by American Baptists.[7] Though spawned in the debate over slavery, the SBC's unique identification with southern history, life, and culture diminished precipitously.

The post-war revival also increased membership in the Methodist Church. However, a more direct challenge to southern Methodists' regional identification came from the 1939 union that returned the northern and southern branches of the church to a single body, repairing the rift precipitated ninety-five years earlier by election of a slave-holding bishop. Though strictly segregated, the new church's national strength and diversity gave many communicants pride. Methodists claimed a history and loyal following in every part of the nation. Their theological viewpoints ran the gamut from the fundamentalism of Mississippi pastor B. K. Hardin to the social gospel radicalism of Harry Ward of Union Theological Seminary in New York. Proudly showcasing their well-educated and professional constituency, Methodists also claimed a strong following among the urban working classes. Pockets of the rural South still employed an updated circuit-rider method of ministry, where several small churches shared one pastor who rotated within the "charge." At mid-century, Methodists managed large outreaches overseas and served a variety of ethnic groups at home. They claimed an erudite and respected leadership, a variety of service and fellowship divisions, and well-regarded educational institutions. In short, only six years old at war's end, the new Methodist Church was also newly grand, complex, and national.[8]

Southern Presbyterians (officially designated the Presbyterian Church, U.S.) remained technically a regionally defined body in the post–World War II period. No dramatic reorganization or membership surge pushed it out of its traditional geographic home, and the church's General Assembly continued to reject overtures from the northern church (Presbyterian Church, U.S.A.) to reunite.[9] Yet, the issue of reunion constituted a central tension in southern Presbyterians' corporate life, bringing the northern and southern expressions of the church into constant conversation and wracking the southern denomination with interminable bickering. Like a couple that cannot decide whether to marry or separate, constant conflict indicated troubled intimacy rather than complete disinterest.

Threats to the Southern Presbyterian Church's regional self-definition lay at the heart of these hostilities. Loss of southern identity in the event of a union loomed as a legitimate concern, since southerners stood to lose 50 percent of their representation in the church's legislative body. The northern church's 2,500,000 members, dominated by a more liberal theology and a social gospel orientation, could easily obliterate the wishes and traditions of the southern church's 700,000 members. Furthermore, union became the lightning rod for a variety of issues that tormented the Southern Presbyterian Church. As Southern Presbyterians debated union, arguments coalesced along a liberal/conservative axis that included issues of theology, social policy, church government—and integration. In this debate, the conflation of conservative religious beliefs with southern identity reached its apex of expression.[10] Though Presbyterians failed to formalize a union in these years—the southern church's General Assembly rejected it in 1942, 1948, and again in 1954—a strong current pushed them toward an ultimate rapprochement.

These new Southern Baptist, Methodist, and Presbyterian bodies nourished evangelicals' connections to national trends and altered the character of local religious communities. Southern Baptists and Methodists in Mississippi now read the same literature, followed the same church news, and used the same educational material as their coreligionists in Michigan and California. And not only did Mississippians drink from pools of religious thought shared by millions nationwide;

they also contributed significantly to the streams that shaped national denominational life. In 1947, in excess of twenty Mississippi Baptists gained appointments to denominational boards.[11] By 1953, both the SBC and the Methodist Church published their Sunday school literature under the direction of former Mississippians, James L. Sullivan of Brookhaven and one-time Millsaps College professor, Henry Morton Bullock.[12] A Hattiesburg academic, Dr. Ralph Noonkester, regularly wrote material used by Baptist Sunday schools nationwide.[13] Mississippians Dr. G. T. Gillespie, Reverend R. E. Hough, and Dr. J. Kelly Unger contributed material for the *Southern Presbyterian Journal.*[14] Thelma Stevens from Hattiesburg worked in New York as an executive in the Methodist Church's Woman's Division.[15] As bishop of Mississippi's two Methodist conferences from 1948 to 1964, Marvin Franklin occupied a seat on the Methodist Council of Bishops, where he served with sophisticated luminaries like west-coast cosmopolitan Gerald Kennedy and the notorious liberal G. Bromley Oxnam. The native Mississippi Methodist Francis Stuart Harmon worked with the National Council of Churches and the New York YMCA.[16] Dr. John D. Humphrey of Grenada served on the Methodist Judicial Council, and the Methodist Press Association elected Mrs. Sam Ashmore as it secretary in 1960.[17] In addition to these luminaries, Baptists, Methodists, and Presbyterians of all ages attended programs with coreligionists from around the country at the denominational retreat centers at Ridgecrest, Lake Junaluska, and Montreat, North Carolina. Further strengthening Mississippians' nexus of national ties, hundreds of messengers and commissioners from the Magnolia State represented their churches at the annual meetings of the Southern Baptist Convention and the Presbyterian General Assembly, and every four years Mississippi Methodists sent a delegation of lay leaders and ministers to their General Conference.

Theology blurred regional lines now, too. Though most southern Methodists continued to send their young men to Candler School of Theology at Emory University in Atlanta or to Vanderbilt's Divinity School in Nashville, seminaries like Drew in New Jersey or Iliff in Colorado now belonged to them, too. Golden Gate Seminary, established as a Southern Baptist institution in San Francisco in 1950, did not seem southern in the same way as the SBC seminaries in New Orleans, Ft. Worth, and Louisville, but Baptists in the 1950s even considered building a new theological school in Chicago. For their part, Southern Presbyterians enjoyed access to several divinity schools. Though the theological inclinations of any minister could be read from his seminary pedigree, regional origins often failed to match theology. Westminster Seminary in Pennsylvania produced the most conservative preachers in the entire communion, while a degree from Union Seminary in Richmond, Virginia, served as a sure-fire badge of neo-orthodoxy and pro-union enthusiasm.

Faith secured Mississippians' ties to the larger world outside the United States as well. As World War II came to its traumatic conclusions, American Protestants witnessed the suffering of a devastated and hungry world. Believing themselves uniquely positioned to fill these needs, they rushed to seize this rare spiritual opportunity, dramatically broadening their already far-flung missionary and overseas benevolent enterprises. Immediate needs appeared particularly acute. As war-ravaged countries struggled to feed their populations, American churches pooled their resources to ship 150 tons of relief materials to Europe and Asia every week.[18] The SBC alone gathered $3.5million for similar relief work.[19]

More significantly however, the denominations boosted long-term foreign ministry by augmenting existing missionary stations and adding new ones. In Africa, the SBC expanded its operations from one country to ten and its missionaries from forty-five to 447 in the space of twenty years.[20] In 1948, the Methodist Church called for 595 new foreign missionaries and simultaneously increased its missions budget by $7.5 million. In an effort to fill urgent missionary needs, the denomination recruited new college graduates as "special term missionaries" who could dive into foreign service with a scant six weeks training.[21] Southern Presbyterians more than tripled their expenditures on international work. By 1957, some of the denomination's mission stations supported more than twice the number of missionaries as before the war.[22]

Mississippians enthusiastically joined this invigorated foreign presence. Mississippi Baptists dispatched fifty new missionaries in the first post-war decade, more from their state than had served in the entire previous half-century.[23] Twenty-five Mississippi Methodists chose foreign missions careers in the same post-war period.[24] Hailing from small towns like Sumrall, New Albany, Lucedale, and Drew, missionaries wrote letters home about their work in the Congo, Nigeria, or Chile.[25] Sponsoring congregations posted these letters along with photographs on

Sunday school bulletin boards or reprinted excerpts in their newsletters. While on furloughs, missionaries often pursued an exhausting schedule of appearances before women's groups, Sunday school classes, and Brotherhood meetings, all to inform the home folks how their mission dollars accrued to great benefit in every corner of the globe. Special offerings for missions—the Lottie Moon Christmas offering named for the nineteenth-century Baptist missionary and the Annie Armstrong Easter offering memorializing the founder of the WMU—kept global religious work ever in Mississippians' minds.

A myriad of other religious activities and rituals raised Mississippians' religious sights outside American borders. Each February, Baptists observed a Sunday for "thinking of fellow Baptists around the world and for prayer that the world be so evangelized so that future wars may be prevented." Each summer the *Baptist Record* reported on the Baptist World Alliance from a different international host city. In 1947, six Mississippians joined nearly 1,000 other Americans who sailed to this gathering in Copenhagen, Denmark.[26] Methodists followed the World Methodist Federation, remembering the words of John Wesley that "Methodists are 'one people in all the world.'"[27] Members of almost all of Mississippi's Protestant denominations participated in the newly organized World Council of Churches, celebrating the global Christian family during World-Wide Communion Sunday in the fall. The state's evangelicals also gobbled up international religious news in the *Baptist Record* and the *Mississippi Methodist Advocate*, where they felt the suffering of Japanese Baptists, wept with German pastor Martin Neimoller over his country's devastated church, and rejoiced when a Kamikaze pilot found Jesus.[28]

No isolated provincials, Southern Baptists, Methodists, and Presbyterians in Mississippi belonged to faith communities in vastly expanded connectional worlds. While many Mississippians still regarded their faith as "southern" in style, theology, history, and practice, these older identities sometimes warred against their new national connections and burgeoning global vision. Mississippi's evangelicals squirmed a bit in these new garments; religion now made them at once parochial and cosmopolitan, insular and expansive. They often celebrated the national dimensions of Southern Baptist, Methodist, and Presbyterian faith and relished the advance of Christian work around the world, even as they pined for the glory days of a southern church.

No East or West: Protestant Progressives and Race

America's racial tensions rose to acute levels as its vast war machinery dismantled and military personnel flocked home. Affronted by the great irony that their own racially troubled nation had dispatched them abroad in a war against racial hatred, black Americans achieved important gains during the war. They continued their struggle at war's end. The declining clout of labor during demobilization inspired black activists in their fight for workplace equality. When Irene Morgan refused to give up her seat on a Virginia bus in 1944, the National Association for the Advancement of Colored People (NAACP) took her case all the way to the Supreme Court and won a ruling against segregation on interstate transportation. To test that ruling in 1947, the Fellowship of Reconciliation staged a two-week integrated bus trip through four states of the upper South.[29] Important activity at the federal level also fueled the hopes of black Americans. President Harry S. Truman's Committee on Civil Rights not only issued a stinging indictment of American race relations in 1947 but also included integration of the armed services and the creation of a permanent Fair Employment Practices Committee (FEPC) among its recommendations.

Black equality found important advocates in America's mushrooming religious communions as well. Though the denominations maintained segregated norms, religious progressives in their midst heard and contributed to the country's most frank discussions about race. From seminaries and denominational offices, in women's groups, among missionaries on foreign fields, and in the black membership, this cadre pointedly condemned American racial practices. Though many stopped short of advocating integration in the hearing of their profoundly conservative constituencies, they did champion concrete changes in legal, political, economic, and social practices, and they identified much in America's racial system as inimical to the Gospel. Deeply influenced by the social gospel and by theologies connected to neo-orthodoxy and Christian realism, none of these racial progressives espoused the narrow biblical interpretations favored by fundamentalists.

On both social and theological issues, the SBC's most liberal voices spoke from the seminaries. At Southwestern Baptist seminary in Fort Worth, professor of Christian ethics Thomas Bufford (T. B.) Maston offered his students an expanded racial consciousness. Influenced by the social gospel and by neo-orthodoxy through his own mentors at Southwestern and Yale, Maston authored three books on race relations after World War II. The first, *"Of One": A Study of Christian Principles and Race Relations,* published in 1946, argued that the notion of spiritual equality demanded qualitative change in racial arrangements. At Southwestern, Maston directed the graduate work of Foy D. Valentine, who completed doctoral work on Southern Baptists and race relations in 1949.[30] In Louisville, students at Southern Baptist Seminary also confronted the racial implications of the Gospel. There, Jesse Buford Weatherspoon taught a course on "Christianity and Race Relations," and his colleague Edward McDowell exposed students to interracial fellowship and ministry opportunities. Their student Clarence Jordan ministered in a black neighborhood while pursuing his doctoral studies in New Testament Greek.[31] According to the SBC's Social Services Commission, by 1947 all Southern Baptist seminaries offered "strong courses dealing with race relations in the light of Christian ethical ideals."[32] In a denomination that harbored a strong fundamentalist contingent, such teachings offered potential for serious controversy. Maston's "Christocentric" theology, for example, rejected biblical literalism and inerrancy, maintaining that all scripture required interpretation in light of the life and teachings of Christ.

Progressive Baptist inclinations did not stay confined to the seminaries. Some racial progressives edited Baptist newspapers or ministered on college campuses. Often reflecting the influence of their seminary professors, a few pastors shared these egalitarian ideals.[33] Perhaps most importantly, however, some denominational officials and convention-level leaders—those who served on the Home Missions Board, the Foreign Missions Board, and the WMU—keenly felt a responsibility to educate Baptists into a new sense of responsibility on race relations.[34] Though none overtly assaulted segregation in the immediate post-war years, these agencies published material aimed to broaden their constituencies' thinking about racial arrangements. The WMU, for example, published Maston's *Of One* under its auspices. The Home Missions Board produced "Ten Commandments on Race Relations," which argued that "there is no such thing as a superior race."[35] Publications from the Foreign Mission Board recommended *A Rising Wind* by NAACP leader Walter White to help "[i]ntelligent Christian people" who wanted an answer to the "race problem."[36] Material produced by the Sunday School Board also challenged Southern Baptist racial attitudes, if often a bit more obliquely.

Southern Baptists' progressive impulses burst into full display in 1947, when the SBC's Committee on Race Relations, itself a remarkable product of the previous year's convention, presented its report to the annual convention meeting. Chairman Jesse Weatherspoon's extensive account lavishly detailed the current scope of Southern Baptist "work with Negroes." The long list highlighted efforts to provide black ministerial education through seminary extensions, and it emphasized the WMU's work with black women. But the committee went beyond congratulating itself for racial outreach; it also issued a call for further and decisive action, citing the common faith of "six million white Baptists and three and one-half million Negro Baptists" in the South, with their mutual belief "in the lordship of Christ and his teachings" as a foundation. "And surely," the report continued, "the initiative and leadership in the solution of [race] problems belongs to those who have the greater advantage." The committee acknowledged its sense that the racial status quo could not long remain: "The tides are moving fast." It recommended a series of "Christian and Baptist principles" as a "basis for Christian action." Though the enumerated principles failed to include integration, they did identify practices that would strike squarely at some of the most blatant injustices routinely suffered by black Americans. The report advocated for "constitutional rights of all citizens irrespective of the origins or racial inheritance," including "the right to vote, to serve on juries, to receive justice in the courts, to be free from mob violence . . . to receive equal services for equal payment on public carriers and conveniences . . . an adequate wage . . . and healthful working conditions."[37]

As if the report's pointed recommendations did not make adequately clear the position of progressive SBC leaders, the Convention then heard an address by Dr. George D. Kelsey. The appearance of a black minister to address the all-white SBC no doubt rankled some, yet none could argue with his impeccable credentials. A Yale Ph.D., Kelsey served as professor of religion and philosophy and director of Morehouse College's School of Religion. Kelsey's message on "Christian Love and Race Relations," while skillfully diplomatic before this white audience, frankly attacked the fallacy that a person could "subscribe to a racial code while at the same time trying to be a Christian." Neither did Kelsey pander to white images of their own benevolence. Rather, he identified black Americans "as the victim in the American racial situation," while comparing them to the Chinese who needed to forgive the Japanese for atrocities committed in the recent war.[38]

As a newly enlarged denomination that had renewed its commitment to segregation in its 1939 union, the Methodist Church seemed an unlikely place for a conversation about race. Yet the new church's theological, economic, social, and ethnic diversity made it ripe for dialogue about change. The denomination's small black membership and its women played critical roles in urging a reconsideration of racial practices. Its significant gender discrimination notwithstanding, the church offered a vast opportunity for women's religious work in a fairly autonomous setting through its Woman's Division, and women who worked in this organization molded it into one of the most racially progressive elements in the Methodist Church. Its most important leaders in the post-war era had deep roots in racial activism. For example, the veteran anti-lynching activist from Georgia, Dorothy Tilly, served as one of only two women on President Truman's Civil Rights Commission. In addition to her work with the Methodist Church's Woman's Division, Tilly served as a field secretary for the Southern Regional Council (SRC), an organization that sought better race relations through a gradualist approach. Before moving full time to the Woman's Division in 1940, Mississippi native Thelma Stevens worked in Georgia with the Bethlehem Center, a community outreach that provided educational and social services to African Americans.[39]

Coming from backgrounds in education, anti-lynching campaigns, missions, and social work, the women who directed, staffed, and participated in the Woman's Division's programs often rejected traditional models of female religious work. Rather than hosting teas and raising money for pew cushions, they initiated serious efforts to foster concrete social change. They also spurned a Gospel that focused narrowly on salvation and evangelism, embracing instead teachings from the likes of the modernist Harry Emerson Fosdick and the noted Christian realist Reinhold Niebuhr, both celebrated enemies of fundamentalism. Motivated by a strong social gospel ethos, these women framed their activities as imitations of the life of Jesus, believing his example offered social principles to guide their actions.[40]

Figure 2.1 The Woman's Division of the Methodist Church singing at the 1950 Women's Assembly in Cleveland, Ohio Methodist Prints, *World Outlook*, July 1950. By permission of the General Board of Global Ministries.

Armed with such principles, these women assertively molded Methodist opinion and policy on race relations. Beginning in 1944, they prodded the General Conference to drop its segregated arrangement.[41] In Methodist publications, they wrote about race relations both at home and abroad, asking pointed questions like "[Are we] eager for world brotherhood in Russia, but not willing to let it come to New York, if its coming implie[s] the lowering of the color bar?"[42] They offered plans for worship services structured around the theme of "World Brotherhood"; in their proposed model, the congregation would sing "In Christ there is no East or West, in Him no North or South" and hear a sermon on the equality of all men. They issued a constant stream of position statements and reports that clearly expressed their intent "to combat all forms of intolerance against minorities." They mobilized their vast army of women to inundate local and national political leaders with information about race-related issues. In Washington, D.C., Woman's Division representative Eleanor Neff lobbied and testified on behalf of civil rights measures, including anti-lynching legislation, anti-poll tax measures, and the creation of a permanent Fair Employment Practices Committee.[43]

Methodism's activist women strove to educate their constituency into new attitudes. Study courses, leadership conferences, and national assemblies under their auspices aimed to raise Methodists' awareness of the broader world, legacies of colonialism, and issues of race. In 1946, Methodist women featured among their offerings one study course on India and another titled "The Christian and Race." Connecting Methodist women's traditional missionary concern to their racial practices, the speaker for the India course explained: "One of the greatest hindrances to the progress of Christianity on non-Christian lands like India is the un-Christian and sub-Christian conduct of Christian nations as regards war, the economic exploitation and political domination of backward people, interracial relationships and relationships between the sexes."[44] Participants who studied "The Christian and Race" read *Blind Spots: Experiments in the Self-Cure of Race Prejudice* by the prominent missionary Henry Smith Leiper, a text that used the author's extended missionary experience to argue for the essential equality of all human beings.[45]

These progressive women practiced the interracialism that they preached. They broke with paternalistic patterns that made whites the spiritual mentors and guardians of African Americans. Black women exercised leadership in their programs and participated on a basis of equality. For some Methodists, Woman's Division meetings provided rare opportunities for the kinds of interracial interaction that remained strictly taboo in their home areas. When six students from Louisiana attended a youth retreat in Illinois in 1946, for example, they waxed glowing about the experience as their first truly interracial encounter.[46]

In addition to the assertive work of Methodist women, challenges to segregation came from the church's roughly 330,000 black Methodists, a tiny minority that shrank steadily against the white membership that rapidly topped eight, then nine million by 1950.[47] Confronting their dissatisfaction almost immediately after reunion, black bishops at the General Conference of 1944 explained that they tolerated the segregated arrangement only because they recognized the low level of whites' spirituality: "We are not at all in harmony with any Methodist or others who think such a plan necessary in a truly Christian brotherhood. We consider it expedient only on account of the Christian Childhood of some American Methodists who need a little coddling until they grow into full grown manhood (and womanhood) in Christ Jesus." Though the

Conference responded with expressions of good intent, it took no definitive action until 1948, when it eliminated the western half of the Central
Jurisdiction, absorbing the African American churches there into the
Southern California-Arizona Conference. This bit of progress notwithstanding, segregation remained the rule in the Methodist Church.[48]

The association between theological orientation and racial outlook
displayed itself most starkly among Southern Presbyterians. A conservative theology that restricted the church's mission to spiritual concerns
had restrained Southern Presbyterian involvement in political, social,
economic, and racial outreach since the denomination's origins. In the
twentieth century, as many ministers and leaders rejected fundamentalism for more moderate perspectives, efforts to push the denomination toward greater social consciousness often foundered as hard-core
conservatives continued to insist that the church should hew strictly
to spiritual concerns. "Our primary interest is in the reign of our Lord
Jesus Christ in the hearts of men," maintained the fundamentalists. "We
must make sure that we get down to the roots of humanity's trouble and
that we do not spend our time dealing with minor, surface ailments that
are but eruptions from poisons that lie deeper down." Even efforts in
1934 to establish a committee charged only to *study* social ills met with
serious opposition from conservatives.[49]

Not surprisingly, then, Southern Presbyterians' racial progressives
collected loosely around the theologically moderate faculty at Union
Theological Seminary in Richmond, Virginia. Seminary professor and
church historian Ernest Trice Thompson spearheaded the effort to move
his denomination away from a limiting view of spirituality and toward
a vision of Christianity that included social action. Among such efforts,
in 1944 Thompson and others launched the *Presbyterian Outlook* as a
counterweight to the conservative and overtly polemical *Southern Presbyterian Journal*, which had begun publication in 1942. Through his own
weekly column, as well as sermons and articles from a wide range of
authors and sources, Thompson made the *Outlook* into Southern Presbyterians' most clarion voice for racial justice and theological moderation.[50]

In addition to their educational efforts, Southern Presbyterian racial
progressives shaped the direction of the denomination at the highest
echelons. During World War II, these leaders introduced a measure at
General Assembly that called upon all Christian citizens "to combat,

with all earnestness and power, racial superiority against Negroes, anti-Semitism and unsympathetic treatment of Japanese in internment areas." In 1946, this group successfully lobbied to create a Division of Christian Relations to deal with racial issues. Equipped with a full-time director, this agency kept social concerns before the General Assembly, in spite of the conservative contingent's wishes.[51]

As in the Methodist Church, Southern Presbyterians' own stark complicity in segregation muted their calls for racial justice. The church's tiny black minority—less than .05 percent of total membership—remained administratively and physically segregated. Until 1950, black commissioners to the General Assembly even entered through a back door and ate at separate tables. That same year, one of the denomination's most eminent leaders, former Union Seminary Professor Walter Lingle, introduced a proposal to abolish the church's all-black synod—a move with great symbolic and administrative impact, if few practical implications for racially segregated worship. The strength of progressive sentiment demonstrated itself in the lively debate that followed. Distinguished layman Colonel Francis Pickens Miller took the floor to urge an end to segregation in the church because "the Church of our Lord Jesus Christ is a community of all believers." The General Assembly responded to Miller's words with "thunderous applause," and the motion to abolish the segregated synod carried overwhelmingly. Yet, this move had few repercussions at the local church level, where congregations continued to worship as racially specific bodies.[52]

* * *

Perhaps nowhere did the vision of Baptist, Methodist, and Presbyterian racial progressives express itself as forcefully as in missionary publications. In a world still reordering itself after the convulsions of World War II, missions magazines offered their subscribers a significant global education. Replete with maps, charts, and photographs, these publications helped readers follow the progress of communism in China, understand geopolitics in Southeast Asia, observe religious persecution in Eastern Europe, and learn about agricultural workers in Brazil. Evangelicals regarded "home" and foreign missions as of a piece, and this material also raised readers' awareness of the many hidden communities in the United States where religious workers served: urban ghettos, rural migrant settlements, Latino enclaves, Asian neighborhoods, and Native American reservations.

Missions publications' overt interracialism contrasted sharply with the assumed segregation in most aspects of American life, and these publications served as rare sites where white Americans routinely saw blacks' competence highlighted and interracial activity treated as unremarkable. The Methodist publication *World Outlook* took racial mixing for granted. On page after page, its photos displayed black and white youth together in interracial institutions, conferences, and retreats. Black and white adults conferred on ministry strategy and mixed in recreation at rural workers' conferences. The magazine regularly ran articles by noted black leaders like Ralph Bunche of the United Nations and Channing Tobias of the NAACP, with photos of the authors included. *Window,* a publication that sought to raise the missionary awareness of young Baptist women, also depicted interracial contacts as utterly routine, even featuring black women on its cover from time to time.[53]

Missions literature served as a prime place to candidly confront America's racial practices and to challenge their arbitrary and oppressive nature. After World War II, missionaries often worked in areas ravaged by political upheavals in which race, discrimination, white domination, and class struggle figured significantly. Some missionaries unthinkingly transferred their racial attitudes to their work with foreign nationals, only to find that indigenous people—especially those where anti-colonial sentiment flourished—would not accept white assumptions of superiority. Other foreign workers dropped the cultural blinders they wore at home and acquired sympathies with the perspectives of the oppressed.

Expanding evangelical missions in Africa provided perhaps the most convincing arena for progressives to argue the case against American racial practices. On returning from a trip to the Congo, the Southern Presbyterian Dr. T. Watson Street reported that Congolese nationals complained bitterly about missionaries who treated them as inferiors. Watson feared that nationals' resentment of the color line would undermine Southern Presbyterian mission work there.[54] Conditions in South Africa also offered a revealing point of comparison with the American South. As white leaders tightened the system of apartheid in 1949, the American Methodist missionary Darrell Randall expressed grave concerns over white South Africans robbing blacks of their political voices and limiting their access to government benefits.[55] When Methodist Bishop W. Earl Ledden toured slums on the outskirts of Johannesburg, he warned American readers about the potential effects of such poverty: "[one] cannot expect them much longer to endure their lot in silence."[56]

Other missionary writers spoke even more bluntly to their coreligionists about the impact of American racial practices on their work. American racial injustices provided useful ammunition for antidemocratic and antichristian forces in emerging nations, and foreign newspapers often purposefully highlighted such incidents. Newspapers around the world flashed headlines of post-war racial brutality in America: the lynching of Willie Earle in South Carolina, the beating of Isaac Woodward in the same state, and the ordeal of the black Mississippian Willie McGee, sentenced to death for the dubious rape of a white woman. A Baptist writer in the missionary publication *Commission* chided American Christians for the crippling effect of such coverage. "When acts of racial injustice in America . . . get spread abroad, we are hanging chains on the hands of our missionaries and weights on their feet."[57] Eleanor Neff of the Woman's Division described how Methodist missionaries had pointed out "glaring inconsistencies between our professions and our practice regarding race. They tell us that it is becoming increasingly difficult to gain the respect of native peoples for our church because of this dualism and they urge us to make our practices Christian."[58] In *World Outlook*, a Methodist writer explained that American racial injustices implicitly called Christian commitments into question: "When we contemplate our own missionary-sending country, what do we see? A vitally Christian civilization? A church spiritually stalwart and aflame with missionary passion? We do not." The writer went on, "[R]acial intolerance and bigotry even within our churches themselves, and racial injustice, discrimination, and persecution undercut . . . both the continued existence of democracy in America and the entire missionary enterprise of the church in foreign fields."[59] Dr. Emory Ross, a veteran of Methodist work in the Belgian Congo, offered a similar assessment: "No amount of talk will convince [colonized] peoples that color as *color* and race as race are not large factors in the maintenance of the colonial system. . . . [But, t]he first additional advance must be made at home. We are sullied abroad in this and every other matter if we are not at home as clean as ever we can be."[60]

In post-war America, the chorus calling for changes in race relations included an insistent strain from the country's most significant Protestant religious communions. Motivated by their conceptions of faith and increasingly by the jangling discord between their global missionary vision and their racial practices, these leaders sought to persuade their coreligionists to rethink their racial practices. Yet, for all the clarity of their egalitarian vision, these progressives often called only for better treatment of black Americans and frequently highlighted individual attitudes, not structural issues, as the essential problems. Even when they did point to systemic inequality, the call for radical change lacked weight when advanced only by this small element—a perceived elite—in these vast and multifaceted religious bodies. Most white Americans seemed fairly content to let the status quo remain, and in Mississippi, they fought tenaciously to keep it.

Mississippians and Conversations about Race

Mississippians' robust global and denominational connections propelled them into these conversations about race. With their newly thick nexus of institutional ties and their heightened world awareness, white Mississippians could scarcely avoid the insistent message that rang from so many religious mouthpieces. Hundreds of Mississippi messengers, delegates, and commissioners listened as their national religious leaders broadcast progressive racial sentiments at denominational gatherings. By the score, Mississippi's young folk at seminaries imbibed the frank teaching of T. B. Maston, Jesse Weatherspoon, and Ernest Trice Thompson. Mississippi Methodist women flocked to the Woman's Division's racially conscious conferences, retreats, and seminars, and Methodist young people traveled out of state for integrated meetings. As missionary literature flooded Mississippi's Protestant homes and church libraries, evangelicals encountered the struggle for equality in foreign lands, witnessed blacks and whites interacting comfortably together, and absorbed the admonition that brutality in their own state undercut their missionaries' work. Indeed, no white Mississippian of faith who participated actively in denominational life could fail to hear this rigorous reassessment of American race relations.

Some Mississippians joined the chorus of religious voices that advocated change in race relations. From his pulpit at Oxford University Methodist Church, Dr. W. J. Cunningham rejected the notion of black inferiority, describing the idea of racial differences as "purely imaginary." Cunningham urged "simple, elemental justice" for black Mississippians, and went on to identify the "race problem . . . as the special point where many of us need to test our own Christianity for its genuineness today."[61] Along with fourteen other women from North Mississippi, Methodist women's leader Mrs. Dan G. Comfort of Durant attended a missions-emphasis retreat at Lake Junaluska in 1946. She found the speaker's connections between global missions and American race relations to be "a revelation" and among the week's highlights. Women at the conference took "The Christian and Race" study course, and Comfort assessed the entire experience in glowing terms: "God was there . . . he would talk to you, were you to listen."[62] When Mississippi Methodists welcomed Marvin Franklin as their new bishop in 1948, his instincts seemed utterly in sync with the denominational progressives. Apparently unafraid of alienating his new constituency, he maintained in an address made in June 1948 that "[a] morally mature majority race will never take advantage of any minority race, but rather will undertake it to guarantee educational, judicial, and economic fairness to that race. Racial hate and prejudice have no place in a Christian nation." Yet in the same sermon, Franklin took care also to reaffirm the principle of segregation: "It would seem natural for each individual to be very proud of the race to which he belongs and do all he can to maintain its integrity and solidarity."[63]

Perhaps no white Mississippi evangelical displayed so cosmopolitan and egalitarian a racial vision as Mrs. Cora Rodman Ratliff. Writing from her hometown of Sherard in the Delta, where black citizens suffered perhaps more cruelly than any place in the country, Ratliff transcended local realities in her Methodist vision. Like other Methodist women who renounced the religious pabulum of "insipid" ladies programs that had "no relation to life," Ratliff issued calls to meaningful action. She boldly connected racial practices in Mississippi to evangelical efforts to reach a global multitude: "We know that the morning papers of Tokyo and Moscow carry the activities of Mississippi of the preceding day. What we do in America affects what we can do in other countries. The greatest affronts experienced by our missionaries today are some of the issues we evade and side-step in our homeland. . . . We are aware that our whole Christian enterprise is in jeopardy on this point." Ratliff drew on Methodist women's legacy of working for "very radical" social change to urge the women of her constituency to tackle racial injustice, which she regarded as "[t]he greatest problem of the next fifty years."[64] Ratliff may correctly have assessed Methodist women as the best point of entry for a radical re-visioning of Mississippi's racial hierarchy. Along with other people of faith in the state, some Mississippi Methodist women affiliated themselves with the Southern Regional Council in early 1946. Identifying the council as "pro-democracy and pro-humanity," these women hoped "to study the many problems of the South and to mobilize the people of the South to solve these problems."[65]

Yet, in spite of their bold assertions and frank understandings of the global implications of domestic racial arrangements, none of these progressive Mississippi voices called outright for an end to segregation in the post-war decade. They may have believed, like many whites, that they could reasonably advocate for equality within a segregated system. Some may have recognized segregation itself as the primary obstacle, but understood how vigorously white Mississippians would close their hearing against a call to dismantle it. Certainly, these few progressives did not represent the mainstream of Mississippi's evangelical community. The basic animus of the state's larger evangelical world displayed itself quite clearly in a dramatic tension with denominational leaders on matters of theology, politics—and certainly, race.

Mississippi Baptists did not often criticize their denominational leaders in the early post-war period, but their publications displayed a fundamentally different approach to race relations. Even as denominational material replete with overt interracialism streamed into Baptist homes, Mississippians' own very popular weekly, the *Baptist Record*, almost never featured black Mississippians in its pages. In spite of the invisibility of blacks in the *Record*, the editor clearly believed the state's African American Baptists would want to read it, and he encouraged white readers to make "a gift of the *Record* to a Negro Church."[66] In 1946, the *Record* ran a rare piece that treated the spiritual lives of black Mississippians. Yet, rather than showing any of Mississippi's hundreds of vibrant black Baptist congregations, the article focused entirely on prison ministry at the notorious Parchman Penitentiary. Neither did the large photo that accompanied the piece feature the confident, competent, well-dressed African Americans of SBC publications. Instead, inmates in stripes waited for baptism, standing waist-deep in a pond.[67]

Such subtle rejections of the denomination's direction did not always suffice, and at least one congregation wanted to clarify the differences between their racial outlook and that of SBC leaders. In a resolution directed in part to the writers of Baptist literature, the Mendenhall Baptist Church acknowledged that "much is being said, written and done about the [race] problem." While many progressive Baptist statements focused on the equality and essential *lack* of differences between peoples, the Mendenhall Church thought such talk ignored a basic truth: "We recognize that there is a difference between the races that the hand of man cannot remove, regardless of the much publicized doctrine of a common origin or brotherhood of man." These Mississippians believed God had established these distinctions and that the races should remain separate in order to preserve them. Lest any in the camp of progressives misunderstand their message, the Mendenhall resolution spelled it out: "we condemn any teaching, doctrine, or example that is biased toward social equality wherever found . . . we call upon our religious leaders and statesmen to strive to keep the races pure that they may serve out the purpose for which God created them."[68]

At the time, the Mendenhall resolution constituted a rarity in the published words of Mississippi Baptists, a group that typically kept their intramural tensions under wraps. In contrast, Methodists in the state fairly radiated anxiety over their leaders' progressive impulses. Not surprisingly, Methodist discomfort manifested itself primarily in complaints about racial views, political orientation, and theology expressed in denominational literature. The controversy went quite public in 1946, when members of three Jackson churches complained about the literature because it "advocated the Fair Employment Practices Committee, and advocated social and political equality between the white and negro races." The Millsaps Memorial Church objected to the suggestion in a youth publication that students get "acquainted with some person or group of another race, seeking their friendship as [they] would that of anyone else who interests [them]." The objectionable lesson had also suggested the NAACP as an "excellent source of information."[69] Critics singled out *Methodist Woman* as especially offending: in "articles too numerous to mention," the material had "been [too] political and social-equality aimed . . . we have lived peacefully with other races for centuries, and perhaps are better qualified to know just how to live with these people in brotherly love than some who prepare the material."[70]

The same literature that offended for its racial progressivism also drew fire for its theological underpinnings; one Mississippian described the material as "the dull platitudes and the puerile negations of a decadent liberalism."[71] Mississippi Methodists' rumblings against theological trends in their church continued beyond the 1946 dispute, and an elderly Methodist explained that the trouble ensued from declining respect for biblical literalism: "all our confessed orthodox Bishops deny or refuse to defend the faith and inerrancy of the Holy Writ." Since the material from his own denomination seemed like "salt that has lost its savor," this Methodist sought out the spiritual nurture of ultra conservative serials like *Methodist Challenge,* published by the strident and oppositional Methodist right-winger Fightin' Bob Schuler of California.[72]

Similarly, Mississippi Presbyterians also displayed an extraordinary lack of consonance with their denomination and its general direction in racial, political, and theological matters. Many Presbyterians in Mississippi preferred *Christian Beacon*, published by the Presbyterian archfundamentalist Carl McIntyre, to their own denomination's fare. Few laymen worked more assiduously against the growing "liberalism" of the denomination than the Hattiesburg businessman L. E. Faulkner. Wherever Faulkner found expressions of Presbyterian compromise on racial segregation, political conservatism, and theological fundamentalism, he opposed these trends. In his seemingly inexhaustible labors to preserve a pure Presbyterian faith, he identified several sources of these odious tendencies: religiously motivated social service agencies, the northern Presbyterian Church, and the Federal Council of Churches (FCC, but after 1950, the National Council of Churches, or NCC). All of these forces could be neutralized, Faulkner believed, if right-thinking southern Presbyterians could rein in or silence its apostates. To that end, Faulkner wrote copiously, authoring by one count over forty pamphlets and many articles that elaborated the danger of the contemporary trend toward "modernism" in the church. From his position as an influential businessman and Sunday school superintendent at Hatties-burg's First Presbyterian Church, he enjoyed a following of like-minded coreligionists in the city, the state, and beyond.[73]

Though conservative discontent with "liberal" trends concentrated heavily in Mississippi, these disgruntled Methodists and Presbyterians expressed concerns felt in many quarters of their denominations. Mis-sissippians participated in strong religious networks and maintained important national connections with others who shared their views and anxieties, and their associations crossed denominational lines and regional boundaries. Mississippi Methodists who organized the Vol-untary Committee of Christian Laymen in 1950 to oppose the liberal tendencies in the denomination joined a network of other such lay-men's groups around the country with similar agendas and aspirations. For his part, Faulkner corresponded with an array of conservatives throughout the country, including the far-right Verne P. Kaub of the American Council of Christian Laymen in Madison, Wisconsin, and the South Carolina newspaper reporter William Workman. Bob Shuler of the *Methodist Challenge* honored the Mississippian as a "mighty Presbyterian" in his own ultra-conservative organ.[74]

Thus, though denominational trends thrust many Mississippians into national religious connections that challenged the racial hierarchy along with its theological underpinnings, others resisted denomina-tional initiatives regarding race, reinvigorated their religious conserva-tism, and reached out to create or join new networks of their own. Yet if Mississippi evangelicals objected to faith-based pleas for racial justice, they had not yet heard any clarion religious voice call for an outright dismantling of segregation. Absent such a demand, denominational leaders' admonitions that Christians should act fairly or "recognize the image of God in every man" fizzled for want of urgency. Certainly many white Mississippians in the daily lived reality of segregation regarded the institution as natural, timeless, and invulnerable to threat—exactly as they had structured it to appear. Those who so wished could easily dismiss the pronouncements of progressive denominational material as mere distant carping. In 1954, however, the situation changed dramati-cally when the Supreme Court issued the *Brown v. Board of Education* decision declaring segregated schools unconstitutional, and all three denominations heartily endorsed it.

3

Responding to *Brown*

The Recalcitrant Parish

Southern Baptists descended on St. Louis for their annual convention a mere two weeks after the U.S. Supreme Court issued its watershed *Brown v. Board of Education* ruling in May of 1954. With the South already seething over the decision, the thousands of Baptist messengers anticipated some sort of convention statement on the subject, as did their constituents at home. Likely few, however, expected that the Southern Baptist Convention (SBC) would endorse the *Brown* decision so resoundingly. The Convention's Christian Life Commission (CLC) declared the decision "in harmony with the constitutional guarantee of equal freedom to all citizens, and with the Christian principles of equal justice and love for all men." Jesse Weatherspoon gave the report a needed boost for adoption, imploring his coreligionist not to signal that America could "count Baptists out in the matter of equal justice." Spontaneous applause filled the hall when nearly 10,000 Baptist messengers approved the CLC resolution, while a negligible minority objected. As if to absorb both the promise and the peril of this moment, the messengers erupted in a stirring chorus of "He Leadeth Me," the traditional Baptist hymn of surrender.[1]

The enthusiastic endorsement of *Brown* in St. Louis, however, contrasted sharply with the censure the CLC report met in Mississippi. The SBC's approval of the decision stunned Baptists in the Magnolia State and riled segregationists of all faiths; indeed, it ignited local indignation like kerosene on fire. Phone calls expressing shock and betrayal inundated the state association's office. A few churches even threatened to sever their connections with the SBC. The *Baptist Record* received so much mail about *Brown* and the SBC endorsement that editor Dr. Arthur Leon Goodrich claimed it would take "a year to print it all."[2]

Bodies representing the Methodist Church and the Presbyterian Church, U.S., also endorsed the principle of racial equality shortly after the High Court announced the *Brown* decision, and their proclamations also elicited fierce objections from their Mississippi constituents. Denominational support for *Brown* confirmed the worst suspicions of these evangelicals, who monitored the progressive racial goings-on at the highest echelons of their fellowships. In their eyes, these institutions had tossed aside all appropriate caution and made official their status as a threat to segregation. In short, the keepers of their own faith had joined the forces arrayed against white Mississippians' way of life.

Post-war conversation about the meanings and implications of the faith mushroomed into a full-blown argument after *Brown*. Faced with official word from their denominations that segregation represented an unchristian social arrangement, Mississippians Christians shot back their own edicts. They found no mandate against the racial hierarchy in their traditions, and they refused to violate their own sensibilities by lowering the color bar. How could the segregation they had practiced for decades suddenly become "unchristian" by fiat? Yet, in spite of strong opposition to the idea of desegregation, a few moderates expressed agreement—even a sense of relief—that their religious leaders had embraced a vision of racial equality.

Some have criticized these denominational dictums as too little, too late, too tepid, and utterly lacking enforcement. Certainly black activists in the trenches could have used more binding action from white Protestants decades earlier. On the other hand, a few have marshaled these statements and other evidence to overstate white religious support for ending the racial hierarchy. When viewed from the eyes of the denominations' Mississippi constituency, however, these endorsements appear neither utterly innocuous, nor do they indicate a pervasive evangelical commitment to black equality.[3]

Even before the *Brown* announcement on May 17, 1954, and throughout the remainder of that spring and summer, the issue of integration—whether it could be avoided, how it might be avoided, why it must be avoided—dominated Mississippi's public discourse. Because the denominations' support for *Brown* appeared, in some cases, within days of the High Court's decision, Mississippians often seemed to conflate the Court with their denominational hierarchy, considering the religious implications of segregation's demise alongside its political and legal aspects. As the state actively obstructed the civil rights quest, the churches contributed considerable energy to the culture and the strategies of resistance. Restive evangelicals needed little encouragement to serve as effective censors of integrationist ideology, and they lent an aura of righteous legitimacy to the state's own methods of defiance.

Soul Liberty: "Each Church Is a Rule unto Itself"

The Supreme Court's *Brown* decision signified a turning point in African Americans' long struggle for equality. In one sweeping gesture, the ruling overturned the legal precedent for "separate but equal" facilities affirmed in the *Plessy v. Ferguson* decision of 1896. With a sense that the law stood firmly on their side, an emboldened black community redoubled their insistence on dismantling the Jim Crow system in all its facets. The ranks of black activists swelled, and the fronts on which they waged their battle multiplied.[4]

Brown also marked a new era for the white South. It signaled a commitment to black equality from the federal government, though that commitment would often prove tenuous in ensuing years. Depriving southern states of the legal foundation for operating segregated school systems—a lynchpin of black inferiority—the decision sounded a death knell for all expressions of Jim Crow. White southerners determined not to relinquish their privileges easily. State governments and private citizens mounted an organized campaign to maintain whites' political, economic, and legal superiority, and Mississippi formed the vanguard of this resistance. This effort to avoid compliance with the High Court's decision, known by scholars as massive resistance, required tremendous political will, canny legal maneuvering, and immense public support.[5]

Once the denominations declared support for *Brown*, national religious institutions appeared as menacing to the southern way of life as the Supreme Court, and the churches thus quickly joined the opposition to integration. Though strongly tied to their national institutions, Mississippi's Christian citizens functioned as valuable lieutenants in the state's program of massive resistance. Baptists, Methodists, and Presbyterians stymied integrationist arguments of religious origins by stifling, drowning out, or contravening both the national church and their local coreligionists of more moderate inclinations. They began by vigorously denouncing the denominational endorsements of desegregation.

The small pool of dissenting votes in St. Louis had included an absentee ballot read to the Convention on behalf of Dr. Douglas Hudgins, already en route back to Jackson, where he commanded the pulpit of one of the SBC's largest congregations. Though he rarely addressed racial issues from the pulpit, Hudgins dispelled his congregation's rampant dismay in his message the next Sunday. He diluted the impact of the Convention report by minimizing the support for it, claiming that "the resolution passed, but with a large dissenting vote." He went on to depict such matters as outside the purview of Baptist concerns: "there were many, many attending this Convention who believed sincerely, honestly and out of conviction and judgment that any resolution on a purely civic matter was neither appropriate nor necessary before a religious body." Hudgins sealed his disavowal of the CLC report with a lengthy explanation of Baptist polity, assuring parishioners that the autonomy of local churches made the decisions of the Convention "actions of subjective co-operation. They are not authoritarian, nor disciplinary. . . . We have within our organization, therefore, the right to say that we will or will not follow cooperatively with our brethren."[6]

As editor of the *Baptist Record*, Dr. Arthur Leon Goodrich also rendered the CLC resolutions meaningless for his readers. Though he employed slightly different language, he based his objections on exactly the same premises that Hudgins used. Portraying the Convention as deeply divided, he ignored the one-hundred-to-one ratio by which the report had passed. Insisting, rather, that the report had caused "the chagrin of many," he dismissed the notion that it reflected "the will of all or most of the people." Goodrich then criticized the Convention for even addressing the issue. The CLC report, in his mind, constituted "the lowest point of the whole Convention, because the Christian Life Commission went out of its field to dip its finger in politics. . . . We are very indignant at any suggestion of a breakdown of the wall of separation between church and state." After so thoroughly condemning the resolutions, however, Goodrich virtually dismissed them on the grounds of Baptist polity: "our readers need not fear any results from this action. No Convention can bind any Baptist church. Each church is a rule unto itself."[7]

Throughout the state, pulpit and pew joined the groundswell of denunciation, indicating that Mississippi Baptists needed little encouragement to resist black equality. Though Hudgins and Goodrich correctly noted that the resolution "could not bind local Baptist Churches," pastors, congregations, and individual laymen still threw it in the SBC's face. First Baptist Church of Grenada and its pastor, Dr. Jack Landrum, drafted a four-part resolution that echoed the main points of Hudgins' and Goodrich's commentaries, and then repudiated the notion "that all Southern Baptists endorse the action of the Supreme Court on this or any other decision." The resolution concluded with a threat: "a continuation of such actions by the Southern Baptist Convention could eventually cause the withdrawal of this and other churches from cooperation with the Southern Baptist Convention."[8] Many applauded the Grenada congregation's "courageous" stand, while others urged their own churches to take similar action.[9] A deacon of a Columbus, Mississippi, church praised Goodrich for renouncing the CLC resolutions, and he asked for continued resistance if the Mississippi State Baptist Convention endorsed the resolutions at its November meeting: "if the proposition pops up, we are depending on a filibuster from men like you."[10] A prominent judge believed that "churches that [endorse the Supreme Court decision] are resting their foundation on sand."[11] One layman encouraged more Mississippi Baptists to join the tide of opposition: "Now is the time for Baptist people to let the leaders know that they made a very unwise and hurtful move at the convention, and that handing down decisions from the top is not the best way to get the cooperation of Baptist people."[12] Some churches announced they would withhold contributions to the CLC.[13]

Mississippi's secular press also chronicled the SBC resolution and its disastrous reception in the state. The *Hattiesburg American* featured the remarks of a layman who warned church leaders against such progressive action: "Southern Baptists violated the very foundation of the South when they said out with segregation . . . your move at St. Louis will be the final blow."[14] The *Meridian Star* sent a reporter to the churches to ask for commentary. Reverend R. H. Fitzgerald of Russell Baptist Church responded, "I do not have any hard feelings toward the Negro race, but I think it is best for both races to remain segregated." When Dr. Walter L. Moore of Meridian's First Baptist Church addressed the issue in a Sunday sermon, he quickly turned to the issue of interracial worship: "I know of not a single [black Mississippian] who would be at all interested in joining this church. They are loyal to their own churches, and they also have some race prejudice."[15] A leading member of Moore's church, "speaking for himself and some other members who . . . had expressed themselves openly," affirmed his fervor for "maintaining segregation for the spiritual good of both races."[16] A few pastors contacted by the *Star*, however, replied with only innocuous platitudes—"[A] solution will require a considerable amount of time with the most competent and Christian thinking to be found in our nation today"—or the even more evasive, "No comment."[17]

Mississippi Baptists' most consistent remonstrance relied on the Baptist traditions of local church autonomy and "soul liberty." Perhaps to an extent greater than any other American faith tradition, Baptists claim the right to follow the dictates of their own consciences against the directives of an ecclesiastical hierarchy. This notion informs Baptist polity, in which local congregations maintain independence in government, doctrine, and ministry. No governing authority oversees Baptist ministers or enforces moral and doctrinal standards. As such, the Southern Baptist Convention exists only for the one week each year that messengers—so called because they have no actual delegated authority—from its member churches gather as a collective body. The system, designed to protect individuals from a dictatorial religious leadership, creates a Baptist ministry that often responds quite thoroughly to local conditions. As Mississippi Baptists' deployed this important principle after the *Brown* decision, their segregationist preferences acquired the legitimacy of a lofty and proud virtue, and their defiance of the SBC appeared only the exercise of a religious principle they claimed with pride.[18]

Baptists' glory in their recalcitrance lent a ring of righteous dissent to the state's insistence that it, too, could plot and follow its own course. Indeed, the notion of local church autonomy bore a strong resemblance to the principle of interposition, one of segregationists' most cherished legal tools. Mississippians had long evoked states' rights to oppose measures that would undermine the racial hierarchy, arguing against anti-poll tax and anti-lynching legislation on the grounds that such laws would usurp the state's authority in its own affairs. After the *Brown* decision, the principle of states' rights found new life in the notion that states had not only the right, but also the obligation, to "interpose" their own sovereignty when the federal government exceeded its constitutional powers. Many southern legislatures passed interposition resolutions in the early months of 1956, and Mississippi's own declaration of this doctrine proclaimed the *Brown* decision "null, void, and of no effect" within its borders.[19] Though most Mississippians no doubt little understood the intricacies of interposition, they eagerly wrapped their racial sentiments with this cloak of high-minded dissent. The preponderance of the white population, Mississippi Baptists nurtured themselves on a religion that relished precisely the same kind of local independence. Little wonder, then, that Mississippi governors and legislators defied the federal government with overwhelming popular support.

"Our Efforts Will Be Fraught with Peril": Mississippi Methodists and the *Brown* Decision

Methodists convene as a national body only once every four years, and the *Brown* case did not fall in a General Conference year. Thus, Methodism's national representative voice did not have opportunity to issue a quick response to *Brown*, as did Baptist and Presbyterian assemblies. Nonetheless, various national Methodist agencies endorsed the decision immediately. In keeping with their already established race relations efforts, the Methodist Women of the Society of Christian Service, meeting in Milwaukee in June, declared their "determination . . . to work with greater urgency for elimination of segregation," and "pledge[d] to work through church and community to speed transition from segregated schools." Later that month, Methodist college students from thirteen southern states—including Mississippi—called for church-wide support of the decision. In July, the National Conference of Methodist Men pledged active support for the Supreme Court's ruling, and only days later the denomination's General Board of Evangelism declared, "We rejoice in the recent decision of the Supreme Court on segregation in the schools. We believe it is in the right direction of a fully integrated Christian society . . . We expect our people everywhere to cooperate with state and school authorities in implementing the decision of the Supreme Court."[20]

But deep cleavages over race vexed the Methodist Church even at the highest echelons, a reality that burst into public view when the Methodist Council of Bishops met in Chicago in November. In a separate caucus preparatory to the meeting, the eight bishops of the Southeastern Jurisdiction specifically asked the Council to keep silent on the High Court's decision: "we are convinced that any statement from the Council at this time will result in no great gain and will make our task more difficult. We therefore respectfully request that you, our colleagues, refrain from making any further statement at this time." Yet the Council ignored the request of their southern colleagues, issuing a firm declaration: "One of the foundation stones of our faith is the belief that all men are brothers. The church is furnished with an unequaled opportunity to provide leadership in support of the principle involved in the action of the Court. We accept this responsibility." The eight southern bishops returned home to take the extraordinary step of publicly disassociating themselves from their brethren. Even the bishops' newly elected president, Alabamian Clare Purcell, announced to the press his displeasure with the Council's action.[21]

As one of the eight dissenting bishops, Mississippian Marvin Franklin immediately issued a disclaimer that put distance between the Council of Bishops and his constituency. Methodist ecclesiastical structure does not emphasize local church autonomy as Baptist polity does, but Franklin nonetheless highlighted the Council's lack of authority over local Methodist life. Reminding his hearers that the Council claimed no legislative powers in the church, he predicted that their statement would "have little or no effect on Mississippi Methodists." Like Baptists who noted the lack of unanimity on the SBC's endorsement of *Brown,* Franklin pointed to the eight southern bishops as evidence that the Council's statement "did not give the full picture." Finally, Franklin repeated a familiar objection by criticizing the statement as "not timely," reassuring his constituents that Methodist polity allowed for sufficient diversity of belief among its members: "The Methodist Church respects the honesty and integrity of all members of our respective areas."[22]

In spite of Bishop Franklin's attempts to preempt panic among Mississippi Methodists, church members—individually and corporately— added their own renunciations of the Council of Bishops' statement and those of other Methodist agencies. Angry parishioners telephoned or wrote Franklin's office to register their disapproval. The board of the First Methodist Church in Lexington, Mississippi, declared: "This board disavows the stand and repudiates any suggestion that this church be bound by their stand." The Cleveland District of the North Mississippi Conference carried the implications of the *Brown* decision straight to interracial worship: "if we permit Negroes to become members and worship in our white churches our efforts . . . will be fraut [*sic*] with peril, resulting in untold bitterness and racial hatred that will result in a serious split in the Methodist Church."[23] Church boards in Starkville and Indianola passed similar resolutions.[24] Mrs. F. T. Clark of Ruleville wrote the *Advocate*'s editor, "I most certainly do not agree [with these statements] . . . . If, however, this is to be the stand chosen by the Methodist Church in intergration [*sic*] then what about our schools like Millsaps? Are they to be opened to any Negro who ask [*sic*] for admission?"[25] Delegates of the annual North Mississippi meeting of the Women's Society of Christian Service (WSCS) overwhelmingly rejected the position of the national WSCS, on the grounds that it "seeks to break down segregation within the women's groups and eventually could result in integration of the church congregations themselves." However, the same women's group in the Mississippi Conference responded to the efforts of more moderate women and they took the opposite step, refusing to rescind support for the WSCS's racial charter.[26]

The presence of an African American constituency in the church, though segregated both administratively and physically, gave concrete foundations to white Methodists' concerns that endorsement of *Brown* might mean integration in local churches. Congregations like Galloway Memorial Methodist in Jackson passed a resolution to maintain racial distinctions in the church. The memorial, adopted by a decisive vote of the congregation's Board of Stewards, urged Methodist leaders to "use all rightful means to oppose any attempt to change the present law of the Methodist church respecting the separate jurisdictions for the White and Negro memberships," and it called on other "congregations, official boards, and organized groups within the church . . . to pass suitable resolutions of a like nature, as memorials to General Conference."[27] Weeks later, the annual meeting of the Mississippi Conference received similar memorials about preserving the segregated jurisdictional system.[28]

While the *Brown* decision and the national church leaders' endorsement of it raised the hackles of many outspoken Mississippi Methodists, others endeavored to steer a less reactionary course. The *Mississippi Methodist Advocate,* under the direction of its moderate editor, Clinton T. Howell, carried articles and news items revealing that Methodists in the South harbored opinions about race and segregation that varied over a complicated continuum. Howell featured the comments of Methodist leaders like Alabama Conference Missions Secretary Paul Duffy, who urged readers to "move forward into a new day of Christian brotherhood." In one issue, Howell endeavored to foster a healthy debate by featuring opposing opinion pieces side by side. One author suggested that racism in American churches hurt the work of missions overseas, while the other argued for continued segregation because black Methodists "preferred their own churches." Both pieces evoked positive responses, and one reader expressed appreciation for the *Advocate's* fair-mindedness: "Those of us who sit in the middle of the situation know that there are two schools of thought, and certainly church people are entitled to be informed on both."[29]

Yet, its very moderation, its commitment to presenting the full range of Methodist opinion, made the *Advocate* appear a potentially threatening conduit of integrationist sentiment to church folk who wanted to stymie any religious condemnation of segregation. Conservative Methodists circulated resolutions that suggested the *Advocate* "praises the Supreme Court decision and approves integration." Howell countered that he only endeavored "to enable the Methodists of the Area [*sic*] to get a clear picture of the thinking and acting of others over the Methodist Church, who either hold the readers [*sic*] point of view or an opposite one."[30]

Mississippi Methodists with strong segregationist inclinations intended to halt any possibility of integration in the church. A contingent of such ministers and laymen joined others from five southern states in Birmingham in December 1954, vowing to halt racial mixing in the church. The following March in Jackson, Mississippians kicked off their own statewide organization, the Mississippi Association of Methodist Ministers and Layman (MAMML). Already alienated by the increasingly progressive orientation of the denomination, this group opposed any change to the segregated jurisdictional system, and they encouraged their coreligionists to boycott official church publications that seemed to promote integration in church or society. While they shared goals similar to segregationist Methodists in other southern states, the leadership of the Mississippi group overlapped extensively with leaders of the Citizens' Councils, a newly formed grassroots organization devoted to preserving segregation.[31]

The church's endorsement of the *Brown* decision exacerbated long-standing fissures among Mississippi Methodists. It galvanized segregationists' commitments to preserve their racially based jurisdictional system, while moderates among them strove to broadcast the voice of the national church and to keep the avenues of thought open. Perhaps most significantly, Marvin Franklin, the titular leader of the Mississippi church, had been unable either to endorse or to explicitly reject the Bishops' statement on the *Brown* decision, and his mousy equivocation would leave a leadership vacuum eagerly filled by those below him. Over the next decade, these burgeoning cracks in Mississippi Methodism would develop into an unbreachable chasm.

A Christian View on Segregation: Mississippi Presbyterians and the *Brown* Decision

Only days after the *Brown* decision, the General Assembly of the Southern Presbyterian Church issued not one, but two, statements that assaulted segregation. A year in preparation, the first document reflected the attitudes and work of progressive leaders. Titled "The Church and Segregation," the report described segregation as "the subordination of one people to another." It urged the removal of racial barriers, asked the General Assembly to condemn segregation as unchristian, and asserted that the church should "lead rather than follow." The second document, "A Statement to Southern Christians" affirmed the principle of racial equality, denied that the Bible advocated segregation, explicitly endorsed the *Brown* decision, and called upon southern Presbyterians "to lend their assistance to those charged with the duty of implementing the decision."[32]

Even as the General Assembly debated the two statements, Mississippians led the charge against them. One pastor pleaded with the Assembly to reject both documents, claiming that "the whole philosophy of our idea of the Negro has been called in question." While claiming that he "d[id] love the Negro," he also insisted that "some of us believe that God made two races."[33] When word reached Mississippi that the General Assembly had adopted the "Statement to Southern Christians" by a vote of 236 to 169, First Presbyterian Church in Jackson issued one of the first and most scathing indictments: "These pronouncements so violate the traditions of the Southern Presbyterian Church and so seriously threaten the peace and purity of the Church that they must not go unanswered . . . this Session unanimously declares that this Church will not follow the recent advice of the General Assembly urging nonsegregation. [*sic*] And declares that segregation of the races is not discrimination and declares that this Church shall, with good-will toward all men, maintain traditional policy and practice of distinct separation of the races."[34] Other Mississippi Presbyterians joined the outcry against the General Assembly. Reverend R. L. McLaurin of Oakland Heights Presbyterian Church in Meridian defended segregation as the will of God: "I am opposed to and think that the recent Supreme Court decision is in violation and contradiction to the Scripture teachings on segregation." At Meridian's First Presbyterian, Dr. J. Kelly Unger invoked the independence of the local church, adding, "[W]e do not have a need for this in Mississippi since our colored people have their own churches. I am sure that the colored people are happier with their people and ministers and are satisfied."[35]

A Jackson Presbyterian pastor privately confided that "feelings were running high" in response to the General Assembly's statements.[36] Certainly strong emotions erupted when each of the state's five presbyteries met that fall. When the notoriously conservative Meridian Presbytery gathered, a member of Bay Street Church in Hattiesburg wanted to condemn the General Assembly, but offered language that "was too strong even for Meridian Presbytery." Though the moderator tried to control the discussion, it "quickly degenerated into racial intermarriage."[37] The presbytery went on to adopt a resolution that "deplore[d] action of the General Assembly in its recommendation concerning segregation" and "refuse[d] to accept said recommendation as wise, or binding upon our consciences." Though fifty-five members of the presbytery favored the resolution of defiance, eight voted against it, and three recorded a protest in the minutes.[38] The presbytery also requested the

General Assembly to "instruct the agencies of our Church to refrain from publishing articles pro or con regarding the abolition of segregation of the races," as well as to abolish the Division of Christian Relations, the denomination's agency that handled all race-relations work.[39] In other Mississippi presbyteries, members wanted to censure the General Assembly, and one requested the General Assembly to "reconsider and rescind" its statement.[40]

At its annual meeting in November of 1954, the Mississippi Synod heard two responses to the "Statement to Southern Christians." The colorful, moderate Reverend Robert Walkup of Starkville urged the Synod to ignore the recalcitrant voices in the state and support the General Assembly's position. However, the highly esteemed Mississippi Presbyterian statesman Dr. G. T. Gillespie objected to Walkup's position and offered a substitute report.[41] Echoing the principles by which Baptists and Methodists rejected their denominations' pronouncements, Gillespie denounced the General Assembly's recommendations. Arguing that segregation, as a social and political issue, lay outside ecclesiastical concerns, Gillespie claimed the Assembly's statements were "in error." He maintained that the Synod "cannot place the stamp of its approval upon [the] recommendation that . . . churches . . . admit persons to membership and fellowship without reference to race." In a final gesture of defiance, Gillespie requested that the General Assembly rescind its "progressive" statements on race.[42] The Synod displayed both its largely conservative inclinations and its willful intransigence by voting down Walkup's report and adopting Gillespie's. Importantly however, moderates in the Synod registered strong disagreement with Gillespie's statements, and thirty-nine of the Synod's ninety-nine members signed a dissent that would communicate this position to the General Assembly. Indeed, Mississippi Presbyterians maintained their recalcitrance over the objections of a sizeable minority.[43]

Gillespie's report by no means delivered his soul of all he had to say on the subject of the Christian faith and segregation. In making his case before the Synod, he launched into a lengthy defense of racial separation. Claiming that America faced a choice between "the Anglo-Saxon ideal of racial integrity maintained by a consistent application of the principle of segregation, and the Communist goal of amalgamation," Gillespie asserted that all of nature respected the laws of segregation:

"under natural conditions . . . bluebirds never mate with redbirds, doves never mate with black birds, nor mockingbirds with jays." Defending segregation as "not unchristian," he launched into a tour-de-force of segregationist proof-texts; the sons of Ham, the tower of Babel, the call of Abraham, the law of Moses, the warnings of the prophets, the day of Pentecost, all found a place in Gillespie's canon of biblical blessings on racial separation and purity, with each example building to a culmination in "that great multitude that bowed before the Lamb in the future celestial city," a throng "of the peoples of every nation, kindred, race and language blended into a beautiful and harmonious unity, and yet each preserving its own distinctive genius and virtues, the better to shew forth the infinite riches and diversity of the Divine glory and grace throughout the ages to come."[44]

Gillespie's segregationist peroration became a much talked-about polemic. The newly formed Citizens' Council reprinted his address as "A Christian View on Segregation" and added it to its arsenal of segregationist apologetics. Though it clearly expressed Mississippi evangelicals' resistance to integration, the pamphlet's appearance as the definitive view obscured its origins as a victory speech after a row with a substantial minority. The speech also traveled extensively outside Mississippi, where it served as the basis for wider Presbyterian discussions about race. The conservative North Carolina-based *Southern Presbyterian Journal* printed it as a "fine and rational" elucidation of the periodical's own viewpoints. The more liberal *Presbyterian Outlook* featured Gillespie's argument alongside responses from Union Theological Seminary faculty who critiqued its scriptural and logical foundations.[45]

Thus, in spite of their denominations' endorsement of desegregation, Mississippi members of the South's three largest Protestant communions registered strong disagreement with the denominational authorities. Choosing between the call of national religious leaders and the tug of local traditions, most Mississippi Christians indicated a clear preference for the southern way of life. Segregationist evangelicals in the Magnolia State regarded their denominational leadership as the source of a surreptitious and pernicious ideology, and they joined the project of massive resistance by turning back the religious critique of segregation at the state's borders.

Sacrificial Lambs

While evangelicals' outcry against their national leadership echoed from the Delta to the coast and back to Memphis, a few religious voices broke with popular opinion. At least some Mississippi pastors affirmed their denominations' critique of segregation. Reverend Jack Southerland of Meridian claimed, "the statement adopted by the Southern Baptist Convention [is] in keeping with Christian principle."[46] The assistant pastor of Forty-First Avenue Baptist Church in the same city argued, "Regardless what one's personal views might be in this matter, he must recognize that Christ would have all men to live together in equality and brotherly love."[47] Dr. Frank M. Cross of Central Presbyterian Church in Meridian announced, "My church affirms that segregation is un-Christian. The State rules that segregation is unlawful. As a Christian and a citizen, I accept and will abide by these decisions of my Church and State."[48] From the Delta town of Belzoni, Reverend Chester Molpus of First Baptist Church watched the heady defiance of the Magnolia parish and found it absurd. Molpus had attended the SBC meeting in St. Louis, where he voted for the adoption of the CLC recommendations. Molpus believed that the Convention "took the painfully right action" in endorsing the *Brown* decision, and that "the voice of Christian leaders ought not be silent" on the issue of segregation.[49]

Molpus' long history with his congregation no doubt spared him the fate of Stanley Smith of Shady Grove Baptist Church. Shady Grove belonged to the Copiah County Baptist Association, which roundly condemned the CLC for "writing and teaching and otherwise pressing for radical departure from the time-tested and proven policy of segregation in local churches."[50] When Smith and four other pastors refused to endorse this statement, the Shady Grove congregation punished their pastor quickly and decisively. Word circulated in both church and community that he "voted to let 'niggers' into the church." The preacher tried "to give my testimony in behalf of racial understanding and in opposition to racial discrimination," but found the "people of such deep-seated racial prejudice" that he could get neither "a sympathetic hearing" nor "a receptive hearing." Though Smith tried to preempt them, the deacons visited on their pastor the consequences of his soul liberty and drove him from the Shady Grove pulpit within two weeks. The high priests of segregation had begun the sacrifice of ministerial lambs.[51]

Indeed, the denominations' endorsements of *Brown* moved Mississippians to draw racial lines even more clearly than before. In Holmes County, Dr. David Minter and Gene Cox ran a farm and a medical clinic for the county's rural poor, both black and white. When a black child, in a panic under interrogation by whites, confirmed rumors of "interracial swimming" at the farm, local white leaders hauled Minter and Cox before a throng of over 500 people that included two state legislators, a number of lawyers, and other "leading people." During a long inquisition, members of the crowd demanded, "Do you believe in segregation?" Cox replied, "I believe that segregation is unChristian." One planter shot back, "This ain't no Christian meetin'," the mob drowning him out in approval. The sensational mock trial came to a crescendo as the interrogators voted to "banish them from the county." During the questioning, the local Presbyterian pastor stood up to protest the treatment of Minter and Cox. The crowd booed the Reverend Marsh Calloway, and days later his small congregation sacked their sixty-year-old minister.[52]

Mississippians axed Smith, Cox, Minter, and Calloway because they advocated a faith that challenged the racial hierarchy. Tellingly, Cox and Minter had run their interracial ministry unmolested for seventeen years. Yet, once the prospect of integration won the endorsement of the South's major religious bodies, Cox's proclamation that "segregation is unChristian" appeared threatening in a way his long-standing and quiet endeavors had not. In the changed context after 1954, these parishioners believed they had done their communities the favor of removing a dangerous heterodoxy from their midst. Upon learning of Smith's fate, the Mississippi Baptist State Association's executive secretary-treasurer, Dr. Chester Quarles, wrote to the executive committee of the SBC: "Friends, these are significant and stragetic [*sic*] days in Mississippi. Pray for all of us. I have no doubt that other pastors will lose their churches in the near future because of their stand against resolutions and motions made by intemperate brethren." Tragically, Quarles comments would prove all too prescient.[53]

4

"A Strange and Serious Christian Heresy"

Massive Resistance and the Religious Defense of Segregation

"During the past two years there has been a deluge of materials spread over the face of the South in which various Biblical proofs are given for divine sanction of racial segregation . . . not only the ignorant wool-hat-hill folk [are] accepting the exegesis of the hate mongers but the more refined as well. . . . The pamphlets, articles, and tracts [are] written by preachers and religious educators well known in the circle of the target audience." Thus observed Will Campbell, the progressive Mississippi Baptist expatriate, in 1957.[1] The writer Lillian Smith confirmed that "[t]here is a great deal of this kind of talk going around these days, quoting chapter and verse, etc."[2] Other religious leaders described how "many segregationists cloak their activities with quotations from the scriptures . . . [and] claims [are] made by certain ministers that the Bible endorse[s] segregation."[3] Indeed, southern Christians seemed so zealous to cite biblical proofs for segregation that Campbell concluded "some of the racial hate being peddled in the name of Jesus Christ" constituted "a strange and serious Christian heresy."[4]

The biblical case for racial segregation enjoyed a renaissance after the *Brown* decision because religion itself seemed a threat to southern apartheid. Religious assaults on segregation included the major denominations' support for *Brown*, the faith-based activism of many black leaders, and the growing conviction in some circles that the Christian faith mandated racial equality. While black activists and their sympathizers wished that white religion would offer a more vigorous call to racial justice, white southerners regarded as dangerous even the limited support religion had conferred on the quest for black equality.

The faith-based indictment of the southern social system, left unchallenged and allowed to grow, could prove disastrous for the project of massive resistance. If Mississippians heeded the voices of their coreligionists outside the Deep South, their energy for the fight against integration might flag. If they heard about the sinfulness of segregation in their churches and religious literature, they might come to doubt the rightness of Mississippi's path of defiance. Surely, they would lack the conviction to resist the Supreme Court, to suffer the closing of public schools, and to visit punishment on their fellows who violated the bonds of white solidarity. Only at great peril could massive resisters forego a religious defense, for the moral challenge to segregation could cost their campaign what it needed most—the enthusiastic and unwavering support of ordinary Mississippians. Because religion now jeopardized segregation, segregationists called on religion to defend it.

The religious case for segregation took a variety of guises and appeared in many places in the form of an influential and pervasive phenomenon Paul Harvey has described as "segregationist folk theology." Though it drew on biblical texts describing the curse of Ham, the tower of Babel, and the example of Israel as a racially exclusive people, segregationist folk theology functioned as an orthodoxy that wove together biblical literalism, political conservatism, and racial segregation, elevating all three to equally revered status. Tugging at any single strand constituted a heretical unraveling of the entire fabric. Those who articulated these ideas took as natural and God-ordained the social world they saw around them, but except for the essential assumption that heaven smiled on the racial hierarchy, the arguments they marshaled displayed little consistency.[5]

Given the thorough blending of its secular and religious aspects, this belief system cropped up in venues outside pulpits, Sunday school classes, radio sermons, and religious literature. Indeed, segregationist folk theology found expression nearly everywhere—in secular newspapers and organizations, at the state's universities and schools, at county rallies, and in legislative chambers. Though it lay dormant much of the time, when segregation seemed imperiled, it erupted with fury through the normally placid surface of life-as-usual.

Mississippi lawmakers in the post-*Brown* era wanted to give a legal and political expression to the divine plan for the races. Thus they offered protection to congregations that perceived a danger to segregation from their own denominations. Yet, here the story takes a curious

turn, for Mississippians disagreed, not about God's will regarding segregation, but about the extent to which the religion of outsiders really
threatened it. Indeed, many white Mississippians, convinced that their
racial system lay safe in the church's uncompromising hands, objected
to this intrusion of the state into religious affairs.

Segregationist Folk Theology

Paul Harvey describes the folk theology of segregation as "handed down
naturally, as confirmed dogma, a set of assumptions about the divine
ordering of the social world."[6] This worldview's informal and unsophisticated character strains categorization as "theology," since it would
have failed the standards of hermeneutics in any seminary classroom.
Nonetheless, those who elaborated its tenets described their most essential assumptions about God, the created order, and the moral laws of
the universe. Their logic followed a sort of callow, common-sense reasoning, drawing support from the natural world, from racial relationships as southerners had long known them, from global political and
economic conditions, and finally, from a reading of the Bible that, not
surprisingly, read the segregation white Mississippians so cherished into
the text as a divine mandate. The multifaceted nature of this religious
defense—its reliance on a variety of extra-biblical evidence and claims—
displayed the strength, rather than the weakness, of these arguments in
the minds of those who espoused them. These expositors believed they
had identified a principle so pervasive in its practice and application
that it extended beyond the Bible. In a world defined by a God-ordained
principle so significant and sacrosanct as they imagined, hierarchies of
all sorts revealed themselves throughout the created order.[7]

Layfolk and ministers without powerful denominational connections articulated this theology far more often than religious elites or
pastors of large and prominent congregations. The leaders of the Mississippi Baptist Convention, the editors of the *Baptist Record,* and the
pastor of Mississippi's largest Baptist church never gave voice to it as
such. Neither did the bishop of Mississippi's two white Methodist conferences and the pastors of large Methodist congregations. At the same
time, however, Mississippi's most influential Presbyterian leader, Dr.
G. T. Gillespie, provides an important exception to this generalization.

President of the Mississippi Synod of the Southern Presbyterian Church, Gillespie authored "A Christian View of Segregation," perhaps the best-known and most representative example of the folk theology of segregation. Gillespie and a few others notwithstanding, the folk theology of segregation came far more often from Mississippi's ordinary pastors and from its eager laymen.[8]

Of extant sermons or tracts advertised as "biblical defenses of segregation," few hewed so exclusively to biblical sources as a 1953 sermon preached by Reverend J. C. Wasson, a Methodist minister in the small Delta town of Itta Bena. Wasson offered classic segregationist readings of two texts often employed for this purpose: Genesis 9:18–27, which details the story of Noah's curse on his grandson, "Cursed be Canaan; a slave of slaves shall he be to his brothers," and Deuteronomy 7:1–6, in which God tells the children of Israel, "You shall not make marriages with [surrounding tribes], giving your daughters to their sons or taking their daughters for your sons." In elucidating the Genesis account, Wasson explained that Noah pronounced the curse because Canaan's father, Ham, having found Noah drunk and naked in his tent, had informed his brothers and so "had on this occasion treated his father with contempt or reprehensible levity." Wasson continued: "The word, Ham, means hot and it signifies burnt or black. Ham's descendants moved southward into Africa, a hot country, without any doubt this was the beginning of the niger [sic] race." Wasson preferred the spelling "niger" because, "the words negro and nigger are not in the Bible. In Acts 13:1 is the only place in the Bible where the black race is designated by its proper name: 'And Simeon that was called Niger,' niger the I is a long I, pronounced Ni-ger, the word means black." The Deuteronomy text prescribed "death" as "the penalty for violating the law of segregation," from which Wasson inferred, "No intelligent Bible student can deny that God is the author of segregation." Wasson then proceeded to identify the law of Moses as a command to "be segregated to keep their race pure" and to elucidate other Old Testament stories—the division of Israel into two kingdoms and the Babylonian captivity—as punishment for the sin of miscegenation.[9]

Another Methodist, the prominent attorney John Creighton Satterfield, elaborated the biblical foundations of segregation at a forum at Millsaps College in 1958. While acknowledging that both segregationists

and integrationists could find biblical support for their views, Satterfield proceeded to dismember integrationists' favorite passages. Explicating a passage from the apostle Paul's sermon at Mars Hill in Acts
17:26, "God has made of one blood all nations of men for to dwell on all
the face of the earth," the Methodist layman argued that integrationists
who used this verse "imply that there are no differences in men and
read into Paul's statement something that he probably did not have in
mind." Furthermore, Satterfield maintained, those who favored racial
mixing stopped reading the verse too soon. "Paul went on to say 'and
hath appointed the bounds of their habitation.'" That last phrase, Satterfield claimed, "justifies the segregation of the races." Satterfield proceeded next to Galatians 3:26–28, another reference favored by religious
enemies of segregation: "In Christ Jesus, you are sons of God through
faith—there is neither Jew nor Greek, there is neither slave nor free,
there is neither male nor female, for you are all one in Christ Jesus."
Stripping this verse of its racially egalitarian implications, Satterfield
observed: "I am sure neither you nor I believe it is necessary to abolish
the differences between male and female in order to live a Christian
life." He went on to explain that the "South's system of segregation is not
based on 'race prejudice' but on 'race preference.'"[10]

Most biblical defenses of segregation, however, did not stick so closely
to biblical texts, and many actually mixed scriptural arguments with
other types of evidence. William W. Miller's sermon, "The Bible and Segregation," presented on radio station WTOK in early March, 1956, followed this model. Even though Miller, pastor of the Bible Baptist Church
in Meridian, declared that "THE BIBLE DOES CLEARLY AND INDIS-
PUTABLY TEACH SEGREGATION OF THE RACES [emphasis in the
original]," only a fraction of his sermon enumerated the classic segregationist texts. He devoted the far greater bulk of his message to assailing
the theological credentials of those who advanced a Christian mandate
for black equality and elucidating the communist-inspired origins of the
movement for racial justice and, especially, of the NAACP. Miller concluded his address with an admonition to the "dear Negro friends and
brethren" who might have been in his listening audience: "renounce, the
devil inspired, Communist supported and directed NAACP as the slith-
ering serpent that it is. . . . Don't imagine that in following the NAACP
segregation line you are walking in the Christian faith. Don't think for a

moment that you can pray to God and get His blessing upon a course of action which is anti-thetical to the Christian faith."[11]

The Hattiesburg Baptist layman, D. B. Red, authored two tracts in the pattern of Miller's sermon. Red's "A Corrupt Tree Bringeth Forth Evil Fruit" took its title from Matthew 7:17, advertising on its cover its purpose as "A plea for RACIAL SEGREGATION Based on Scripture, History and World Conditions." The first half of the tract traced the history of Israel as a people commanded to remain distinct from those around them. Moses, Ezra, Nehemiah, and Hosea had all admonished the Israelites not to intermarry with neighboring tribes. In this rendering, as in Wasson's, the children of Israel failed to obey, sought integration, and reaped dire consequences. Red then turned from biblical texts to world politics, history, and geology. He cited turmoil in Africa and India as a result of integration, explained the role of communism in instigating the movement for racial equality, offered the example of Reconstruction as a moment when the South almost lost its way in the face of forced integration, and finally, detailed the beauty of the created order: "Was it not wise to separate the various minerals instead of pouring them all together?" Mississippi's Senator James O. Eastland endorsed the tract for its "masterful job in marshalling both biblical and secular arguments." Red's other self-published tract, "Race Mixing A Religious Fraud," used much of the same material as an attempt to answer religious "race mixers" who advocated integration. Red admonished in his closing paragraphs: "Is your denomination helping to push us down the Devil's highway of racial integration? If so, remember who is paying the bills and whose civilization is going down the drain. . . . The best way to be heard is to speak through the ballot box and collection plate."[12]

Mississippians contributed to and drank from the stream of tracts and sermon reprints with similar themes, content, and format that circulated throughout the South. While probably the most famous and well-traveled biblical defense of segregation came from the Mississippi Presbyterian divine, Dr. G. T. Gillespie, his polemic also leaned heavily on secular as well as religious arguments, though its Citizens' Council promoters circulated it under the title "A Christian View on Segregation." The piece began by describing white southerners' abhorrence of racial intermarriage as part of their elevated culture and depicted segregation as a universal law of nature that resulted in improvements wherever it was applied: "The phenomenal development of the race horse, the draft horse, the beef and dairy breeds of cattle furnish impressive evidence that segregation promotes development and progress . . . whereas the intermingling of breeding stock results invariably in the production of 'scrubs' or mongrel types, and the downgrading of the whole herd." When Gillespie turned to the Bible for evidence, he cited many of the same passages and examples as those developed by Wasson and Red, and then finished with a quick tour of American history, calling on statements by Thomas Jefferson, Abraham Lincoln, and Booker T. Washington to argue that segregation "represents the best thinking of representative American leadership." Though the treatise ostensibly qualified itself by asserting that "the Bible contains no clear mandate for or against segregation," Gillespie nonetheless clearly intended to identify segregation as in keeping with the will and plan of God: "[the Bible] does furnish considerable data from which valid inferences may be drawn in support of the general principle of segregation as an important feature of the Divine purpose and Providence throughout the ages."[13]

The fine distinctions of hermeneutics and exegesis that drew fire from Gillespie's theological critics outside the state (and that still invite the musings of scholars) failed to concern the white southern layfolk who served as the pamphlet's primary audience. Gillespie and his promoters likely did not hope to convert integrationists. Rather, they primarily wanted to assure southern segregationists that the Bible did not condemn the practice. Erle Johnston, publicist for Ross Barnett's successful gubernatorial campaign and later director of the state's Sovereignty Commission, understood the goals of Gillespie's sermon and explained that it gave "those segregationists who needed some kind of Biblical inspiration to feel comfortable . . . what they wanted."[14] The address suited the purposes of the racial hierarchy so well that it became one of Governor Barnett's "favorite moral sources" when he cited "pastors and ministers of various faiths [who] supported his position."[15] Indeed, the Brandon, Mississippi, editor who claimed that "Dr. G. T. Gillespie . . . can convince anyone that segregation is neither immoral nor un-Christian and is God's will," demonstrated that legions of Mississippians understood the intent of Gillespie's message.[16]

Such pamphlets, tracts, and sermons represented the formal articulation of the biblical case for segregation, but white Mississippians more often expressed their belief in the divine nature of the racial hierarchy in less structured and formal settings. Segregationist folk theology announced itself in the ordinary operations of life; it wove itself into workday exchanges, peppered private ruminations, and bubbled up in conversation. Charging a grand jury in Scott County, Circuit Judge O. H. Barnett explained: "Segregation is right, it is Christian, and it ought to be taught in the homes and preached from every pulpit in the state and nation."[17] A Presbyterian confided to his diary that "the pure white race and the pure black have been bred naturally and by Divine Providence over a long, long period of time."[18] Similarly, a state highway patrolman demanded that a civil rights worker use his Bible to "[l]ook it up where it says about mongrelizin' of black and white degeneratin' the races." When the activist asked for the exact reference, the patrolman replied, "I don't know, but it's in there."[19]

Beliefs are "quiescent most of the time, [but] activated in crisis," as the anthropologist Michael Jackson maintains; thus Mississippians little needed to go about in ordinary times with this doctrine tripping off their tongues.[20] Yet in the changed atmosphere of the post-*Brown* challenge, the folk theology of segregation grew vigorous and strident, and it amplified still further when a special religious danger appeared on the horizon. Ole Miss's 1956 Religious Emphasis Week presented just such a moment. Here the Christian faith seemed to put segregation under threat, and the conviction that God willed white supremacy sprang roaring to life.

Policing Religious Thought: Religious Emphasis Week at Ole Miss

In February 1956, the University of Mississippi yanked the welcome mat from Reverend Alvin Kershaw, canceling his scheduled appearance as a guest speaker for Religious Emphasis Week. The institution took this step after months of pressure from segregationists who objected to the Ohio minister's support for the NAACP. Scholars often regard this affair as essentially political: it marked the final descent of "the Magnolia Curtain," as Will Campbell dubbed it, a moment of purposeful turning away from the principles of a free society in an effort to safeguard segregation. Yet Kershaw's status as a minister and representative of the Episcopal faith provoked a narrative spin-off that demonstrated the centrality of religious questions in the racial orthodoxy. Thundering their belief that God ordained racial segregation, Mississippians rejected Kershaw because he seemed the living embodiment of a dangerous heresy.[21]

While the controversy unfolded over several months late in 1955 and into early 1956, Mississippians honed in on the religious message implied in Kershaw's endorsement of the NAACP. In particular, segregationists objected to Kershaw's explicit assertion, made to the press as the affair unfolded, that "the core of religious teaching is love of God and neighbor," as well as to the more implicit suggestion in his NAACP membership.[22] A fellow Episcopal priest captured the crux of the matter by explaining to Kershaw that "the NAACP . . . is [the southerner's] open enemy and . . . as a priest of the Church, you imply that the Church . . . is also his enemy."[23] The suggestion that God might endorse the black quest for equality smacked of blasphemy to those who claimed divine sanction for the other side of this struggle; in Mississippi's enthusiastically Christian culture, practitioners of the faith rushed to protect the orthodoxy of white supremacy.

In urging revocation of Kershaw's invitation, a legislator from Brandon vigorously contravened the notion that Episcopal faith mandated a commitment to black equality: "I belong to the Episcopal church in Brandon and I can assure you the people in our church do not condone any such remarks by this preacher as symbolizing our feelings one bit. I do and will continue to believe in segregation, no matter what my religion or any preacher may say to the contrary, and I know every other redblooded [sic] Mississippian feels the same."[24] Other Mississippi Episcopalians defended the segregationist preferences of their coreligionists with traditional decorum. A Jackson woman thought their shared Episcopal heritage rendered her "a kindred spirit" with Kershaw, but asked him to change his mind about the intended gift to the NAACP because, she believed, "God created us as we are."[25] "I am appealing to you as a Christian," wrote another Episcopalian, a Jackson physician. "If you are a Christian, a true minister of Christ's gospel, and wish as He did, to promote peace and good will on earth, you will cancel your engagement at the University of Mississippi."[26]

More colorful segregationists thought Episcopal restraint too good for the likes of Kershaw. "I wouldn't want your kind of religion, and if you continue at the rate you are traveling I doubt that I will be running into you on the streets of heaven," warned one communicant.[27] After informing Kershaw that he "should not be addressed as 'Reverend' because [his] actions ma[d]e a mockery of the word," a Gulf Coast resident elucidated the divine origins of segregation for the Ohio minister: "God created and SEGREGATED the races and no individual, executive, court or Congress has either the moral or spiritual right to defy His Will by ordering or allowing racial integration. . . . The South intends to follow the Will of God and the Traditionally [sic] established right of the states, regardless of you and all of the brainwashed pro-communists like you and those in control of our present Government in Washington." The writer went on to recommend for Kershaw a rigorous course of penance: "You and all like you should discard your churchly robes that you have disgraced, clad yourselves in sackcloth, get down on your knees, grovel in the dust and humbly beg God to forgive you for your past great sins and for helping the NAACP upset the tranquil, serene communities by agitating and stirring up continuous unrest among our people."[28]

The *Jackson Daily News* and the *Clarion-Ledger* took for granted and defended both the heartfelt faith and the segregationist commitments of their readership. Their commentaries made Kershaw's religion and the implications of his actions an issue not just for Mississippi's Episcopalians—a small percentage of the state's white population—but for the vast majority of white Mississippians who claimed a Christian identity. They painted Kershaw as but one of a broader ilk of northern clergy educated in liberal, overly cerebral seminaries—institutions that had strayed from the pure, more soulful traditions of a biblical faith. Kershaw and others like him appeared simple-minded dupes who had failed to fully consider the implications of their do-good impulses. In particular, the editorialists relished the apparently strange incongruity of a Christian minister with a penchant for jazz: "This old sin-soaked world needs a lot of things but one thing it does not need is a jazzed-up Jesus," admonished the editor of the *Daily News*.[29]

Once the University had ceremoniously uninvited Kershaw, the other speakers on the program withdrew both as gestures of protest against the institution's failure to uphold free speech and to demonstrate solidarity with their ministerial colleague. The ensuing effort to rescue REW demonstrated how profoundly disturbing segregationists found it

Figure 4.1 When the Reverend Alvin Kershaw of Ohio openly supported the NAACP, Mississippians challenged the authenticity of his Christianity. By permission of the *Clarion-Ledger*.

that an argument for integration based upon the tenets of Christianity nearly cropped up in Mississippi. Some endeavored to use REW as a forum for segregationist perspectives, recommending a slate of ministers known for their vocal support of segregation. Dr. G. T. Gillespie, Dr. David M. Nelson, president of the Southern Baptist-affiliated Mississippi College, and the Reverend John Reed Miller of Jackson's First Presbyterian Church all agreed to offer vigorous doses of old-time religion that included segregationist commitments.[30] The REW committee instead chose several moderate Oxford-area ministers, but again had to redraw the plans when even these five local clergy refused to participate.[31] Organizers finally reduced that year's Religious Emphasis Week to a pristine observance: for three days, Director of Religious Life Will Campbell led participants into the University's Fulton Chapel at 10 a.m. and for thirty minutes sat in silent meditation and prayer.[32]

Though the shouts of segregationists received the far greater share of media attention, the five local ministers who refused to participate demonstrated the presence of moderates among Mississippi's clergy. Indeed, segregationists so loudly insisted that all white Christians abhorred the prospect of integration precisely *because* a cadre of Mississippi ministers and layfolk embraced the churches' commitment to desegregation. One such minister, Reverend Emile Joffrion, the rector of St. Peter's Episcopal Mission in Oxford, admonished his congregation in the midst of the crisis unfolding in their backyard: "so far as the Church is concerned Mr. Kersha[w] has done nothing with which the Church cannot agree in giving part of his money to support the cause of de-segregation of the races."[33] Joffrion believed other Mississippi Episcopal ministers shared his sentiments.[34] His young colleague, Reverend Duncan Gray, cancelled his appearance at REW at Mississippi State College in Starkville because organizers asked participants not to discuss segregation. Gray explained that he could not promise to avoid the issue because "segregation is incompatible with the Christian faith."[35]

Significantly, when segregationists sought two years later to convince Mississippi's Institutions of Higher Learning Board that Ole Miss constituted a dangerous challenge to the state's way of life, their twenty-six-page complaint also wove conservative religion into the defense of segregation. They claimed that Ole Miss subverted "[b]elief in one omnipotent God; that the Bible is true; that we have souls which are immortal." They thought, furthermore, that the university failed to uphold the "belief in the ethnological truth that where races of different color mix with each other socially that intermarriage inevitably results and that we have the obligation, and the inalienable right, to preserve the identity of the white race." The chancellor responded by defending his beliefs in "God, the Bible, and the immortality of the soul; in state sovereignty; in private property; and in the deleterious effects of racial intermarriage and the importance of racial integrity." In civil-rights-era Mississippi, commitments to evangelical Christianity, political conservatism, and racial segregation came "of a piece."[36]

The Kershaw affair joined the ranks of other such episodes when religious advocacy for racial equality revealed a deep and active well of conviction that the Creator sanctioned segregation. A similar debacle unfolded in the spring of 1958 at Millsaps College, the highly esteemed Methodist school in Jackson. Dr. Ernest Borinski, white sociology professor at Jackson's historically black Tougaloo Southern Christian

College, announced at a Millsaps forum that segregation amounted to a "rejection of Christian principles." His comments set off a geyser of talk about God's love for racial separation.[37]

If Kershaw's actions especially challenged Mississippi's Episcopalians, the Millsaps affair called forth segregation's Methodist defenders. *Clarion-Ledger* columnist Tom Etheridge held up models in Mississippi Methodism's ancestral architects—twice-wounded Confederate Major Reuben Miller Millsaps and revered Methodist Bishop Charles Betts Galloway. By Borinski's logic, Etheridge maintained, these notables and all the good Methodists of Mississippi required classification as "unchristian."[38] "So much for the asinine argument that real Christians do not believe in segregation," he concluded. Other layfolk objected to Borinski's remarks in ways that revealed a firm grounding in the biblical foundations of the racial hierarchy. Miss Clayton Mikell of Silver Creek asserted that "to the Christian viewpoint, there is only one angle, and that is segregation so far as the races are concerned. . . . That's God's way of life, the Bible teaches it, therefore it's the Christian way of life."[39] Another writer claimed that integration "is a deadly evil such as God does not approve of. Our reason for so believing is our Bible . . . any individual or church or school that wants to join with the Communists and atheists and practice integration and intermarrying may do so [but] . . . I am not coming with you."[40] From Belzoni in the Delta, Mattie D. Womack described segregation as "only the response to divine and natural laws. Segregation threads through the Bible." After explicating the curse of Ham, Womack explained how this "thread" continued: "God directed the genealogy of Christ that the bloodline might be kept pure. He forbade association of his covenant people with the Canaanites (Canan was the fourth son of Ham) as well as many other groups." Those who believed otherwise, thought Womack, should "study the Bible and study history."[41]

The Millsaps controversy spilled over into congregational life in small towns. The First Methodist Church in Durant cancelled the revival appearance of Reverend Noel Hinson, a district superintendent in the North Mississippi Methodist Conference, because he had congratulated Millsaps' president for "airing both sides of the racial issue."[42] Just days before the revival opened, the Durant Church informed Hinson that "Our members had anticipated an inspirational revival with you as guest preacher, however your . . . approving the [Millsaps]

program of Racial Relations disagrees so completely with our belief in
Christian ideals and principles, we feel it is best to cancel your engagement for this revival."[43] One layman even claimed that Hinson penal-
ized Methodist ministers under his charge by appointing them to small,
low-paying pastorates if they supported segregation.[44]

In an effort to reign in the radicalizing potential of the Gospel, Mississippians slammed shut the doors of hospitality on other religious
leaders from outside the state. In each of the four years following 1954,
at least one such spiritual leader met similar, flagrant censorship. The
Detroit Methodist clergyman Henry Hitt Crane so riled the Hattiesburg community when he spoke during REW at Mississippi Southern
College in 1955 that one local minister suggested those responsible for
Crane's invitation "should be shot."[45] Crane's "dangerous talk" included
not race, but pacifist and pro-labor union language, prompting the legislature to pass a "speakers test" resolution that urged all public colleges
and universities to "screen speakers and weed out those advocating
policies foreign to our way of life."[46] This very resolution emboldened
the legislature to behave so proactively in the Kershaw case the following year. Radical segregationists among Mississippi Baptists tried to
shun even the president of the Southern Baptist Convention, moderate
Arkansas Congressman Brooks Hays, in 1957. And the Millsaps controversy in 1958 precipitated the cancellation of a talk by Dr. Glenn Smiley
of the Fellowship of Reconciliation, a New York-based Christian group
devoted to achieving racial justice through non-violent, direct action.[47]
Indeed, Mississippi evangelicals diligently policed Magnolia State pulpits to disable them as vehicles for integrationist notions, while promoting segregation as part of Mississippi's Christian orthodoxy.

"God Separated the Races": The Citizens' Councils
and the Religious Defense of Segregation

Immediately after the *Brown* decision and in direct response to the
threat it posed, leading citizens from the Mississippi Delta organized
grass-roots support for segregation. As the South's most avid promoters of the case for segregation, the Citizens' Councils flourished, and
the religious argument figured importantly in their program. The
organization attracted 25,000 members among the state's middle and

upper-middle classes within months after its birth in July 1954. In two years, it grew to 85,000 members in sixty-five chapters in Mississippi alone. In its wild nascent success, the movement spread quickly to other states, reaching a national membership of 250,000 by the end of 1956. By 1960, the Citizens' Councils promoted the gospel of racial purity through annual rallies, a regional paper with a circulation of 40,000, weekly television programs broadcast by twelve stations, and radio shows aired on more than fifty stations. The organization's success owed, in part, to its disavowal of violence, its pledge to maintain segregation by legal methods, its polished and sophisticated use of public media, and a somewhat socially elevated constituency that included senators, lawyers, and prominent businessmen.[48]

In their capacity as self-appointed defenders of "racial integrity and states' rights," the Citizens' Councils recognized that ignoring religious arguments would leave potentially dangerous streams of thought unguarded. Understanding both religion's danger and its possibilities, the group's original mastermind, Robert Patterson, exhorted laymen to "straighten these churches out" and secure their cooperation in the fight against integration.[49] The Mississippi Gulf Coast chapter purposefully solicited "all clergymen occupying pulpits in this community," appealing "for their continued support of racial segregation in our churches." As fellow Christians, the councilors explained, "we . . . feel ourselves entitled to the honest support of our own pastors in this frightening situation."[50] Reverend J. L. Pipkin of Blue Mountain urged the organization to pursue the religious argument more aggressively: "I believe this may be the Christians['] greatest challenge, to get up and tell the truth against these great odds."[51] Indeed, conspicuously Christian councilors, frightened for the future of segregation, militantly advanced an understanding of their faith and segregation as mutually linked.

While the Citizens' Councils deployed an army of Christian spokesmen, they regarded ministers as a prize catch. One chapter proudly boasted "the accession to its ranks of five very fine men of God from the local clergy."[52] Clergyman occupied prominent places in the organization, as did laymen with very public religious commitments. Local pastors commonly offered the invocation at rallies, and prominent ministers served as keynote speakers.[53] Presbyterian ministers who performed these tasks included Dr. G. T. Gillespie, the aforementioned Reverend

Miller of First Presbyterian Church in Jackson, and Reverend William Arnett Gamble, stated clerk of the Central Mississippi Presbytery, who served on the board of the Jackson Citizens' Council.[54] Among Baptists, Dr. David M. Nelson spoke for Council events and wrote literature for the organization; Baptist Reverend Charles C. Jones of Mendenhall, along with the laymen Louis Hollis of First Baptist Church, Jackson, and D. B. Red of Hattiesburg, also occupied a variety of posts in the organization.[55] Methodist pastors who served the organization included Reverend B. K. Hardin of Jackson's Boling Street Methodist Church, and Delmar Dennis, who spoke at rallies and other events.[56] By showcasing this phalanx, the Councils sought to create the impression that they had unanimous support among Mississippi's religious leaders. In 1957 the group claimed that "only two ministers in the state are not with us," an assertion that smacked of hyperbole.[57]

Ministerial participation afforded the Councils a symbolic religious imprimatur and an aura of respectability, but the organization understood that religious *thought* constituted the real battleground for Mississippians' hearts and minds. Thus, to its arsenal of printed segregationist polemics, the Councils added a subset designed specifically for its Bible-reading audience. These Christian defenses of segregation offer prime examples of segregationist folk theology and its multi-faceted foundations. In addition to Dr. Gillespie and his "A Christian View on Segregation," Mississippi College president Dr. Nelson endowed the Citizens' Councils with considerable prestige. Though his pamphlet on "Conflicting Views on Segregation" seemed to suggest a concern with open-mindedness and fair play, the piece aimed primarily to contravene the moral case for integration as a well-intentioned but naïve and unsophisticated perversion of God's divine plan. The text ostensibly reproduced Nelson's correspondence with "Tom," a pseudonymous Mississippi College alumnus. Nelson repeatedly challenged Tom's understanding of segregation as a "moral question" and repudiated his conviction that Christian faith required that "there should be no racial differences." Nelson argued that, in striking down legal segregation, the Supreme Court had attempted "to do what the good Lord in His infinite wisdom did not do. He made the people into races, with racial characteristics, with inherent likes and dislikes, similarities and dissimilarities, and it would be as fallacious for mere man to try to improve upon the work of the Lord as it proved to be in his attempt to build a tower to heaven." When Tom countered that "The promotion of the Missionary Work in the Baptist Church and the teaching [of Christianity] at Mississippi College . . . seemed to be out of line with our practice of excluding Negroes from our colleges and churches," Nelson replied, "Again we demur and call for the chapter and the verse of the Bible. The whole tenor of the Scriptures is against mixed marriages and the pollution of the blood of distinct and separate races."[58]

The Citizens' Councils did not confine their religious defense of segregation to the tract publications and sermon collections that they advertised for sale in their weekly paper. Nearly every issue of the organization's paper, The Citizens' Council and its refurbished successor after mid-1961, The Citizen, contained an article, op-ed piece, cartoon, letter to the editor, or news item calculated to establish, elucidate, and defend the orthodoxy that God himself had established segregation to spare whites from contamination by blacks and that any attempt "to destroy these God-given distinctions . . . opposes God's plan." A multipart "Manual for Southerners," aimed at school-aged children and printed over several issues in 1957, developed the case for God's blessing on segregation, as indicated by the subheadings "God separated the Races," "God Doesn't Want Races to Mix," and "Segregation is Christian."[59] Many issues of The Citizen included segregationist sermon reprints among its articles. The authors of these included spokesmen from Mississippi's religious communions—the Presbyterian pastor Al Freundt, the Baptist deacon Louis Hollis, and the Methodist Sunday school teacher Dr. Medford Evans. Mississippians, however, represented only part of the team of southern religious spokesmen who made similar arguments in the organization's journal. The paper pulled in the commentary of religious leaders from across the South, including Dr. Bob Jones, Sr., president and founder of Bob Jones University in Greenville, South Carolina, North Carolina Episcopal minister James Dees, and the Texas Episcopalian rector Robert T. Ingram.[60]

Though the Citizens' Councils advanced several different and even contradictory religious arguments for segregation, the organization probably made its most effective faith-based case by tying religious advocacy for racial equality to liberal theology. A corollary line of reasoning maintained that only the proponents of segregation remained loyal to biblical truth and the old-time Gospel of salvation. Council literature repeatedly advanced the trope of liberal ministers as effeminate, deluded, and educated beyond their own capacities to understand or communicate. Such ministers, they argued, were not harmless, over-zealous, do-gooders, but apostates and heretics who flirted dangerously with socialism, if not outright communism, in emphasizing equality and social engagement. The abstruse theology of racial justice preached by such ministers bore little resemblance to the easily understood evangelical Gospel that issued from southern pulpits. Thus, the Council argument made a short leap from advocacy for racial justice to the kind of religious liberalism Mississippians had decried for decades, and the religious defense of segregation remained intimately tied to a defense of conservative, evangelical Christianity. Commitment to segregation became part and parcel of Mississippians' own cherished faith, and they could fear for their own souls if they accepted the argument for racial equality.

Thus, in the religious and racial worlds of white Mississippians, churches and ministers who advocated racial equality dangerously perverted both the Bible and the divine plan, and they constituted an evil worthy of the Christian's most vigorous opposition. As if to confirm the dangerous status of denominations that had endorsed racial equality, the Citizens' Councils included the Episcopal Church and the Methodist Church on a list of organizations under the jarring heading "Here is the enemy." Other Citizens' Council material decried apostasy in the Catholic Church, the Lutheran Church, and the American Baptist Convention. Almost the entire May 1958 issue of *The Citizens' Council* explored the pernicious "doctrine" of integration in American religious communities. Under the heading "Southern Churches Urge Mixing," the issue featured articles condemning Southern Baptist and Presbyterian literature and documenting the rise of communist influence within the churches. Dr. Nelson closed the issue with a defense of the place of race in the divine plan: "races are different, radically different, and man is not responsible for this difference, but God [is] . . . [to] attempt to merge them in the crucible of miscegenation . . . is the height of blasphemy."[61]

Will Campbell understood the genius of tying the religious defense of segregation to the conservative faith of Mississippians. When he wanted to draft a short series of publications aimed at "Mississippi Cockle Burrs and Georgia Crackers" as a riposte to the Citizens' Council argument, he planned to approach Mississippians with the same kind of chapter and verse method they favored.[62] Though he did "not believe in the Biblical method of proof text," he "want[ed] to encounter them . . . using their own language, own Biblical methods." Wrote Campbell, "If they want to believe a big fish swallowed Jonah, I won't argue with them."[63] Yet he also knew that even "good fundamentalism [c]ould as successfully deny the racist biblical claims" as more modernist or historical-critical methods.[64] Such a tract series as Campbell envisioned might have been Mississippi's only prayer for changing its resistant trajectory, for Mississippians who wanted to keep the faith that had been delivered unto them could find no resonance with the idea that God would champion the cause of black equality.

Defending Segregation: The Mississippi Legislature and the Church Property Bill

Perhaps unremarkably in a Mississippi that consistently blended the sacred and the secular, the Mississippi state legislature gave political form to the religious case for segregation, just as it had to other important evangelical tenets, like the belief in creation and the abhorrence for beverage alcohol. The legislature took this step at the very same time it provided other protections for segregation, and the perceived threat from religious institutions again constituted the motivating force. Yet here, Mississippians' disagreements about the real danger that the denominations presented set them arguing amongst themselves.

Almost exclusively, Mississippi's legislature comprised Protestant men deeply committed to preserving segregation. In several remarkable rounds of law-making—a special session in the fall of 1954, two frenzied stints during J. P. Coleman's gubernatorial term in 1956 and 1958, and then in a renewed delirium during the early months of Ross Barnett's administration in 1960—the two houses passed with near unanimity a slate of measures to bolster segregation. The 1956 legislative session proved particularly stunning for the extremity of its enactments. One bill repealed the state's compulsory school attendance laws—a necessity for the subsequent reconstruction of a system of private education that could still take advantage of state funds. In other measures, the legislature prohibited interference with the state's segregation laws—effectively offering local school districts the choice of defying state law or ignoring the High Court. Finally, a series of bills increased the state's power to thwart civil rights activity. The most far-reaching measure of this sort effectively made civil rights organizing a misdemeanor, as efforts to "encourage disobedience to any law of the State of Mississippi, and nonconformance with the established traditions, customs, and usages of the State of Mississippi" became punishable by a $1,000 fine and a six-month jail term.[65]

As lawmakers abandoned themselves to this spree of anti-integration measures, two proposals and the debates over them demonstrated how dangerous religion appeared to segregation. The two separate measures—one in the Senate and the other in the House—would have deprived religious institutions of their ad valorem tax exemptions if they "practiced integration." In arguing for the measure's necessity, one lawmaker identified religious institutions as the only groups in Mississippi "that offend[ed] against segregation." Since the debate clarified that no one "knew of [any actual] religious integration in Mississippi," this assessment of religion's threat no doubt primarily reflected an awareness of the strong support for desegregation issued by every major denomination, the increasing efforts in some communions toward abolishing their administratively segregated structures, and the disaster that would ensue for massive resistance if these trends found expression in Mississippi's heavily church-going citizenry.[66]

Inasmuch as the debate clearly identified the threat to segregation from Protestant churches, many legislators and observers regarded the Catholic Church as the bills' primary target. Often regarded as religious outsiders, Catholics in fact constituted the third largest denominational group in Mississippi. By 1954, the Roman church operated parochial schools in addition to its three hospitals and many parish churches, and the two bills would have affected all of these institutions. Though Mississippi's Catholic schools and churches practiced segregation, black and white priests generally did enjoy closer working relationships than ministers of different races in the Protestant denominations. Most likely, however, events just over Mississippi's southern and western borders in heavily Catholic Louisiana instigated the legislature's concerns about the Roman church. New Orleans' Archbishop Joseph Francis Rummel had already begun working toward desegregation of that parish's schools and had threatened to excommunicate Catholics in the Louisiana Legislature if they attempted to forbid integration. While the Louisiana controversy had not fully played out by the time Mississippi's church bills came up for debate—the church would cast out several southern Louisiana Catholics shortly thereafter—the turmoil in their neighboring state caught Mississippians' attention.[67]

Regardless of their personal commitments to segregation, few of Mississippi's clergymen of any denomination seemed to favor the church bills. Baptists' traditionally strong commitments to separation of church and state elicited their objections to the measures on principle. In the Delta town of Greenville, ministers from the Baptist, Methodist, Presbyterian, and Disciples of Christ traditions all expressed grave concerns about the bills and their implications, and the local Catholic monsignor called them "dangerous." Others bristled at the implications of legislating segregation in the churches; to some, such a notion seemed to violate the important belief that "Christianity is for everybody."[68]

The church bills drew heated debate even in Mississippi's die-hard segregationist legislature, marking an exception to the group's solidarity in support of segregationist measures to that point in the 1956 session. Lawmakers who had voted "down the line" in support of other measures in the anti-integration package now broke ranks to demonstrate that fears about the integrationist potential of religious institutions could lose out when pitted against loyalty to those institutions, regard for separation of church and state, and commitments to religious freedom. The sole female member of the Senate and a converted Catholic, Mrs. John Farese, rose as the most forceful opponent of the church bill. Farese choked visibly as she presciently lamented, "I'm touched almost to tears, but this puts me in a position where I might see a colored soul come into church and be told to get out of the house of God." Though an avowed segregationist, Farese thought "religious integration is another matter. I don't want . . . [to] keep anyone from worshipping God." A representative from Columbus, Mississippi thought the house bill meant only to "take a slap at the Catholic Church." Still others, Governor J. P. Coleman included, opposed the bill on the grounds that it violated separation of church and state. Though the bill died in Mississippi's House of Representatives, its 24–20 victory in the Senate augured well for future attempts.[69]

The Mississippi legislature did not wash its hands of religion after 1956. Four years on, the faith connections of its citizens evidently seemed simultaneously less sacrosanct and more dangerous. Like its predecessor, the 1960 Church Property Bill constituted but one piece of legislation in an entire session devoted to increasing segregationist safeguards at the outset of a new gubernatorial term. The accession of Ross Barnett marked a departure from the more "moderate" segregationist methods of J. P. Coleman, whose perceived lack of rigor had garnered criticism and political opposition. With the spirit of defiance at a rolling boil under the new governor, the Mississippi legislature dropped whatever reservations it once held about interfering in religious life.

The debate over the 1956 bills had identified the Methodist Church as only one of several threatening religious institutions, but the 1960 Church Property Bill took aim squarely—some said uniquely—at Methodist churches. However odious to segregationists that denomination had appeared in 1956, by 1960 the threat seemed to have grown in intensity and immediacy. Steady condemnation of segregation in the church's literature and continued development of plans to absorb the all-black unit, the Central Jurisdiction, into the existing geographic jurisdictions seemed particularly troubling in the spring of 1960, for the Methodist General Conference sat just on the horizon as the Church Property Bill controversy unfolded. In Mississippi, Methodists had worked many years to hold the "integrationist tendencies" of the denomination at bay, but each new general conference seemed ripe with the potential to sweep away their efforts. Methodist Sunday school classes and board meetings condemned church literature with rhythmic regularity, and some congregations adopted material from other sources. Perhaps most significantly, an aggressive organization of conservative Methodists, the Mississippi Association of Methodist Ministers and Layman (MAMML), increased its opposition to the church, its denunciations of Methodist literature, and its criticisms of Methodist leaders. This group held out the possibility of forming a breakaway movement in the event that the national organization went too far in pressing the racially egalitarian demands of the Gospel.

The 1960 Church Property Bills offered protection for congregations' property rights, enabling them to break away from their denominations. When first introduced in both houses of the legislature in late

January of 1960, the bills encountered wide opposition from Catholics, Presbyterians, and Episcopalians, but Methodists especially jumped into the fight against it.

Tellingly, though fears about the integrationist tendencies of the church had prompted the legislation, the divisions among Methodists did not revolve around the advisability of mixing races in the churches. As the bill sat pending an open hearing, Methodists' arguments about its implications illuminated the various points in the continuum along which racial sentiments in Mississippi lay. No Mississippi Methodist voiced a desire to end their long-standing practice of all-white worship. Their disagreements turned, rather, on whether or not the Methodist hierarchy could force them to integrate and, consequently, on whether Methodists needed legislation such as the Church Property Bill. In fact, leaders who spoke out against the measure assured their coreligionists that the practice of all-white worship would remain safe in the Magnolia State for a long time to come. "No law of the church nor any decree of one of its administrators will change racial practices in Mississippi churches unless and until the great majority wills it," vouched Reverend Roy Clark of Capitol Street Methodist in Jackson.[70] Rather than worry that the denominational hierarchy might force them to integrate, ministers in the Brookhaven district opposed the bill because "we do not believe that the situation against which this proposed law is aimed will take place in Mississippi at any time in the foreseeable future."[71] Reverend Johnny A. Dinas of Columbus, Mississippi, assured his congregation that "Methodism . . . guarantee[s] . . . the present status in our Churches." These Methodists cherished the "strong pillars [of the church's] connectional framework," and to them, the more significant danger lay in the bill's potential to enable segregationists of the most extreme ilk to dominate and ultimately divide Mississippi Methodism.[72] Even the usually mealy Bishop Franklin spoke out to condemn the measure as "a dangerous proposal [that] will promote disunity and division at a time when all Mississippians should stand united to build a greater state."[73]

Yet, for some Methodists, constant reminders about "integration propaganda in church literature" outweighed the assurances of more moderate leaders.[74] The MAMML took out a full-page ad in the *Times-Picayune* to warn Mississippians about the threat to their

churches. Claiming that "the Methodist Church expect[s] to integrate all Methodist Churches," the ad advised, "[o]ur legislature has
worked diligently to provide laws to maintain segregation. Mississippians have spent many millions of dollars to provide separate school
facilities. ARE WE NOW TO ALLOW OUR CHURCHES TO BRING
ABOUT MIXING OF THE RACES [emphasis in the original]?"[75]
Such concerns moved some congregations to urge legislators to enact
the Church Bill.

Methodists and other white Mississippi Christians brought these
arguments into a crowded open hearing on the bill. As in debate leading up to the hearings, that night's fiery deliberations did not involve a
consideration of the appropriateness of segregation in churches. Opponents and advocates both seemed to take the desirability of all-white
congregations for granted. Dr. W. B. Selah, long-time pastor of Mississippi's largest Methodist Church, Galloway Memorial in Jackson, testified that "the council of bishops can't force integration. Whether white
churches in Mississippi have Negro members is up to the white members." The Methodist lay leader Dr. J. P. Stafford gave an impassioned
plea to "Kill this vicious scheme. It will widen the breaches within
our churches." Though the bill theoretically would have no impact on
Southern Baptist congregations, since church property under Baptist
polity already belonged to the local congregations, *Baptist Record* editor
Joe Odle logged opposition to the measure on the grounds of Baptists'
historical commitment to separation of church and state, arguing that
"the bill sets a dangerous precedent in that it opens the door to state
control of the churches." Episcopal and Catholic laymen also testified
against the legislation.[76]

Supporters who packed the session insisted that opponents underestimated the danger to segregation represented by the denominations.
"The issue," claimed Representative Stanny Sanders, "is whether we
will continue to fight integration even though it is sponsored by our
churches." In spite of the bill's ostensibly broader application, proponents in the house "proceeded to attack . . . the Methodist Church,
her leaders, her institutions and agencies, claiming that the Methodist Church plan[ed] to force integration on Mississippi's congregations."
After the diatribes against Methodism, Louis Hollis, chair of the deacons at Jackson's First Baptist and a Citizens' Council staffer, returned

to the theme of the wider threat, claiming that integration also threatened Baptist churches because the "Southern Baptist Convention has taken a left wing trend." Senator Edgar Lee brought the debate to a dramatic conclusion by claiming that "God segregated the races" and then shouting the by-then-hackneyed segregationist prophecy that if lawmakers failed to enact this legislation, they would one day "waken to the screams of a mulatto grandchild."[77]

During the roughly nine weeks that the measure wended its way through the two houses of Mississippi's legislature, public opposition ran overwhelmingly against the bill. Large lay organizations, Sunday school classes, many agencies of the church, a Methodist student organization, and often entire congregations under unanimous vote registered their disapproval. The scattered and unofficial support for the bill came from only a minority of churches that often mustered barely enough votes to pass a resolution. Yet, in spite of the measure's very limited public approval, the Church Property Bill passed in the Senate by a vote of 29–10 and in the House by a comfortable margin of 87–13. Governor Ross Barnett signed the bill into law, without comment, on April 1, 1960.[78]

*　*　*

With religious discourse on task with the project of resistance and the path clear for churches to separate from the denominations in the event of imminent integration, Mississippi's most committed segregationists had taken important steps in the struggle to keep hearts and minds enthusiastic about preserving the racial status quo. Mississippians' religious impulses seemed safely tucked into segregationists' back pockets. But religion is hard to predict and difficult to control. Segregationists could never satisfactorily manipulate Mississippians' strong religious ties to communities larger than their own. These ties would prove all-important tethers as the state pursued an ever-more defiant course.

5

"Ask for the Old Paths"

Mississippi's Southern Baptists and Segregation

In November 1954, just six months after the announcement of the *Brown* decision, white Baptists performed their yearly ritual of gathering for the state convention in Jackson. In his opening address, state association president Dr. John E. Barnes affirmed the wisdom of doing things in familiar ways with a text from Jeremiah 6:16: "Thus saith the Lord, Stand ye in the ways and see, and ask for the old paths where is the good way and walk therein, and ye shall find rest for your souls." While Barnes made no direct mention of the Supreme Court decision, the Christian Life Commission's (CLC) recommendations, or Mississippi Baptists' reactions to them, he referred to all of these obliquely when he acknowledged that the state sat at a critical juncture: "the people of Mississippi are facing a momentous question [as] to which path we shall take." His recommendation, "it is well for us to follow paths that are tested by years of experience," evoked the same comforting sense of stability, familiarity, and history as other favored euphemistic references to segregation. As 1954 drew to a close and Mississippians planned strategies to preserve the racial hierarchy at all costs, Baptists found support for their traditions even in the words of a radical Old Testament prophet.[1]

While Mississippi Baptists determined to stay the old path of segregation, this intent put them at odds with progressives in the Southern Baptist Convention (SBC). In particular, preserving the racial hierarchy meant warding off the measured critique of racial subordination that issued from denominational agencies, leaders, missionaries, and literature. While Mississippi Baptists' most public leaders almost never spoke about race, their constituents engaged in an intense struggle with the SBC over civil rights initiatives. An extraordinary polarization developed between

Deep South Baptists and their more socially conscious coreligionists at SBC headquarters in Nashville and in other parts of the country.[2]

Most Mississippi Baptist pastors did not regularly harangue against integration from their pulpits, in part because their congregations required no convincing. Yet many did preach a set of religious and political ideologies essential to white supremacy without ever mentioning race, race relations, or segregation. As the civil rights years progressed, they articulated these ideologies ever more purposefully. The state's most influential pastor, Reverend Douglas Hudgins of First Baptist Church in Jackson, mastered this approach. Offering unabashed enthusiasm for the leading architects of massive resistance, he preached a Gospel message that construed morality in entirely individualistic terms and rendered the structures of inequality invisible. Perhaps more importantly, contrary both to depictions of Baptists as apolitical and to his own admonitions for coreligionists to stay out of politics, Hudgins forcefully advocated a vision of a Christian America built on a specific political ideology. In this view, a federal government strong enough to mandate racial equality also promoted moral weakness. If the preaching of Douglas Hudgins is any indication, the ideology of the Christian right sharpened its teeth in the defense of segregation long before the Moral Majority.

Moreover, as black activists forced a dramatic awakening of the nation's racial consciousness, Mississippi Baptists could hardly appear as practitioners of compassionate Christianity if they ignored the sufferings of their black neighbors. Thus, in the civil rights years, they dramatically expanded their interracial outreach, developing the most extensive such program of any state Baptist convention in the country. They eagerly promoted this ministry as evidence of their racial good will and of their seriousness about the demands of the Gospel. Yet in spite of their efforts to suggest otherwise, the Mississippi Baptist State Convention's Department of Negro Work stayed firmly on the old path of segregation. It operated entirely within accepted racial parameters and gained favor with Mississippi Baptists largely because it seemed a foil for civil rights activity.

Mississippi Baptists and the SBC

To many Mississippi Baptists, the threat to the racial hierarchy seemed to come from within their own faith tradition, and this peril seemed especially acute after 1954. The SBC's endorsement of *Brown* put it on the side of the enemy, a fact for which segregationists found ample confirmation in the reports, statements, tracts, pamphlets, and Sunday school literature issued by denominational agencies. As they defended segregation against an assault from their own religious leaders, Mississippians' relationship with denominational leaders acquired an especially combative character.

As a body, the Mississippi Baptist Convention Association never issued a public pronouncement regarding race or integration until 1964, when violence in the state grew most acute. With the exception of Dr. A. L. Goodrich, the *Baptist Record* editor who made clear his commitment to segregation in 1954, Mississippi's state-level Baptist leaders maintained an almost uniform silence on the issue. Committed to denominational unity and institution building, subsequent *Record* editors W. C. Fields (1956–1959) and Joe Odle (1959–1976), along with Convention Executive Secretary-Treasurer Chester Quarles (1950–1968), believed controversy would sabotage Baptist work in the state. These men endeavored to keep discussions of race and integration out of public Baptist discourse, a strategy that required quieting both the reactionary voices of their constituents as well as progressive pronouncements from denominational agencies. Both Goodrich and Fields refused to publish inflammatory letters from segregationists, and the *Record's* advisory committee supported this policy. The committee members, all pastors of Mississippi Baptist churches, believed such letters might serve as "the beginning of unwholesome discussion of the race question"[3] Yet importantly, this refusal reflected comfort with the status quo rather than interest in black equality. One advisory committee member advised against publishing a segregationist missive because he regarded the NAACP and the Citizens' Councils as the "two radical groups which are antagonizing the racial situation in Mississippi."[4] Another thought that the segregationist sentiments expressed by a writer "may be true" and that "later on it might be necessary . . . to publish [such a letter]."[5] These same leaders who silenced enthusiastic segregationists also urged a complementary caution on denominational agencies. For his part, Joe Odle implored SBC leaders to restrain their socially conscious instincts: "when actions are taken or statements made that upset large segments of our people . . . there must be careful consideration of it."[6]

The SBC's racial initiatives required stifling precisely because so many Mississippi Baptists cared passionately about preserving the racial hierarchy; even mild statements provoked an outcry that rippled through the state's congregations, as segregationist enthusiasts purposefully stoked their coreligionists' fears. These incendiaries included prominent laymen like Louis Hollis, a Citizens' Council officer as well as Superintendent of Sunday Schools and Chair of the Board of Deacons at First Baptist Church of Jackson. Hollis elaborated the pernicious nature of the SBC before the Mississippi legislature, in Citizens' Council publications and on its television talk-show, as well as in deacons' meetings at his church. Among other items, he objected to apparently pro-integration statements in SBC literature and to its evangelistic cooperation with black Baptist denominations, which he regarded as "Hot beds [sic] of NAACP Activity."[7] Hollis believed that denominational leaders were "compromising our traditional doctrines and beliefs as Southern Baptists," and he "found plenty of evidence that the Southern Baptist Convention is moving more and more to the left."[8]

By no means unique, Hollis had a counterpart in Hattiesburg layman and Citizens' Councilor D. B. Red, the author of two self-published segregationist pamphlets. Like Hollis, Red sounded the alarm about the dangerous racial instincts of Southern Baptist leaders, especially those associated with the Christian Life Commission.[9] Another eager Baptist segregationist, Reverend Charles C. Jones, hoped to "warn our Baptist people where they sorely need to be warned" through extensive letter-writing campaigns. A retired pastor of Mendenhall Baptist Church and local Citizens' Council president, Jones thought that "the drift toward desegregation in our literature and from some of our pulpits is too strong to go unchallenged by those who see the danger of it."[10] In a missive to Baptist leaders all across the country, he argued that "the strange doctrine that the races of mankind must become one to save civilization, or to do mission work, is a man-made scarecrow to mongrelize the races. The Bible reveals that mongrel races have never honored nor glorified God."[11]

But resentment against racial progressives in the SBC ran far deeper than revealed by a few vocal segregationist die-hards. Indeed, similar distrust seemed to percolate in nearly every congregation in the state, and the complaints frequently identified a single agency within the Convention—the Christian Life Commission. In blaming public statements about race on the CLC, Mississippi Baptists had correctly identified one important matrix of the SBC's social conscience. In the wake of the *Brown* decision and the rising southern resistance to it, the agency stepped up its campaigns to educate Southern Baptists about the problems of racial discrimination. This educational program included "race relations" packets the agency mailed unsolicited to pastors. The packets included tracts and pamphlets written by pastors, agency executives, and seminary professors. The brief essays—"Is Segregation Christian?" "The Unity of Humanity," "The Racial Problem is My Problem," and "Some Quiet Thoughts on a Turbulent Issue"—sought to dismantle the biblical defense of segregation, to defend the necessity and the appropriateness of the Supreme Court's decision, and to affirm the incompatibility of Christian teaching and legislated segregation.[12] Though the pamphlets acknowledged the difficulty of bringing integration to the Deep South and made no recommendations for how it should be accomplished, they did advocate racial equality as a Christian principle. "Is Segregation Christian?" for example, argued unambiguously that "It [is] wrong to classify some human beings as inferior."

The CLC's race relations packets especially angered some Mississippi Baptists. Upon receiving "The Unity of Humanity," Jackson pastor Douglas Hudgins wrote "to register [his] opposition to the distribution of this tract."[13] The Silver City Baptist Church withheld funds from the CLC because it produced such material.[14] A Delta pastor protested "after receiving [the CLC's] latest 'propaganda' booklet," the third he had received that year. He explained, "[I] resent your using mission money to tell me something that I do not believe. I further resent the fact that the Christian Life Commission is seemingly trying to 'ram this matter down our throats.'"[15] By 1958, Mississippians' voluminous complaints about the CLC's use of their monies to print and distribute race relations literature forced the agency to assure them that outside grant sources, not denominational offerings, funded the material.[16]

Other CLC initiatives elicited storms of fury. The agency's 1957 annual report, which denounced violence against black Americans and recommended "that law enforcement agencies bring to justice those who perpetuate violence against negroes in the cause of segregation," provoked a special outcry. "All the members of my church are disturbed," wrote a Leflore County deacon and member of the state legislature. He wanted to know the exact content of the resolution because the local paper indicated it would "tend to integrate all the churches."[17] Reverend Otis Seal, a Citizens' Council spokesman and pastor of First Baptist Church, Itta Bena, noted that the report had "created a great deal of talk in our strong Baptist area." Reverend Seal suggested that the CLC's continued insistence on speaking to the race issue might cost the SBC in its pocketbook: "Our Church is a strong believer in the cooperative program and we strain our local program in order to support it. Just how much longer we will be able to keep them following I do not know." A constant critic of the CLC, First Baptist of Grenada published a strenuous remonstrance, canceling its financial allocations to the agency and calling for its permanent dissolution. Others applauded and mimicked this action.[18]

Though the CLC garnered special vituperation, Mississippi Baptists attacked other SBC agencies as well. The Sunday School and Home Missions Boards rhythmically drew denunciation. G. W. Simmons of Utica complained that "much of the literature from Nashville insinuates that it is un-Christian to believe in segregation."[19] From Columbia, Vernon H. Broom thought that SBC literature "cunningly includ[ed] modernistic social doctrines."[20] The Board of Moss Baptist Church refused to use any more SBC literature because it failed "systematically to teach the Scriptures" and gave too much attention "to racial issues—which we believe communistically influenced."[21] In 1957, anticipating a barrage of such condemnation, the Home Missions Board withdrew *The Long Bridge,* a missions study book already in Baptist bookstores. Though the material did not discuss the relative merits of segregation and integration, Baptist leaders worried that its frank depiction of the board's work among black Americans might foment "harmful debate and divisive discussion."[22] In spite of their caution, SBC agencies raised Mississippians' hackles with even the mildest material, such as an adult Sunday school lesson titled "Red, Yellow, Black, and White," words borrowed from a well-known children's hymn. The piece made a Vicksburg layman's "blood boil," and a Training Union director from Columbus thought the author deserved classification "as an agitator along with Martin Luther King and others of his kind."[23] Though Mississippians poured money into missions by the thousands, they abhorred the cover of a 1963 Sunday school booklet depicting an African in native dress.[24] By 1964, these complaints reached a crescendo such that Joe Odle felt compelled to write a lengthy defense of the Sunday School Board.[25]

The integration of Central High School in Little Rock, Arkansas, in 1957 offered Mississippi Baptists a special opportunity to demonstrate their hostility toward the SBC's racial progressives. Violence at Little Rock shocked American citizens and galvanized Mississippians, but the affair assumed heightened significance for Southern Baptists because their newly elected president, Arkansas congressman Brooks Hays, played a mediating role in the crisis. Many southerners condemned Hays as a traitor to the entire region, since he declined to support Arkansas' recalcitrant governor. While a majority of Baptists nationwide applauded Hays' efforts on behalf of racial justice, a significant minority identified him as the symbol of a dangerous trend in religious life. This minority included many Mississippians, who linked Hays' mediation at Little Rock to his just-relinquished chairmanship of the CLC and painted him as the chief of a left-leaning religious cabal bent on betraying white southerners to integration.[26]

An accidental arrangement of events raised the stakes for Hays. Well before the Little Rock crisis, the Mississippi Baptist State Convention had selected him as the special speaker for their annual convention in November 1957. Yet once he garnered his new infamy in the crisis, many believed his appearance at this gathering implied their endorsement of his position, and they wanted to set the record straight.[27] Six Baptist congregations passed resolutions that urged the State Convention to withdraw the invitation. First Baptist Church of Utica cut to the heart of the issue: Hays was "an avowed integrationist."[28] Though the six congregations represented only a tiny fraction of Mississippi's Baptists, Hays himself thought that they represented the "general sentiment of the people." In his many years in the thick of Baptist life, he had never known of a similar effort on behalf of local congregations to prevent a speaker—least of all the president of the SBC—from appearing before Baptist audiences.[29]

Mississippi Baptists could scarcely declare the president of the Southern Baptist Convention persona non grata, and Hays' appearance went ahead as scheduled. But the Mississippi audience displayed a stubborn resistance.[30] When the State Convention president stood to introduce him, Hays expected to hear the litany of his impressive professional and Baptist credentials usually invoked on such occasions. Instead, the emcee offered only a brief "Ladies and gentlemen of the Convention, the President of the Southern Baptist Convention," and sat down.

Stunned by the terse introduction, Hays knew the gentleman intended to avoid "bragging on [him] or saying anything that would make him appear to applaud [his] position." Though Hays found some friendly faces in the audience, others—identified by a friend as "Ku Kluxers and council members [who] were against [his] coming"—showed their resistance in body and facial language.[31]

While Hays' charm and humor ultimately won the crowd over that November evening, segregationists continued to eye him suspiciously. An old family friend acknowledged that Mississippians "say ugly things about you and against you as our Southern Baptist Convention President."[32] Another Mississippian begged him "not to lend your aid to integration."[33] A year after his tense Mississippi appearance, Arkansas voters punished Hays for his efforts at Little Rock by rejecting his bid for re-election, a move that boosted his status as a pro-integration symbol. Some tried to capture the momentum against him and deprive him of his leadership within the SBC as well. The segregationist Baptist Laymen of Mississippi wired Hays: "We believe you have outlived your usefulness as president of the Southern Baptist Convention and urge your immediate resignation." The group believed that "such action would help to restore the solidarity to Southern Baptists who are firm believers in Southern tradition." A group in Alabama that claimed a membership of 1,500 followed with a similar plea.[34] Yet, at the same time that strong disapproval of Hays emanated from some Baptist strongholds, the state conventions of Maryland and Virginia heaped praise upon the Arkansas leader. The following spring, a runaway majority re-elected him to the SBC presidency.[35]

And on and on it went. Mississippians howled their objections upon learning that the CLC had received a substantial grant from the Fund for the Republic, an agency of the Ford Foundation that supported left-leaning organizations and causes.[36] They went up in arms over a training union manual that suggested class members read a book by the African American writer James Baldwin.[37] They made a ruckus when college students from Mississippi attended a retreat with a few black internationals.[38] State-level leaders and agency heads in Nashville grew weary of quelling the agitation in Mississippi congregations.

Yet, for all the deep commitments to white supremacy expressed by Mississippi Baptists, a very few demonstrated that they read the implications of the Christian faith differently than the majority of whites in the state. Like the few pastors who had spoken in favor of the *Brown* decision in 1954, an isolated Mississippi Baptist occasionally challenged the state's dominant racial ethic. Thus, for example, even as he refused to advocate integration, Reverend Clyde Gordon of First Baptist Church in Poplarville preached a remarkably bold sermon that debunked most favorite segregationist tropes. He repudiated biblical arguments for the racial hierarchy by objecting to attempts "to take the Bible and prove by it that God is color conscious. . . . Some say that Noah placed a curse on Ham and he became black. That is not the truth. It is not so stated in the Bible." Gordon also went on to challenge the notion of black inferiority: "[the Negro] is a human being made in the image of God. . . . I will never consider myself better than any human being that God has created upon this earth." Placing the blame for "yellow negroes" firmly on the sexual predations of white men rather than on black men or women, Gordon condemned the exploitation of black Mississippians, with an admonition to his hearers to "remember that there is a just God on the throne."[39] A few other Baptist pastors made similar arguments, but not without considerable risk to their livelihoods. The pastor of a Baptist church near Indianola, Reverend R. B. Smith took a "forthright stand on the race issue" that cost him his pulpit in late 1961.[40] Bradley Pope left his church in Shelby over a similar incident in 1963, and in the Delta town of Belzoni, Pastor Chester Molpus left First Baptist Church in 1964 because his faith-based belief in racial equality offended the congregation.[41]

Such mavericks raised their voices rarely, however. Most Mississippi Baptist pastors employed strategic silence on racial issues as much as possible. Laymen did not necessarily require a minister who would defend segregation, for when it came under threat, they would step up to defend it themselves. A pastor skilled at endorsing the racial hierarchy in more subtle ways often better served the purposes of white supremacy. No one performed such tasks better than the Reverend Douglas Hudgins.

Scaffolding for Segregation: Reverend Douglas Hudgins

Like most Mississippi Baptists, Reverend Douglas Hudgins preferred the old paths. Like many Mississippi Baptist preachers, he rarely spoke about race in the pulpit. Indeed, segregation little required a white supremacist sermon to support it, and such preaching may have seemed unconvincing for its superfluity. Though absent such harangues, Hudgins' homilies nonetheless offered a way of thinking about religion and politics that disqualified the racial hierarchy as either a moral wrong or an offense against democracy. Even as Americans increasingly found the race issue morally compelling, Hudgins' preaching demonstrates why that same moral clarity eluded many Mississippians.[42]

First Baptist Church in downtown Jackson, the largest church of any denomination in Mississippi, occupied the premier position among the state's Baptist congregations. Spanning a half city block across the street from the state capitol building, its stately gothic sanctuary usually filled to its 1,800-seat capacity on Sunday mornings. First Baptist's entire complex of buildings boasted seven assembly halls in addition to the main sanctuary, more than 140 separate rooms for a Sunday school that regularly enrolled 2,200, and a kitchen that served more than 500 meals every Wednesday evening. Even its impressive facilities, however, failed to convey the extent of First Baptist's reach. Through television and radio ministries, First Baptist multiplied its influence by twenty times, according to some estimates. First Baptist's members followed their spiritual commitments with their pocketbooks, and the congregation consistently ranked as the state's top donor to denominational causes. The church's highly visible ministries, its prominence in state religious affairs, its beautiful and ample facilities, and its location near the state's political and geographic center made First Baptist the ideal place to host Mississippi Baptists' annual convention each November. Indeed, in some respects it appeared the very epicenter of Baptist life in Mississippi.[43]

First Baptist Church of Jackson thrived as the crown of Mississippi Baptist congregations, and Douglas Hudgins sparkled as its brightest jewel. Observers thought he had "the beguiling facility of translating penetrating theological truths into every man's language and experience." Tall, svelte, and fashionable, he cut an impressive pulpit figure as he used elegant gestures to "carve his message out of thin air." Hudgins' activity extended beyond his work with his congregation; he served in so many civic and community organizations that one observer called the occasion of his fifteen-year anniversary in Mississippi "an event statewide in significance." And few could compete with Hudgins for national stature in his denomination. A member of several SBC committees and on close terms with many Convention executives, he ran for Convention president in 1957 and garnered sufficient votes to become first vice president.[44]

Though Hudgins almost certainly never preached a sermon that explored the biblical or theological case for segregation, he revealed his lack of inner conflict about southern apartheid as a valid system in a Christian society in both his private statements and in his actions. He dismissed religious controversy over racial equality as mere difference of opinion, writing to one SBC executive, "I know you and I do not hold social questions in the same light," and he regarded segregation as an acceptable social system to which "must never be appended the label 'UnChristian' [*sic*]."[45] Hudgins joined other Mississippi Baptists in castigating the CLC for its efforts "to impose upon Southern Baptists the idea that anyone who opposes integration is narrow, prejudiced, provincial, and un-Christian."[46] Hudgins chaired the SBC's finance committee, a position from which he sought to hamstring the CLC by curtailing its budget. CLC chairman Arthur Miller identified the cause of Hudgins' behavior: "Douglas is violently opposed to anything we do or say about the racial issue and permits his deep and undying prejudices on that question to control him and to keep our Commission on a very limited budget."[47]

Leading apologists for white supremacy and primary architects of massive resistance worshiped at First Baptist, and they saw in Douglas Hudgins an amiable pastor, a great pulpit orator, and an unabashed supporter. Mississippi's most illustrious segregationist governor, Ross Barnett (in office 1960–1964), taught Sunday school and worshiped at First Baptist. Barnett campaigned for governor on the promise that Mississippi would never integrate under his administration, and on the eve of Barnett's inauguration, Hudgins and the congregation of First Baptist staged a special ceremony to honor the newly elected governor with a pulpit Bible.[48] Hudgins additionally served as pastor to several generations of Mississippi's powerful media magnates, the Hederman family. The Hedermans' holdings included the state's two most widely read daily newspapers, the *Jackson Clarion-Ledger* and the *Jackson Daily News* (after 1954), as well as the *Hattiesburg American* and Jackson television station WLBT. These outlets enabled the Hederman empire to serve as "segregation's most potent voice in Mississippi," according to one scholar.[49] Hudgins and the Hedermans gushed their mutual admiration. Hederman staffers waxed effusive in their papers about Hudgins' ministry, claiming that "[f]ew among our theological leadership equal his power in exposition and amplification of the gospel message."[50] For his part, Hudgins gave unqualified adulation to the press and its editors, eulogizing the *Clarion-Ledger*'s editor as a man who "had wrought a great deal of good by turning his artillery of words on idealistic enemies while espousing worthwhile causes."[51]

Parishioners like Ross Barnett, the Hederman family, and the Citizens' Councilor Louis Hollis would hardly have welcomed any moral reflection on Mississippi's racial hierarchy. Yet, neither did they seem to hunger for the strained exegesis of segregation. White supremacy did not always require such expositions, and strident haranguing would have little suited the genteel, gracious, and urbane congregation that worshipped there. Furthermore, such tirades would only have provided activist-minded clergy and liberal Christians throughout the nation just the fodder they sought to bolster the charge of hypocrisy they lobbed at Magnolia State Christians with ever-increasing frequency. Instead, near-complete silence about race seemed better to suit the leaders of massive resistance who worshipped at First Baptist Sunday after Sunday.

Douglas Hudgins regarded himself as a standard-bearer of the Christian faith—one who roused his people to meet the challenges of soul-searching with spiritual courage. He identified himself within the long tradition of Baptist preaching and professed deep respect for the homiletic responsibilities of pastoral ministry. "It is not particularly pleasant for a comfortable, prosperous, and self-satisfied Christian community to submit to a rigorous spiritual analysis and examination," he told his congregation, "but I would be false to the God whom I serve and a spiritual coward and traitor to you, my people, if I did not seek, in the spirit of a loving and divine urgency, to bring you God's truth as I see it."[52] Yet in making such calls for a searing spiritual examination, Hudgins promoted the same individualistic spirituality advanced by most Mississippi evangelicals. The evil effects of segregationist systems disappeared, and blacks' own shortcomings seemed the glaringly obvious reason for their sufferings. Listeners accustomed to this highly individualistic morality with its restricted understanding of sin would find little resonance in the understanding of corporate morality embodied in liberal theology or in the message of civil rights activists.

Hudgins expressed alarm about the contemporary state of moral decay in America. He decried "religious apathy, spiritual indolence, and moral decadence," asking rhetorically, "What about the staggering increase in the number of alcoholics in our nation and the frightful repercussions of illicit traffic in narcotics? What about our dreadful sag in moral convictions, the indulgent attitude of society toward promiscuous sex indulgence, the rise in perversion, the mania for gambling, the wild abandon in revolt against authority?"[53] Though he attacked such behavior with quasi-voyeuristic fervor, Hudgins chose carefully the sins suitable for excoriation, always identifying those that concerned the individual's heart, mind, and body. Alcohol consumption, prideful self-sufficiency, greed, and sexual licentiousness assumed a corporate dimension only insofar as many people practiced them, but the ways in which white Christians cooperated to erect systems of inequality simply failed to register in Hudgins' moral vision.

Hudgins' preaching, heavily focused on personal morality, differed little from the homilies that had distinguished Southern Baptists for decades. Yet, his preaching took its service to white supremacy even further. Though Baptists often claimed to eschew politics, and Hudgins himself excoriated other Baptists for involving themselves in political matters, he thoroughly entangled politics and religion in the pulpit. On everything from labor unions to taxes, he made abundantly clear his sympathy with political ideologies that elevated the efforts and rights of individuals—usually invisibly privileged individuals—above all else. In fact, he articulated a notion of a Christian America deeply imbued with moral and spiritual value, casting left-leaning conceptions of government as utterly evil and presenting a right-of-center politics as the best promoter of individual morality.[54]

Hudgins described expanded governmental power as America's greatest moral peril. Like his friend Billy Graham, he excelled at expounding on current events in ways that revealed far-reaching and distressing spiritual blight. Hudgins, however, presented a variation on the theme of spiritual declension that cast the government as the morally corrupting force on otherwise good and hard-working individuals. In this framing, a virtuous government embraced strict limits, local control, and individual rights. He believed America's federal government had dangerously amassed power, a trend he claimed "no one but a moron could fail to see," and thus encouraged the spiritual decay of its people.[55]

Hudgins traced America's political and spiritual apostasy to the presidency of Franklin Roosevelt, when the size and role of government expanded dramatically to mitigate the effects of the Great Depression. During the New Deal, "America swapped its birthright of individual freedom and liberty for the bread of economic improvement." This trend had continued unabated in the ensuing decades, dangerously amassing both power and responsibility at the federal level. While Hudgins saw evidence of a too-heavy federal system at every hand, nothing better represented this trend than recent rulings of the Supreme Court. Since the epochal shift of the 1930s, the High Court had "taken unto itself by unprecedented presumption the actual task of governing." After 1962, his criticisms of the High Court tended to focus on two decisions regarding public expressions of faith: the 1961 decision against requiring belief in God for holding public office and the 1962 ruling abolishing the practice of prayer in public schools. Importantly however, he not only objected to the substance of these decisions; he also framed them as part of a general and pernicious arrogation of power in federal hands. Accordingly, the two decisions represented but the latest installment in a series, of which *Brown* had also been one.[56]

White supremacy had long relied on the trope of an aggressive and intrusive federal government and the narrative of political declension, but these notions acquired increased significance in civil–rights–era Mississippi. As the basis for the doctrine of interposition as well as the Citizens' Council slogan that united "states' rights" with "racial integrity," claims that the federal government erred in insisting on integration injected a tone of righteous defiance into Mississippi's defense of its social system. Hudgins converted politics into religion by decrying the moral effects of an overreaching federal system on American citizens and describing its opposite—a small, limited government—as the very foundations of virtue. He thought the political tendencies of recent decades had produced a populace that sought sustenance from government rather than from their own resources, undermining notions of individual responsibility and hard work: "We have unconsciously allowed ourselves to shrink from many of the harsh problems of individual, community, and state life and turn expectantly to the Federal Government for help. To provide such help—aid for the farmer; aid for the unemployed; aid for the dependent; aid for the aged . . . government has grown to gigantic proportions . . . Our entire economic philosophy seems to reflect the feeling on the part of the individual that the nation owes him a living whether he is willing to work or not." This new mindset, he thought, emboldened groups of aggrieved peoples to advance dubious claims for redress: "Minority groups . . . thrust their wills upon the great majority and . . . the will and welfare of the mass of Americans seem to be forgotten."[57]

This version of political history and philosophy directly contradicted and undermined the suppositions of civil rights leaders, who wanted the government to exercise its power to guarantee fair systems and remove race-based obstacles to social, economic, and political advancement. Such use of governmental power would equip black Americans to move on their own out of poverty and dependency. Yet, the very obstacles black activists hoped to tear down remained absolutely invisible in Hudgins' version of constitutional government. In fact, by tying an overly powerful government to increased immorality, a growth in dependency, and individual laziness run amok, Hudgins appealed to whites' established prejudices and worst fears about blacks and depicted the civil rights challenge as an opportunity for blacks' already debilitating personal traits only to worsen at taxpayer expense. Hudgins remade African Americans' legitimate appeals for federal protections as encouragement for their own degeneracy. More subtly but more powerfully than a sermon on the curse of Ham, Hudgins' explication of Christian America offered blacks no effective path for ending the oppression they suffered. Indeed, Hudgins' articulation of these themes so aptly fit the political thinking of Mississippi's leading segregationists that Congressman John Bell Williams twice had his sermons inserted in the Congressional Record.[58]

Hudgins best elaborated these themes in early 1960, a mere five days after the January 19 inauguration of Ross Barnett as Mississippi's fifty-second governor. Evidently, so many people requested a copy of the sermon on "A Decade of Destiny: The 1960s" that the church made it available for distribution in pamphlet form. As suggested by its weightily worded title, the sermon pulsated with the message that Hudgins and his listeners stood at a decisive moment in history. The 1960s, Hudgins argued, would decide the path America would take—whether it would return to its proper political foundations and nurture the virtue of its citizenry, or reap the frightening consequences of social chaos. Indeed, as he and his congregation basked in the ascension of one of their own to the governor's chair, Hudgins expounded the spiritual version of the political philosophy with which Ross Barnett, nearly three years later, would mount his famous defiance of the Kennedy administration in an effort to deny James Meredith admission to the University of Mississippi.

Mississippi politicians embraced Douglas Hudgins enthusiastically because his message worked well to keep Mississippi on task in its program of resistance to the federal government. He capped his message of Christian America with an appeal to challenge federal leadership and to stay the South's familiar courses: "maybe we had better look carefully to see if the 'New Frontier' is actually the brink of disaster! If we are citizens of 'One Nation Under God,' it could well be that we should be more concerned in seeking 'Old Paths' than in scouting 'New Frontiers.'"[59] Week after week, as Hudgins addressed thousands in his church, through radio and television ministries, and in many public venues throughout the state, he delivered a gospel that strengthened and renewed the underpinnings of racial subordination. And as white supremacists pushed resistance to new heights during the years of racial crisis, Douglas Hudgins held a steady hand on the scaffolding.

Mississippians had heard and celebrated such political truths before, but in the defense of white supremacy these political notions developed into extraordinarily effective tools, especially when wielded by a polished and urbane religious leader like Hudgins. Mississippi's overwhelmingly evangelical white citizenry, desperately hopeful to maintain the privileges once guaranteed their race, emerged from the civil rights years with strong religious commitments to just this political philosophy. In fact, these ideas assumed an even greater importance in the second half of the 1960s, when federal legislation destroyed some of the framework for white supremacy. A well-honed and thoroughly sanctified political philosophy worked best to perpetuate racial privileges when the structures of inequality grew less pervasive, though more invisible.

"Asking White Christians for Only a Lift": The Department of Negro Work

Mississippi Baptists found yet one more way to stay the old path of segregation, even as that system came under vigorous attack. Understanding that Christians outside their state increasingly regarded segregation as sinful and often considered Mississippi Baptists as a hypocritical lot, they answered potential condemnation by expanding their Department of Negro Work (DNW). Tellingly, the DNW's most active years correspond closely to those of the racial crisis, suggesting both its purpose as a segregationist stop-gap measure and its character as the desperate grasp of an embattled religious paternalism. No other religious denomination in Mississippi managed so vast or multi-faceted an outreach to the state's black population. In fact, the Mississippi Baptist Department of Negro Work outpaced any similar ministry in the southern states.[60]

The DNW became an official department of the Mississippi Baptist State Convention in 1953, though its origins date to a women's outreach program from the 1930s. The agency remained small, however, until Dr. William Penn (W. P.) Davis assumed the helm in 1959 and carried the operation to new heights of visibility, institutional support, and financial viability. The DNW focused the bulk of its attention and finances on the Mississippi Baptist Seminary, a center for training black ministers. This institution provided educational programs ranging from rudimentary reading and writing to Sunday school training for Mississippi's black Baptists. From its Central Center in Jackson, the school ultimately grew to twenty-seven extensions around the state. The seminary remained the centerpiece of the program, but the acquisition of a 119-acre campground for hosting conferences and retreats considerably enlarged the DNW's capacity for ministry after 1958. The DNW also established Baptist student unions on Mississippi's black college campuses, implemented Bible distribution programs, and offered vacation Bible schools for African American children.[61]

The program's vast and multifaceted nature proved a useful defense for white Baptists to deploy when agitation for black equality increased and outsiders criticized Baptists for their apparent indifference to black suffering. Mississippi Baptist Convention Executive Secretary-Treasurer Chester Quarles complained that outsiders focused too much attention on racial strife while ignoring Baptist work among African Americans. "We are seeking to tell the story of our work among the Negroes of Mississippi . . . To our amazement we are finding that our friends across the nation have heard all about the instancies [sic] of violence and blood shed in Mississippi, but have not heard one single word about the work of Christian groups."[62] Ironically, white Baptists congratulated themselves for stepping in to amend the educational deficiencies of Mississippi's

African Americans, even though such weaknesses clearly stemmed from the segregated schools these same Baptists insisted on preserving.

Though white leaders seemed to believe that "missions to Negroes" absolved them of aspersions on their racial goodwill, the DNW found favor among white Mississippi Baptists precisely because it operated firmly within the accepted practices and structures of segregation. Promoted as "the great adventure in interracial education," the Mississippi Baptist Seminary took its "interracial" template from already well-established social patterns. The seminary's constitution called for a twenty-one member board of trustees with a rigidly prescribed racial composition—ten black, and eleven white. Rather than hide this effort at white control, the DNW highlighted it; promotional material frequently reminded that "there must be a majority of one White [sic] trustee," as if to assure whites that the outreach constituted no challenge to racial norms. Both white and black faculty members instructed the all-black student body. Other departmental programs, like pastors' conferences, Sunday school conferences, and women's retreats, though often presented as "interracial," actually featured the same structure: black Baptists attended conferences organized and led predominantly by whites.[63]

Though leaders took pains to describe their efforts as "interracial" and "not paternalistic," the DNW sold itself to Mississippi whites as an agent of black control and a foil to civil rights activity. Accepting the notion that blacks' desire for integration came only at the urging of outside agitators, spokesmen for the DNW suggested that the ministry would render its black beneficiaries less vulnerable to such influences: "[unchurched] minds and hearts furnish the battleground for many ideas and ideals detrimental to Christian faith and unity."[64] When W. P. Davis spoke about the DNW before local Baptist groups, he warned that "if we as Mississippi Baptists do not teach the Negro Preachers, the Communists will," and he assured white audiences that none of the black Mississippians with whom he worked "approv[ed] of the NAACP."[65] Others repeated such promises, promoting the seminary as a means of protecting Mississippi blacks from the influence of outside agitators: "would [you] rather see. . . [your] pastor teaching Negroes or Negroes going up North to school or being taught here in Mississippi by strangers who have come from far places?"[66]

Additionally, the DNW gained popularity with white Baptists because it reinscribed the myths about African Americans upon which the racial hierarchy rested. The Department of Negro Work advertised the training of black leadership as a primary goal—an ostensibly empowering agenda since it implied nourishing black independence and promoting responsibility within the black community. Yet in the southern culture of segregation, authentic black leadership constituted a serious conundrum. Maintaining the myth of black inferiority required continued black infantilization; dependence confirmed blacks' putative low potential and kept them under white control.[67] White Baptist leaders thus chose their black disciples carefully, eschewing those who displayed any intention of breaking ranks with white domination and pursuing those who would accept subservience and compliance as the price of white benevolence. Black ministers involved with the DNW obviously grasped the role required of them. They appear to have rarely questioned white control and to have accepted inferiority as a condition of the financial support white Baptists conferred.

The black Baptist minister Dr. H. L. Lang, who had originally established the seminary at the core of the DNW, worked most closely with Davis. Davis gave Lang a great deal of credit for the ministry's work and seems often to have welcomed him as an equal. At the same time, however, he paraded Lang before the Mississippi Baptist Convention, where he used him to reiterate rather than challenge the fundamental tenets of white supremacy in making appeals for a large budgetary allotment. A bit like blackface performers of earlier in the century, Lang confirmed for his white audiences their most cherished beliefs about blacks and about themselves—notions all the more satisfying when articulated by a black man. Lang confirmed the depravity of blacks and juxtaposed this degradation with the benevolent generosity of his white hearers, as in this recounting of an inspired dream: "I saw a white soldier pull a black soldier from a gutter. The black soldier was drunk. I asked the white soldier why he did it. 'He's my buddy. I could not leave him there,' he said. I'm asking white Christians for only a lift. Just give a lift. Lift us! Dear Christian friends, don't leave us in the ditch." Lang deployed a similar strategy in other fundraising talks, evoking the mythological black beast rapist and suggesting that the DNW offered a possible solution: "Think of the value of a man educated in the Mississippi Baptist Seminary! . . . He respects and protects your wife and mine, your daughters and mine."[68]

A pivotal civil rights event in Jackson demonstrated the parameters to which black ministers tacitly agreed when they joined forces with the DNW. In March of 1961, police arrested students from the all-black Tougaloo College as they attempted to integrate the public library. Large numbers of black Jacksonians staged a sympathy prayer meeting and later marched to the city jail. A large crowd of African Americans applauded as the "Tougaloo Nine" arrived at the courthouse a few days later, and law enforcers reacted violently. In the unprovoked attack, police beat onlookers with clubs and pistols and unleashed German shepherd dogs. One dog bit the black vice president of Mississippi Baptist Seminary, Dr. S. Leon Whitney.[69] Dr. Whitney's connection—however tenuous—to a civil rights demonstration set white Baptists into an uproar. As pastor to several of the defendants, his presence at the trial fell entirely within the purview of his ministerial duties. Nonetheless, white Baptist outrage issued forth upon both Dr. Whitney and Davis. Inundating Davis with phone calls, white Baptists demanded to know why that "nigger [was] connected with [this] work," and they insisted that Davis fire him immediately. Whitney, for his part, knew instinctively that supporting the arrested demonstrators constituted a serious transgression of acceptable behavior by a black minister beholden to white support. Hoping to preempt the crisis, he wired his resignation to Davis and the trustees even before the news became public, though Davis intervened to keep Whitney in the job.[70]

If the DNW applauded its own paternalistic character, its director, W. P. Davis, presents an extraordinarily complicated and contradictory figure. A white man in the inner leadership circle of an ardently segregationist constituency, he had strong personal convictions about racial injustice. Even as he applauded the compliance and submissiveness of his own black associates, he decried the paternalism of Mississippi whites. He presided over a ministry that reinforced the inferiority and dependence of Mississippi blacks, though he identified segregation as an evil. Such contradictions seem inevitable, however, in an outreach both defined and confined by commitments to segregation. As a native-born Mississippian with deep family roots in the church, Davis envisioned himself working with black Mississippians from early in his life. The absence of established paths for working with blacks when he entered the ministry in 1923 indicates the paucity of interracial religious work. Among white Baptists in civil-rights-era Mississippi, a paternalistic ministry such as Davis ultimately administered probably represented his best opportunity for such outreach.[71] Chester Quarles' caution that "The people are not ready, don't push us," suggests that clear limits were established for him.[72]

Though Davis observed all the conventions of segregation, he formed a close relationship with his black ministry partner, Dr. H. L. Lang. Davis and Lang traveled together throughout the state, affording Davis the opportunity to experience directly the ways that segregated restrooms and hotel accommodations often meant no restrooms or accommodations for blacks. The black man occasionally stayed overnight in Davis' home, and Davis frequently enjoyed hospitality in Lang's home and in other black residences and churches. Davis occasionally pushed the limits of acceptable behaviors even further. Once, he eased segregation's tension with a bit of comical deception. Meeting Lang at the railroad station, Davis chose to walk with him through the "colored" waiting room, rather than going alone through the "white" waiting room. He even stopped for a drink of water at the water fountain. As he drank, a policeman tapped him on the shoulder and said, "Don't you know you aren't supposed to be in here, in this nigger room?" Davis quickly invented a clever reply, "Now, Mr. Policeman, a lot of people think I'm white." The astounded policeman stared at Davis for a few seconds before muttering, "Well, I'll be damned," as he turned to walk away. The two ministers continued through the waiting room, suppressing their laughter until they were out.[73]

Importantly, however, though most Mississippi whites seemed relatively comfortable with the interracial elements of Davis' ministry, in the civil rights era, rabid segregationists could no longer tolerate even the paternalistic interracial exchange that had characterized the South for decades. White supremacists tampered with Davis' car and burned crosses on his lawn. Night-time callers threatened his life. Once, as he returned from a meeting with black Baptists, eleven men with covered faces dragged him from his car, beat him, and urinated in his face. Indeed, as tensions in Mississippi escalated, those who failed to observe rigid lines of racial separation jeopardized their own claims to white privilege.[74]

Davis showed an awareness of the DNW's paternalism, and he seemed to understand that relationships of power—such as those encouraged by the DNW—hindered the advance of racial justice. Nonetheless, he appreciated the constraints of the time and chose to work within the parameters imposed on him.[75] Whatever effect—for good or ill—Davis' ministry had on the course of race relations in Mississippi, it seems to have worked its most notable transformation on him. Davis grew into a severe, vocal, and courageous critic of white Mississippians' behavior during the years of racial crisis. In 1965, he testified before the United States Commission on Civil Rights when it held hearings in Jackson. While his appearance before the commission in and of itself would have invited the retribution of Mississippi's racial extremists, Davis boldly denounced both white supremacy and Mississippi's strategies for perpetuating that system: "A power structure designed to deprive citizens of their voting rights and to discriminate in the administration of justice because of race or creed is tyranny."[76] Yet Davis' insights mark him as a rarity among the state's white Baptists. The majority of them remained committed to preserving that power structure to the fullest extent possible.

* * *

As the religious group most closely identified with white Mississippi's culture, it surprises little that Southern Baptists in the state strove so tenaciously to preserve white supremacy. Their strategies for staying on that old path—near silence on racial issues from their leaders, deep and chronic opposition to initiatives of the SBC, the embrace of a political philosophy that reinvented black appeals for government intervention as a path to moral weakness, and a vigorous outreach to black Mississippians that reinforced rather than challenged the racial hierarchy—may have spared Mississippi Baptists the turmoil that wracked their Methodist counterparts. That fractious body passed the civil rights years in confusion, frustration, and distress.

6

"Born of Conviction"

The Travail of Mississippi Methodism

On an early January day in 1963, an irate townsman stormed into the office of Pisgah Methodist Church near McComb to scold Pastor Bill Lampton: "You've messed yourself up real good, boy!" He announced that church members planned to meet that night to "throw [him] out." The following Saturday, Reverend Lampton awoke to find his car tires slashed. Still intending to conduct worship services the next day, he reconsidered when two sympathetic parishioners brought warnings that an angry mob threatened violence to the church and parsonage. Fearing imminent danger, Lampton quickly removed his family to the safety of his parents' home in Columbia. Pisgah Methodist Church held no services that Sunday. Lampton sent for his possessions a few days later and never returned to that pulpit.[1]

Lampton's troubles ensued from the "Born of Conviction" statement that he and twenty-seven other young pastors had placed in the *Mississippi Methodist Advocate*. Their declaration began with an endorsement of the Methodist Church's position on the *Brown* decision: "Born of the deep conviction of our souls . . . We affirm our faith in the official position of the Methodist Church . . . Our Lord Jesus Christ teaches that all men are brothers. He permits no discrimination because of race, color, or creed." The statement's other four paragraphs expressed opposition to the closing of public schools and affirmed the pastors' belief in the right of ministers to speak their conscience—a notion dubbed "freedom of the pulpit" by those religious Mississippians concerned about the increased circumscription of thought in their state. Though the statement hardly seemed radical to the ministers and they intended it only for the state's Methodist community, secular papers picked up the story, and "Born of Conviction" stirred up a hornet's nest.[2]

The grapevines in Mississippi's secular and religious communities fairly crackled with word of the audacious young clerics, and Methodist congregations unleashed fury on the twenty-eight pastors. A church member stopped by the home of an unsuspecting James Rush, pastor of three rural churches in Neshoba County. Finding the minister absent, he heaped verbal abuse upon Rush's wife, so traumatizing her that she required a hospital stay. A second angry church member sought out Mrs. Rush even in her confinement and administered yet another tongue-lashing. While his wife languished, Reverend Rush tried desperately to fend off a coup at two of his churches, but to no avail. At one, he interrupted a clandestine meeting of board members who shocked him with vicious taunts: "Get him a nigger church; bet his son marries a nigger." When Rush refused to recant the affirmations in "Born of Conviction," the board took a vote—contrary to the stipulations of Methodist polity—and fired their pastor then and there.[3]

At the rural Byram Methodist Church near Jackson, angry members demanded Pastor James Nicholson's resignation just days after the statement appeared. Nicholson proposed that he and the board work to hold the church together until June, when he could request a new appointment, but the board would have none of him. With his salary suspended and the specter of an empty church looming, Nicholson accepted the futility of further negotiations and stepped down.[4]

The furor over the "Born of Conviction" statement dramatically illustrates the turbulence of Mississippi's Methodist community in the civil rights years. While Baptists preserved a placid exterior that masked their frictions with the SBC, Methodists passed the civil rights years in chronic, debilitating turmoil. The fractiousness that beset Mississippi's Methodist community arose from several sources: the very real prospect of racial integration in Methodism, the greater theological variety among Mississippi Methodists, and many Mississippians' loyalties to an extraordinarily diverse national denomination. In a sense, their battles represented one theater in the larger national struggle to redefine the meanings of American Christianity with respect to race relations.

"Born of Conviction" also revealed a widening of the chasm between die-hard segregationists and more moderate whites after the fall of 1962, when resistance to James Meredith's admission to the University of Mississippi produced embarrassing and deadly violence. Spurred by the Meredith debacle, moderate representatives of white religious communities began to condemn Mississippi's resistance to federal directives more forcefully; a very few went so far as to convert that critique into an argument for desegregation. As this small circle of religious voices called Mississippi's path of defiance into question, segregationists strove ever harder to keep religion on board with white supremacy. Segregationists had thought all their white enemies lay outside the state, among "liberals" in their denominations, but after Meredith, Mississippi's evangelicals increasingly found themselves torn internally by the racial crisis. Mississippi's white religious communities no longer appeared only as chaplains to the armies of segregation. Rather, they became battlegrounds in the struggle for black civil rights. The call for racial justice could hardly ring with clarity over the din of such a conflagration.

The Varieties of Mississippi Methodism

For the most part, Mississippi Methodists' commitments to white supremacy looked identical to those of others in the state. Well-credential ministers and prominent laymen openly defended segregation. Dr. Felix Sutphin, for example, applauded Mississippi's racial arrangements before his Grenada congregation in 1956.[5] In 1957, Reverend Robert Hunt of Harperville Methodist Church recommended that local churches establish private schools rather than submit to integration. His counterpart at Forest Methodist Church, Dr. Gilbert Oliver, defended segregation even more vigorously: "Segregation of races is not—as we have been told—evil, unchristian and barbaric."[6] The Methodist layman and award-winning journalist Oliver Emmerich of McComb even defended segregation in a head-to-head argument with Thurgood Marshall at a Methodist Conference in Dallas, Texas.[7]

Unlike Baptists, however, Mississippi Methodists belonged to an institution with a black constituency. The denomination's embrace of the principle of racial inclusion in 1944 heightened concerns about integration in the church. In the western United States, portions of the all-black Central Jurisdiction dissolved and joined existing conferences, and a church integrated at the congregational level appeared a looming possibility. In 1956, Mississippi Methodists' commitments to segregation burst forcefully into view when they considered Amendment IX,

ecclesiastical legislation designed to facilitate the administrative transfer of black Methodist churches into previously all-white conferences.
Amendment IX portended no changes in the racial composition of
local congregations; it aimed simply to place black and white churches
within the same administrative structure. Furthermore, the amendment did not mandate these transfers; it made them a matter of local
option, and both white and black churches in a given conference had to
approve the change. Optimistic national leaders believed the measure
would allow southerners time to adjust their attitudes and absorb the
black churches at their own pace, but the most zealous segregationists
regarded it as nothing less than compromise with the forces of evil.[8]

The fate of Amendment IX provoked acrimonious debate when the
Mississippi and North Mississippi conferences convened their annual
meetings in June 1957. The fault lines did not reflect divisions over the
desirability of a segregated church; all present agreed about that. Rather,
the controversy hinged on how the legislation might affect their pros-
pects of retaining race-based Methodism in Mississippi. In supporters'
eyes, the amendment's voluntarism made it a safe arrangement because,
as one layman insisted, "Our brethren of the Central Jurisdiction prefer
to be there, by and large." By contrast, those who opposed the amendment did so because they believed it lacked sufficient strength to stop
integration. "I think you are opening the door to integration. I think
you are ruining this church," argued a bitter opponent. Another maintained, "The (Negroes) seek an official foot in the door, and once the
foot is in they will not be content. While I appreciate the sincerity of
those who believe this is the thing to do, I must vote against the foot
slipping in the door." The amendment ultimately passed because a sizeable majority of Mississippi Methodists accepted the argument that it
protected segregation.[9]

Again in October 1957, Mississippi Methodists defended segregation
as they streamed to Montgomery, Alabama, for hearings before the
denomination's Committee on Interjurisdictional Relations. Conven-
ing one month after the Little Rock school integration crisis, the committee hosted hundreds in packed sessions where over eighty people
asked to speak their minds about the prospect of changing Methodism's
jurisdictional system. No speaker favored even the slightest tinkering
with the church's segregated structure; instead, all revealed the depth to

which fear of such alterations utterly destabilized local congregations. "There is hardly a Sunday that passes that somehow or another the lesson does not deviate from what the lesson intended and get on this subject [of integration]," observed a Natchez pastor. A layman warned that others he knew "possibly without exception" would "consider the destruction of the Jurisdictional System . . . a betrayal." Some declared their intent to withdraw from the church if it abandoned its segregated arrangement. Representatives of a Delta congregation informed the panel that "Methodism in the Mississippi Delta will not be a party to integration in the local church," and for his part, Bishop Franklin "feared what would be the consequence if there is any material change made in our jurisdictional set up."[10]

Yet in spite of their near unanimity on preserving segregation, the racial crisis significantly exacerbated Mississippi Methodists' existing subtle fissures over theology and over attitudes toward the larger national Methodist community. While nearly all Mississippi Methodists embraced a fairly conservative theology, the less rigid proclivities of a minority clashed with the dominant fundamentalist outlook. Mississippi Methodists also differed dramatically in their outlook on their own denomination. Since the union of the northern and southern churches in 1939 had joined conservative evangelical southerners to theological and political liberals, the most conservative Mississippi Methodists sometimes felt threatened in this new body and adopted a combative posture toward it. The more moderate among them, by contrast, felt proud of their identification with America's largest Protestant communion.

To combat the "liberal" trends in their denomination, conservative Mississippi Methodists created the Voluntary Committee of Christian Laymen in 1950. Initially the group seems to have done very little, but when the Methodist Church endorsed the *Brown* decision in 1954, the organization found a fresh raison d'etre and reorganized itself as the Mississippi Association of Methodist Ministers and Layman (MAMML). As the voice of conservative Mississippi Methodism, the group appeared something of a baptized Citizens' Council, advocating continued racial segregation in the Methodist Church and linking this concern to right-wing politics, conservative evangelicalism, and biblical literalism. Significantly, MAMML's membership overlapped considerably with the Citizens' Councils and with the vanguard of white supremacist leadership in the state. Noted segregationist attorney John Satterfield and Jackson Citizens' Council President John Wright lead the organization. Citizen Council spokesman Dr. Medford Evans wrote articles and spoke at MAMML gatherings, and John Kochtitzky, who rendered occasional services for the Sovereignty Commission, served in several MAMML offices.[11]

The MAMML's devotion to segregation transformed it from a simple advocacy organization to an out-and-out attack group. In MAMML's view, the Methodist Church's official embrace of racial equality rendered it the enemy of white Mississippians. Smelling aggression, evil intent, and even apostasy in nearly every official Methodist utterance, the MAMML focused on church literature as a conduit for integrationist propaganda. Complaints about Methodist publications had initially surfaced in the 1940s, but they increased in intensity, volume, and focus after the *Brown* decision.[12] Some congregations argued intently over the merits of Methodist church school material. Others, more united in their rejection of official publications, adopted alternate literature programs.[13] The MAMML both gave voice to and stoked these concerns, citing offensive features that included short fictional stories about interracial friendships or reading lists that recommended works by black authors.[14] In 1957, a group representing nearly every Methodist church in Jackson petitioned the General Conference to rid church literature of "integration propaganda." Though not lodged under MAMML's auspices, this complaint bore the organization's unmistakable fingerprints: MAMML's treasurer, Garner Lester, opened the protest meeting in prayer, John Satterfield addressed the group, and John Kochtitzky drafted the resolution.[15] Two years later, MAMML's successful nourishing of this discontent brought action when the Mississippi Methodist Conference lodged a formal protest with the General Conference; the complaint claimed Methodist publications "tr[ied] to force integration of the races throughout the entire country."[16]

The MAMML united its conservative political concerns to its fundamentalist theology in its attacks on the National Council of Churches (NCC). The NCC had evolved from the Federal Council of Churches (FCC), adopting the new name and an altered organizational structure in 1950. Despite the new arrangement, however, the NCC carried over the social-gospel orientation of its predecessor, advocating policy positions that it hoped would create a more equitable social and economic order. Until 1963, the NCC generally confined its work on race relations to simple pronouncements that affirmed the principle of racial equality, but even such mild statements rankled southern segregationists. As members of denominations who belonged to the NCC, southern conservatives deplored the fact that their financial contributions funded an organization they regarded as both theologically apostate and politically radical. Criticisms of the NCC from southern religious voices multiplied as the civil rights years unfolded, and the MAMML amplified these complaints. Church leaders and theologians who over-intellectualized the old-fashioned faith of the Bible, they believed, had perverted the gospel of salvation through faith into a gospel of social amelioration through political action. To MAMML leaders and other southerners it seemed little wonder that misguided ministers, having discarded the message of spiritual regeneration, would advocate the dangerously perverse doctrine of racial equality. Though evident from early in the post-war era, Mississippians' criticisms of the NCC peaked in 1961, 1962, and 1964.[17]

The MAMML counted sympathizers among pastors, important parishioners, Sunday school teachers, deacons, and ordinary layfolk. Though the organization remained unofficial and never garnered sanction from any agency of the church, many of Mississippi's most influential Methodist leaders shared its concerns. Yet importantly, many Mississippi Methodists regarded the MAMML with deep suspicion. These more moderate Methodists worshiped in the same churches and held the same offices as their counterparts. They included prominent laymen like the Tupelo businessman Jack Reed, state legislator from Washington County, Joseph Wroten, and McComb newspaper editor Oliver Emmerich. Younger pastors, including Maxie Dunnam of Gulfport, Gerald Trigg of Pascagoula, Jim Waits of Biloxi, and Jerry Furr of Jackson, often displayed a more moderate outlook, as did some prominent church officials like the Conference Lay Leader, Dr. J. P. Stafford. Perhaps most importantly, moderates sat at the helm of two of the state's most influential Methodist institutions: Sam Ashmore edited the *Mississippi Methodist Advocate* and Dr. W. B. Selah pastored the large and prestigious Galloway Memorial Methodist Church.

Many of these moderates preferred, and some argued for, continued segregation, especially in the early years of the racial struggle. Some shared MAMML's concern about the liberal drift in church publications and eyed the NCC with suspicion. Yet they differed from MAMML's supporters in two primary respects. Perhaps most important, these moderates displayed a strong loyalty to the Methodist Church. Simply put, they valued their faith tradition more dearly than segregation, and they refused to regard as an enemy the very institution they deemed so essential to their spiritual identity and so vital to religious work in the world. Thus, even as Felix Sutphin expounded the virtues of segregation before his Grenada congregation, he tempered this praise with a defense of the church. Indeed, reasoned moderates like Sutphin, the Methodist Church's embrace of racial equality, however unwise, did not render it irredeemably apostate. Institutional loyalty, a commitment that for many Americans in the mid-twentieth century defined spirituality, simply trumped devotion to legal segregation.[18]

Moderate Methodists also approached the Bible and theology differently from arch-segregationists. In a religious culture that took the truth of Scripture for granted, these moderates certainly held the Bible in high regard, but they stopped short of an unyieldingly literalist approach, rejecting the kind of fundamentalism that the MAMML and its followers embraced. Jim Waits, who pastored Epworth Church in Biloxi, agreed that "the Bible is the Word of God," but he condemned "the selective picking and choosing of isolated texts to prove a point."[19] Similarly, Maxie Dunnam revealed his flexible theology: "We are not forms and creeds, though we have both. . . . A systematic theology satisfactory to the Methodist world has never been written. It never will be because Methodism is life, and there is no way to regiment human and divine experience."[20] This more pliable stance helped moderates embrace a Christianity that spoke directly to political and social questions. Reverend Prentiss M. Gordon rejected the "narrow, non-social interpretation of salvation." Claiming that Methodism offered a "much broader interpretation of salvation," Gordon argued that "I am afraid Christ would be considered . . . a wild-eyed liberal today."[21] Their less rigid outlook led these moderates to take their spiritual truths from a wide variety of sources. The poems of John Donne and Paul Lawrence Dunbar, the writings of Henry David Thoreau, the meditations of the

Wesleys, and even the lyrics of Rogers and Hammerstein songs all found their way into moderate Mississippi Methodist sermons.

Moderates did not openly advocate for integration, and they often remained damningly silent in the face of segregationist initiatives. Yet, their institutional loyalty and theological flexibility put them on a decidedly different trajectory during the racial crisis, as devotion to Methodism ultimately came to mean recalibrating racial attitudes. Even if their own personal instincts ran contrarily, such Methodists often lashed their convictions to the church's official policy while riding through the turbulent times. Yet perhaps even more importantly, though moderates often declined to contend actively for racial equality, some did raise their voices against segregationist orthodoxy. In particular, as the atmosphere grew more and more restrictive, they opposed Mississippi's formal and informal mechanisms for limiting free speech.

No moderate served in a more influential position than the editor of the *Mississippi Methodist Advocate*, Sam Ashmore. Though his own instincts seemed largely in sync with the church's more liberal national leaders, Ashmore took seriously his obligation to serve Mississippi Methodists of all persuasions. He thus gave space in the paper for articles, sermons, or local church resolutions that favored segregation, and he sometimes reported dispassionately on the activities of the MAMML. Yet he balanced segregationist voices by printing the national Methodist agencies' progressive resolutions and featuring sermons from denominational leaders who promoted racial equality. While local ministers generally did not defend the Supreme Court's *Brown* decision or endorse integration, their contributing columns and Ashmore's own editorials urged reason and caution on Methodists—a valuable exercise as the state pursued an ever more radical approach in the defense of segregation. In particular, the *Advocate* frankly condemned Mississippi's anti-civil rights legislation, criticized the state's practice of banning books, defended the Methodist publishing house, praised the work of the National Council of Churches, and championed free speech.[22]

Even Ashmore's oblique approach, however, provoked the archsegregationists of the MAMML, who wanted a church paper that more forthrightly embraced their views. Segregationist leaders expressed appreciation for the *Baptist Record* as a wholesome and spiritually nourishing publication, but controversy constantly swirled around the

Advocate.[23] Conservatives regarded it as but another example of the official Methodist literature they found so disturbing. The MAMML circulated resolutions that censured the paper and urged a boycott of it. By 1963 subscriptions had fallen so drastically that the *Advocate* faced serious financial losses.[24]

Thus, confusing and conflicting messages dinned in the ears of white Mississippians who sat in Methodist pews during the civil rights years. The conservative incantations of the MAMML jangled against pleas for moderation in the *Advocate*. Some Methodists' racial fears clashed uncomfortably against the denominational loyalties of others. Congregations buzzed with intrigue, and disoriented flocks looked to their pastors for help negotiating the haze, but sometimes these ministers found their own convictions shifting as the racial crisis unfolded.

"The Actualities of Life": William Bryan Selah

Galloway Memorial Methodist Church in downtown Jackson contained the diversity of Mississippi Methodism in a microcosm. MAMML stalwart John Wright worshipped there, as did Citizens' Council boosters like Jackson mayor Allen Thompson. The congregation also included a few layfolk with deep commitments to racial equality, such as Tougaloo College physics professor John Garner and his Swiss wife, Margrit. The moderate pastor, Dr. William Bryan Selah, occupied a position between these two poles. Like the overwhelming majority of Mississippi Methodists, Selah supported segregation during much of his career. Yet, because he resigned from Galloway in 1963, when the church rejected black Mississippians who attempted to worship there, many have regarded him as a white hero of the civil rights era. As the following portrait will demonstrate, Selah presents a far more complicated figure. A consummate moderate with a practical rather than ideological commitment to segregation, Selah's devotion to the Methodist Church and his supple theological outlook reshaped his position over time.[25]

Bill Selah enjoyed extraordinary success in his chosen profession. Entering the ministry in the 1920s as part-time pastor of small churches in his native Missouri, he graduated quickly to larger, urban charges in Kansas City, Memphis, and Oklahoma City. He came to Galloway in 1945 at forty-eight years of age, planning to finish his career there.

During Selah's eighteen years in the Galloway pulpit, membership swelled from 2,000 to nearly 4,000. While keeping the church free from financial encumbrances, he increased the staff to twenty-one persons and raised some budget items by ten-fold.[26] In spite of his divinity degree from Yale, Selah maintained a folksy humor and a down-to-earth preaching style that endeared him to the congregation. Parishioners felt he had the "ability to reach everyone"; some called his sermons "deep," their simplicity notwithstanding.[27]

Selah did not come to Galloway as a critic of southern racial mores. To the contrary, he repeatedly demonstrated support for the principle of segregation. In sermons, he made no effort to hide his disagreement with the *Brown* decision, explaining: "[a friend of mine from the North] said that the schools should be integrated at once all over America. He sincerely believes that justice and right demand it. I told him that I could not share his views. I told him I thought it would be tragic for both races in the Deep South to put black and white children in the same school."[28] He supported the bishops of the Southeastern Jurisdiction when they voiced objections to the *Brown* decision. Along with 321 other Mississippi Methodists, he approved Amendment IX as a means to protect segregation in the church, citing the common belief that black Americans' preference for worship with their own race made the maintenance of the Central Jurisdiction a good arrangement.[29] He vigorously opposed the Church Property Bill in 1960 because he doubted that his denomination would ever force an end to segregated worship.[30]

Like many white Mississippi Christians, Selah did not seem to think segregation demonstrated racism, as he denounced "little racial prejudices" and called bigotry the "biggest sin of our generation."[31] He encouraged personal kindness, charity, and generosity of spirit toward black Mississippians, admonishing his parishioners to behave like the Good Samaritan, who "saw the wounded man [and] helped. [H]e did not ask what church he belonged to or what race he was of or what flag flew over him."[32] Such interracial mercies conflicted little with segregation in the minds of many white Mississippi evangelicals who did not believe their faith demanded integration. Yet Selah differed from hardline segregationists in that he treated the racial hierarchy as a practical accommodation to the "actualities of life" in the South, rather than a principle worth preserving at any price. In fact, lacking a fanatical devotion to keeping blacks and whites apart, he argued that integration might make practical sense in some circumstances: "What should a white church do in a community that contained only a few colored families—not enough to support a church of their own? The white people should invite the colored people to come in with them."[33]

Even while endorsing racial segregation in church and public life, Selah rejected the biblical literalism so often married to white supremacy. He characterized questions of biblical inerrancy as distractions from larger, more important truths: "Did the whale swallow Jonah? That question has often blinded men to the message of the book of Jonah, which is that God loved Ninevites as much as Jews and wanted them also to know the joy of salvation."[34] Without ever naming his approach the social gospel, he argued that real faith made qualitative demands on human relationships and social behavior: "It is more important to love our neighbor than it is to believe all the creed . . . the faith that Christ requires involves an investment of life in the direction of his teachings."[35] Selah's sermons often emphasized the brotherhood of man, human compassion, and personal freedom—all unremarkable as Christian themes in ordinary times, but potentially dangerous triggers as Mississippi's atmosphere grew more charged in the civil rights years.

Before 1954, such sentiments fit well within the framework of the white Christian paternalism to which Mississippians were so accustomed. However, the *Brown* decision and Mississippi's increasing circumscription of civil liberties in the pursuit of continued segregation changed the realm of acceptable religious discourse. In particular, Mississippi's leading segregationists drastically limited the space for discussing racial questions in any fashion that challenged the racial orthodoxy. Selah, like Sam Ashmore, served as an important voice of moderation and a pointed critic of the climate of conformity and restrictiveness that characterized Mississippi's culture in these years.

In the spring of 1958, Mississippi Methodists reeled from a debacle reminiscent of Ole Miss's Alvin Kershaw affair at their denominational college, Millsaps, in Jackson. A group of students and faculty invited a white religious advocate of black equality, Dr. Glenn Smiley of the Fellowship of Reconciliation, to speak at a forum on "Christianity and Race Relations." After a huge outcry against Smiley's scheduled appearance, the college administration cancelled the talk.[36] This fiasco garnered immense publicity and attention, especially in Mississippi's Methodist circles, where the college became the focal point in a debate over the relative merits of academic freedom and segregation.

In the midst of this imbroglio, Selah preached a Sunday sermon that frankly discussed the racial crisis and its impact on freedom of speech in Mississippi. His six-point message affirmed his own support for segregation, but argued no correlation between moral character and racial sentiments: "Most people who believe in integration are good Americans and good Christians. . . . Most people who believe in segregation are good Americans and good Christians." Significantly, however, Selah vigorously defended Mississippians' right to free speech in their churches, in the press, and in the academy. They could best respond to the racial crisis, he argued, by "[c]ontend[ing] earnestly for [their] beliefs and allow[ing their] neighbors the same privilege."[37] In a Mississippi writhing under censorship and intimidation, Selah's words had meaning beyond their face value. Given that members of the segregation-besotted state legislature, the Citizens' Councils, and the MAMML—all groups responsible for the restricted climate of expression—filled Galloway's pews, his admonitions no doubt caused considerable squirming. Threatening phone calls in the days following the sermon, he thought, came from just these parishioners.[38]

Yet again, in 1961, the waves of racial controversy crashed down on Galloway, and Selah strode into the waters. Jackson's citizens steeled themselves that June as the "Freedom Riders" headed toward their city.[39] Many of the riders claimed a religious motivation, and black churches sheltered and encouraged them along their journey. Since the riders purposefully integrated as many venues as possible, church boards worried that they might try to attend worship services once they arrived in Jackson. Like other congregations, the Galloway Board convened a special session to consider a motion to refuse admission to black individuals or integrated parties: "the greeters or ushers of the church are hereby instructed to decline to admit any person or persons, white or colored, who in the judgment of the greeters or ushers, seek admission for the purpose of creating an incident, resulting in a breach of the peace."[40]

Selah addressed the board before it voted on the proposal. He affirmed the principle of racial equality, but also allowed for the validity of segregation: "[I]t is not sinful for white people to prefer to worship with white people or for colored people to prefer to worship with colored people. The sin comes when a church seeks to put up a color bar before the Cross of Christ. As Christians we cannot say to anybody, 'You cannot come into the house of God.' To discriminate against a man because of the color of his skin is contrary to the will of God." As to the Freedom Riders, Selah revealed both his own savvy about their strategy as well as a fair amount of scorn for it: "In my judgment the Freedom Riders hope to be turned away. If we do it, we will be playing into their hands, and they will cry to high heaven that Galloway bars colored people." Selah offered a method for depriving them of this opportunity: "let them in." He then read a prepared statement, which he planned to read to the Freedom Riders once they were seated in Galloway's sanctuary: "If you came at the urging of the Congress of Racial Equality or some other organization, I am convinced that you did not come in a sincere spirit to worship God with us. If you came to embarrass us by flouting an old custom, you have not succeeded. If you hoped to be turned away so that you could use the incident for propaganda purposes, you have failed." Selah's proposed statement ended with words that echoed a common Mississippi interpretation of the effects of black activism: "In my judgment your coming here today has not increased interracial goodwill or helped in the solution of the race problem. My advice to you is to go home and let the southern people, black and white, work out their own problems by orderly and constitutional means."[41]

The board ignored Selah's advice and passed its resolution by an overwhelming margin. Selah responded inwardly by determining that he would resign if Galloway ever refused admission to anyone, but Jackson city officials' orchestration of events failed to test that commitment in the summer of 1961. The buses carried the Freedom Riders into an eerily quiet downtown Jackson, where law officers herded them directly from the bus station into waiting police wagons. After summary trials, a number spent the remainder of the summer at Mississippi's infamous Parchman Penitentiary. For his part, Selah sensed that he served as Galloway's pastor on borrowed time.[42]

The confrontation with his board over the admission of black worshippers seemed to have worked a change on Selah. Just a few months later, in November of 1961, he delivered a sermon that dispensed with any ambiguity about segregation. Repeating a principle he had affirmed since arriving at Galloway, Selah told his congregation that Christian love means "we will seek for all men, black and white, the same rights, the same justice and the same opportunities that we seek for ourselves." This time, however, he applied that principle directly to the racial crisis. "Forced segregation is wrong," he argued, and doubly wrong in the church, because "race prejudice is a denial of the basic Christian doctrine of brotherhood." Perhaps he hoped to preempt attacks from fundamentalists when he added, "we will not be judged by our theological opinions, but by the way we treat men."[43] Given the heavy contingent of segregationists among his hearers and the tension that permeated public life, some members admired his courage, but they also wondered why the congregation "didn't rise up in arms."[44]

James Meredith and Mississippi Methodism

In late September 1962, segregationist intransigence thrust Mississippi to the center of national attention. A black Mississippian, James Meredith, successfully registered at the University of Mississippi after President Kennedy called out federal troops and a riot engulfed the campus. Like all civil rights events in the state, the Meredith affair reverberated in Mississippi's religious communities. Yet this fiasco—the state's most headline-grabbing to date in the civil rights era—initiated a turmoil that only grew as event piled upon event and did not abate for over two years. This distress pressed the already evident breaches in Mississippi's Methodist community into yawning chasms.[45]

When the Fifth Circuit Court of Appeals ordered Meredith's enrollment on September 13, Mississippi's segregationist leaders swung into action. Joined by most of the congressional delegation and all but two of the state's legislators, Governor Ross Barnett called for resistance to the federal directive.[46] For the next two weeks, Barnett elevated his defiance to the level of martyrdom, depicting the preservation of Ole Miss's all-white status as an urgent and righteous cause. White Mississippians roared approval. On September 30, as Meredith sat safely in a dormitory under federal protection the night before his first class, a crowd of students and armed outsiders numbering over 3,000 swarmed the campus and the tiny town of Oxford. The crowd set fire to a few vehicles and pelted the small force of federal marshals sent to protect Meredith.

Emboldened by the obvious inability of the marshals to contain them, the mob grew increasingly menacing. When they began firing on the lawmen, who were initially denied permission to fire back, it became clear that only the army could put down the swelling violence. A contingent of 26,000 soldiers from Memphis finally arrived in Oxford at 2:15 a.m. and restored order by dawn, but by then, two persons had died and over 160 federal marshals sustained injuries, many of them gunshot wounds.

Oxford jolted Mississippians of every persuasion. The fiasco dramatically belied proud claims about peaceful race relations in the state. Yet segregationist spinmasters would not accept that the violence stemmed from an absurd enthusiasm for white domination or from the open encouragement of law-breaking that issued from Mississippi's public officials. Instead, they cast their own white residents as the victims of an overbearing and repressive federal government. Praising the bravery and tenacity of Governor Ross Barnett, who had "stood in the schoolhouse door" in an effort to stop Meredith's registration, Mississippians blamed the rioting on the Kennedy administration and its sending federal troops to "occupy" Mississippi. Though their huge expenditure of energy and resources to resist school integration had failed, many white Mississippians grew more strident in their condemnation of excessive federal power, and they entertained serious discussion about closing public schools.

The Meredith debacle sent shockwaves through Mississippi's white religious communities, too. After the affair turned so savage on the night of September 30, a few no doubt grew reflective enough to hear moderate ministers from the Oxford area call their fellow citizens to observe the following Sunday—October 7, 1962—as a "specific time for repentance for our collective and individual guilt in the formation of the atmosphere which produced the strife at the University of Mississippi and Oxford." Crowds filled churches in the university town that Sunday. At St. Peter's Episcopal Church, listeners heard Reverend Duncan Gray explain why Mississippians needed to repent: "You and I, along with every other Mississippian, are responsible for the moral and political climate in our state which made such a tragedy possible." Addressing the action he thought must follow collective repentance, Gray admonished, "[W]e must accept the fact that the color of a person's skin can no longer be a barrier to his admission to the University of Mississippi."[47]

The Oxford community heard several sermons like Gray's that Sunday after the riot. Around the state, a few other religious voices called for a new climate, and some condemned the behavior of their segregationist leaders and fellow citizens. The district superintendents of the North Mississippi Methodist Conference "wholeheartedly" endorsed the Oxford minister's call for responsibility and repentance.[48] In an *Advocate* editorial, Sam Ashmore echoed Gray's call for collective responsibility: "Yes, the church is partly responsible for what happened at Ole Miss. Because we were not more vocal and outspoken; because we were not true to our Christian Convictions, we aided anarchy."[49] In a fiery sermon to his Caswell Springs Methodist congregation, Gerald Trigg compared the frenzied atmosphere created by Governor Barnett to Hitler's Germany.[50] Galloway's Associate Pastor Jerry Furr urged: "Hatred and scorn for those of another race cannot be justified."[51] In Biloxi, Jim Waits preached on the sovereignty of God, blasting Governor Barnett's careless use of the concept: "Sovereignty seems to be in these days a very relative thing, tailored to satisfy the personal whims and ambitions, and the political fears of elective officials."[52] From his pulpit at Jones Memorial Presbyterian Church in Meridian, Reverend Charles Stanford, Jr., also stressed corporate complicity in the events at Oxford: "Those of us who have remained silent on a great and grave moral issue have lent support to those who have spoken out on the side of error and evil."[53] In Starkville, Presbyterian pastor Robert Walkup offered a similar assessment: "The blood is on my hands! For I, together with too many of our people, helped to create the impression that we wanted [these] men of violence."[54] In his sermon and prayers, Dr. Moody McDill of Fondren Presbyterian Church in Jackson also suggested that Mississippians shared responsibility for the deaths and injuries at Oxford.[55] Even the *Baptist Record* offered two brief editorials that "utterly condemned" acts of violence, though the otherwise tepid pieces would not identify any responsible parties: "it is very difficult accurately to place blame."[56] The *Record's* editorials in fact proved less forceful than the statements of some secular groups, for even a group of Mississippi businessmen asked for a halt to violence and for vigorous prosecution of the riot's perpetrators.[57]

Yet, despite these urgings, many Mississippi Christians displayed their long schooling in notions of individual morality and took umbrage at talk of collective responsibility. A Methodist laymen thought it "mis-taken judgment" that "somehow Mississippi was the cause of the vio-lence."[58] After Reverend Stanford's sermon at the Meridian service, an elder refused the elements at communion, and the congregation later presented their pastor with a resolution of censure, calling his sermon "untimely and the references made to alleged sins of the congregation uncalled for."[59] A listener at the Fondren service confided, "I resented Dr. McDill's blaming all of us for the deaths of the two men at Ole Miss., for I feel that the person or persons who fired the shots were wholly respon-sible."[60] In Jackson, a Methodist objected to the district superinten-dents' statement. "We all regret the unfortunate incidents at Oxford," he claimed, but "I cannot see what the good Methodists of the North Mis-sissippi area have to repent for about this."[61] Baptists in Kemper County went further, praising the governor for "his faithful stand for freedom and liberty of the Southern tradition and heritage," and, in Sunflower County, they "protest[ed] the illegal use of federal forces . . . to impose federal will over state authority."[62] Eight parishioners walked out of the service in response to Gerald Trigg's sermon, and later that week his two-year-old son found the charred remains of a cross on the parson-age lawn.[63] Perhaps no Mississippian more forcefully rejected the call for collective repentance than the Presbyterian minister Al Freundt, who asked his congregation at Forest: "Just how repentant should people of Mississippi be for the violence that resulted from the efforts of the Fed-eral Government to enroll the negro James Meredith in the University of Mississippi? . . . [O]ur people do not care to shoulder the sins of others or, even if it were possible, to repent for someone else's errors." The Citi-zens' Councils' magazine featured Freundt's sermon in its next issue.[64]

Most white Mississippi ministers, however, favored the silence that normalized the absurdities of Oxford. At many of the largest churches in the state, Sunday services proceeded without comment. A group of Presbyterian pastors in Meridian voted down a proposal for a public statement about the Oxford riot.[65] When the Mississippi Baptist Con-vention Association convened in late November, it tabled even a moder-ate motion "Concerning Human Relations and Modern Tensions."[66] As Baptist county associations convened for their annual meetings in the weeks following, most passed resolutions against alcohol and pledged to support missionaries, but remained mute about the deadly riot.

No silence resounded more thunderously, however, than that of Methodist Bishop Marvin Franklin. The North Mississippi Conference statement could appropriately have carried his signature along with the others, yet his name was glaringly absent. Neither did he mention Oxford in his weekly *Advocate* column, leaving it instead to Ashmore to offer a Methodist voice of reason. Some moderate Methodists craved a word from the bishop on the fiasco and the general racial climate; at a minimum, a condemnation of violence and of defiance of federal law seemed in order. Even Methodists outside Mississippi noted the omission. Among the telegrams that poured into the bishop's office, one implored: "Does the silence that we hear from the Methodist Church in Mississippi mean that it condones what is happening there please please speak out [sic]."[67] Disgusted with their state's flouting of the law, with the atmosphere such brash intransigence engendered, and with the intractable passivity displayed by Franklin as the state careened down a path of headstrong defiance, a cadre of four young ministers recognized that leadership would have to come from below. Maxie Dunnam, Jim Waits, Gerald Trigg, and Jerry Furr arranged to meet at a campground retreat to discuss ways to offer spiritual guidance to their fellow Mississippi Christians.[68]

That meeting produced the "Born of Conviction" manifesto. The ministers' statement began with an introduction that referred explicitly to the moral dimensions of the racial crisis: "Confronted with the grave crises precipitated by racial discord within our state in recent months, and the genuine dilemma facing persons of Christian conscience, we are compelled to voice publicly our convictions. Indeed, as Christian ministers and as native Mississippians, sharing the anguish of all our people, we have a particular obligation to speak." The four points that followed described the purpose of the church, highlighted Methodism's commitment to the principle that "God is Father of all people and races, that Jesus Christ is His Son, that all men are brothers, and that man is of infinite worth as a child of God," attested to the ministers' support for public education, and, finally, vouched for their "unflinching opposition to Communism," an important affirmation in a paragraph that simultaneously maintained "[Jesus Christ] defends the underprivileged, oppressed, and forsaken." Though "Born of Conviction," notably, did not call for an end to segregation, Mississippi Methodists could rightly regard its several references to "the official position of our church" as a clear rebuke to the critical and separatist stance of the MAMML. Mississippians would also certainly understand that the statement meant to critique their leaders' reckless commitments to segregation.

"Born of Conviction" appeared in the January 2, 1963, issue of the *Advocate* with the names of twenty-eight young Methodist ministers— all Mississippi natives—attached. In an effort to contravene the common assertion that outside agitation created the state's racial problems, the authors invited only native Mississippians to sign it. Perhaps ironically, the statement appeared right next to the bishop's rather innocuous weekly column about the excitement of a new year. Ashmore's editorial on "Freedom of the Pulpit" on the facing page may have sought to preempt the trials the twenty-eight would endure. Though the ministers revealed their awareness of the risky nature of this enterprise in their pledge "to stand together in support of these principles," none likely expected the ferocity of public censure that followed.[69]

Reaction moved so quickly that, only eight days after the statement's appearance, news reports identified the "Born of Conviction" signers as the "now famous twenty-eight." Church members forced three pastors from their pulpits almost immediately, but other congregations reprimanded their pastors by less spectacular means. Many urged their ministers to recant. Others sent resolutions, statements, or letters to Methodist officials and to local papers. Almost all twenty-eight churches suffered a drop in attendance. Community members visited the ministers with abusive phone calls or threatening letters. Sometimes the outcry took only mild and irritating forms, as for one pastor who discovered his lawn strewn with liquor bottles.[70] Perhaps most telling, within six months, seventeen no longer served the same churches as when "Born of Conviction" hit the newsstands; within a year and a half, eighteen had forsaken the state entirely, finding new venues for ministry in other states.[71]

Even Methodist congregations whose pastors did not sign the statement registered their objection to it. Many avowed that they would never accept one of the twenty-eight as pastor. First Methodist Church in Canton thought that "Born of Conviction" constituted "one of [Mississippi Methodism's] greatest blows since its illustrious beginning many years ago." The board of Lumberton Methodist Church agreed that the statement struck a "staggering blow" to the church and suggested that ministers who insisted on too much freedom of the pulpit ought to remember that church members could exercise "freedom of the pew" by taking their membership and their money elsewhere. Mississippi State Senator John McLaurin suggested that the manifesto did "not reflect the thinking of Mississippi Methodists," and he called on other Methodists not to "let a few men destroy our great church."[72]

In spite of the great outcry against the "Born of Conviction" signers, other reactions demonstrated that some Methodists regarded the statement with appreciation. The Mississippi Conference Lay Leader, Dr. J. P. Stafford, characterized the statement as "very worthwhile." An associate lay leader publicly endorsed the statement, and a group of twenty-three ministers and their district superintendent from Tupelo sanctioned it "enthusiastically." One woman wrote a personal letter of support to each of the twenty-eight, grateful "that, at last, the Methodist Church was beginning to speak out." Several members of Maxie Dunnam's congregation in Gulfport wrote Bishop Franklin to express admiration for their minister's courage and leadership.[73]

The "Born of Conviction" story traveled widely, revealing how intensely the rest of the nation observed events in Mississippi. Indeed, stories about the statement and its aftermath appeared in the *Denver Post,* the *Atlanta Constitution,* and the *New York Times,* as well as in a variety of denominational papers. While Mississippians had overwhelmingly rejected the young ministers' statement, outside the state's borders the twenty-eight appeared as heroes. A Methodist minister from New York wrote, "I . . . look upon ["Born of Conviction"] as one of the most promising things that has come out of the Christian Church since the issue of integration has moved into the stage of the hot war. . . . [The twenty eight] deserve the full backing of our official leadership and the machinery of our church organization." Articles in the *Christian Century* and other publications cited the manifesto as a hopeful sign of change.[74]

Though several among the twenty-eight regarded Bill Selah as a mentor, they had not invited him to sign "Born of Conviction," since he was not a Mississippi native. Yet, when he issued a statement in support of the signers—one of whom served as his own associate pastor—a new and secondary center of conflict quickly developed over his solidarity with the young ministers. Selah seemed emboldened by their stance, but in the mercurial climate after Meredith, his words carried inflammatory potential: "To discriminate against a man because of his color or his creed is contrary to the will of God. Forced segregation is wrong. We should voluntarily desegregate all public facilities. We should treat men not on the basis of color, but on the basis of conduct. In the light of Christian principle, there can be no color bar in a Christian church . . . the sin comes when a church seeks to erect a color bar before the cross of Christ."[75]

The board of Galloway Memorial, however, responded to their pastor's statement with a disclaimer: "The recently published statements by the pastors of this Church are their personal opinions and are not necessarily the views and opinions of the individual members of Galloway Memorial Methodist Church. It is not un-Christian that we prefer to remain an all-white congregation. The practice of the separation of the races in Galloway Memorial Methodist Church is a time-honored tradition. We earnestly hope that the perpetuation of that tradition will never be impaired." Though Selah knew full well his congregation did not share his views, this latest round of discord took its toll on the sixty-five-year-old pastor's health. By the end of January, he required a hospital stay.[76]

Though the majority and certainly the most vociferous of Mississippi Methodists expressed outrage, the diversity of reactions to "Born of Conviction" put Bishop Franklin in a difficult position. He tried to distance himself from the situation entirely, but his silence appeared to repudiate the young ministers under his charge. Just days after the release of "Born of Conviction," Franklin and his six district superintendents faced a perfect opportunity to endorse the twenty-eight, Selah, and the official position of the Methodist Church when they issued their annual statement. Yet they only acknowledged the recent upheaval by stating that "[T]ensions of many kinds are in the world today, among them is that of race relations." When pointedly asked by members of the press for comments on "Born of Conviction," Franklin replied that he would not like to be quoted on the issue.[77]

Bishop Franklin's tepid words invited yet another maelstrom that demonstrated how firmly the man was pinned between a powerful clique of segregationists and others who craved to hear a clarion voice of opposition to segregationist extremism. The Millsaps College faculty found it "particularly disappointing that the public statement recently made by you and the cabinet of the Mississippi Conference contained no reference to this crucial issue. We sincerely believe that the prevailing mood of our state would be greatly improved if it were more generally known both within the churches and in society at large that you have the deep concern you do for a free pulpit in a free society."[78] An executive from the National Council of Churches suggested to Bishop Franklin that he might do more for the twenty-eight: "It should not be left to the least affluent and most vulnerable of the servants of the Church to dare to express what the Methodist Church believes. I trust that you are giving these brave and conscientious young men your firm and unfailing support and protection." Other correspondents urged Franklin more forcefully. A long-time ministerial colleague from Atlanta intimated that the bishop had not done enough: "The church must speak; it cannot remain silent. Now that this issue has been opened and Methodist ministers have stepped out and stated their convictions in good faith, I feel that we must not allow them to stand alone." An Episcopal priest from Meridian frankly reprimanded the bishop: "You have failed in your responsibility to your Clergy."[79]

Some of the twenty-eight had entertained no hopes about the bishop's support, but others felt deeply disillusioned. Reverend James Conner expressed his sense of betrayal: "We considered the [bishop's] statement . . . as a repudiation of what we had done." Another, safely relocated to a new church in Indiana, felt free to describe the exact form and context of Bishop Franklin's lack of leadership: "The situation in the conference [of the Methodist church in Mississippi] is impossible to describe. The power clique which dominates the conference has aligned itself with the Mississippi Methodist Ministers and Laymen and with the Citizen's Council." Bishop Franklin evidently gave free reign to segregationist Methodists, and his "hands off" approach in this situation betrayed his real sentiments. One insider thought Mississippi Methodists lay in the clutches of a grotesque evil: "The Mississippi Conference is so far gone in alliance with satanic powers I wonder who can and will save her."[80]

* * *

If anything, the MAMML redoubled its own efforts in response to the daring of the twenty-eight. The young pastors had made their appeal a matter of principle by presenting it as "conviction," and MAMML officer Medford Evans claimed a similar authority in his response, "A Methodist Declaration of Conscience on Racial Segregation." In possibly the organization's strongest assertion of its argument for continued racial apartheid in the church and other venues, Evans argued that "the system of segregation has worked," as it made the same sense as "enforced segregation by sex and by age." Evans refused to depict civil rights activity as a legitimate expression of black discontent, but rather condemned its disruptiveness: "We do not believe [God] was the author of the 'Freedom Rides' or the Meredith case. . . . We urge all integrationists to search their consciences and to reexamine their arguments. We believe they are pulling at one of the pillars which support our nation and civilization. We do not believe that in doing this they are carrying out the will of God. We pray that they will repent." Though less well-known than Dr. Gillespie's "Christian View of Segregation," Evans' piece also traveled extensively outside its original venue. The *Jackson Daily News* reprinted it and the Citizens' Council published it as an article in the January 1963 issue of the *Citizen*.[81]

As if to further challenge the views expressed by "Born of Conviction," about 600 Methodists flooded MAMML's annual March gathering in Jackson. As featured luncheon speaker, John Satterfield laid out the objectives of the organization in a speech that quickly devolved into a tirade on black inferiority. After referring to Mississippi blacks as "almost one million of the finest Negroes in the world," he insisted that Mississippians had failed to spread the truth about blacks because "we have had entirely too much consideration for our colored friends." Satterfield went on to explain this truth as he saw it. Negroes "were in the inferior mental groups," prone to criminality, violent, disruptive, and of low character and morality. Other states that had tried integration, Satterfield maintained, had incurred disastrous results. Satterfield described the evils of integration to warn anew against the dangers of abolishing the Central Jurisdiction in the Methodist Church. Such an action would, in his view, "destroy the Methodist Church."[82] Also on the program, John Wright suggested that if the national body persisted in its progressive trends, Mississippi Methodists should be prepared to pull out of the church. In the event of such secession, he hoped that the Mississippi conference might separate as a unit. However, if separation en masse lacked adequate support in Mississippi, individual congregations could take comfort in the Mississippi Church Property Bill, enacted three years earlier for such a time as this.[83]

The talk of separation was not idle. Indeed, just weeks before, a church in the Meridian district had severed its ties with the Mississippi Methodist conference. They offered clear reasons, according to the Methodist official who investigated: "They are tired of 'liberalism' and . . . do not like the integration emphasis in the literature." This congregation "visualized multitudes of churches doing what [they] have done. They believe that a majority in almost every local church would go into the Southern Methodist Church." The official assessed the entire situation grimly: "My opinion is that it is too late to prevent trouble. Mississippi Methodism is IN trouble [emphasis in the original]."[84]

Selah: Making Good

Reeling still from "Born of Conviction," oscillating between the seductive voice of the MAMML and the "brotherly love" preached by Bill Selah, the entire Mississippi Methodist communion teetered in confusion. Nowhere did this anguish manifest itself more than at Galloway Memorial. Yet, on any given Sunday, all appearances might belie the agitation within, as the sanctuary's magnificent organ droned its usual serene prelude, and gloved ladies, starch-collared gentlemen, and squirming children gathered for worship. On one such Sunday in June 1963—only six months after "Born of Conviction"—Selah pulled into the church parking lot and noticed a large group of people on the street in front of the church. Sending his associate, "Born of Conviction" signer Jerry Furr to investigate, Selah entered the sanctuary from the back door and took his seat on the platform. Furr slipped in beside Selah just as the choir finished the anthem, whispering that five black worshippers had attempted to enter the sanctuary and been turned away.[85]

In their own minds, the events of that morning presented Selah and Furr with the ultimate test: they had to repudiate their convictions or leave the Galloway pulpit. Both had often made clear statements about their positions on racial justice. Selah had repeatedly asserted that he could not serve a church that refused admission to anyone. In keeping with these statements, the two had laid a plan for just this occasion, and the gauntlet had been cast. Walking resolutely to the podium, Selah

shortened his prepared sermon and announced his resignation, bringing eighteen years of pastoral labor to an abrupt and dramatic end. Furr
followed with similar comments.[86]

If black civil rights workers had staged the incident in order to put
white southerners' apparent religious hypocrisy on national display, they
succeeded magnificently. For the second time in less than six months,
the national press featured stories about Mississippi Methodists' turmoil, their tenacious resistance to social change, and the martyrdom of
moderate ministers. Newspapers from the *Los-Angeles Herald Exam-
iner* to the *New York Times* and the *Atlanta Constitution*, and even *Look*
magazine carried reports about the incident. Though a total of twelve
black worshippers had been turned away from four different downtown Jackson churches that Sunday—the others had been First Baptist,
Calvary Baptist, and Capitol Street Methodist—the press focused overwhelmingly on the Galloway visitation and Selah's resignation. To the
chagrin of some Mississippi Protestants, the papers also noted that St.
Peter's Catholic Church, just across a downtown park from Galloway,
admitted five black worshippers that Sunday without incident.[87]

A groundswell of support poured out for Bill Selah. Readers who
learned of the incident in the *Los Angeles Herald-Examiner,* Montana's
Great Falls Tribune, and the *Rocky Mountain News* of Denver wrote to
commend his stand. Fellow Methodists and fellow clergymen from all
over the country sympathized with the difficulty of Selah's decision.
Pastors and laymen who had seen racial tensions flare in their own cities of Nashville and Little Rock registered their admiration. Methodist
missionaries, including one from the Congo and a pastor in Argentina,
expressed appreciation. Scores of people from Selah's past—college
friends, ministerial colleagues, parishioners from his previous pastorates, couples whose marriages he had performed—applauded him.[88]

The most poignant letters, however, came from Selah's own Galloway constituents. Clearly, the deacons who had refused to seat the
black worshippers did not express the will of all church members. The
letters from Galloway members reveal the wide regard in which Jackson's citizenry held Selah, a deep appreciation for his approach to Mississippi's racial difficulties, and considerable agreement with his pronouncements. Effusive church members expressed heartfelt affection
and appreciation: "If there ever was [*sic*] a true servant of God on this

earth, you are that man, and I shall never forget you." Some affirmed the effectiveness of Selah's strategy of preaching brotherhood and love; as one writer testified, "You have done so much for Jackson, the Methodist church, and individuals. . . . You have certainly made me feel differently about this whole mess." One college student went so far as to implore, "Please, Dr. Selah, don't leave now. You're one of the few who have, during the racial strife, expressed sentiments consistent with the Methodist beliefs." Apparently, segregationist pressure had beaten into silence those of more moderate or progressive inclinations, for parishioners assured Dr. Selah that "more people than you know think as you do" and "You . . . have the support of many, some of whom are afraid to speak out, however."[89]

Selah and Furr distanced themselves from Mississippi's segregationists at an opportune time for, within days, the state's already beleaguered reputation plummeted still further. A mere two days after white downtown Jackson churches turned away black worshippers and just hours after President Kennedy delivered an historic speech introducing federal legislation to guarantee black civil rights, a gunman shot and killed Mississippi NAACP Field Secretary Medgar Evers. The same national papers that described how white Jacksonians turned away black worshippers on Sunday reported confrontations between Jackson police and the thousands of Evers' black mourners the following Saturday. To outsiders, the ironies of the state had never loomed larger.

7

The Jackson Church Visits

"A Good Quarter-Time Church with a Bird Dog and Shotgun"

On Easter Sunday 1964, Charles Golden and James Matthews planned to worship together at Galloway Memorial Methodist Church. The two knew that, for the previous ten months, white Jackson churches had systematically rejected integrated parties that came to visit. As a native black Mississippian, Golden understood the rigidity of racial lines in his home state, but he still expected welcome as a bishop of the Methodist Church. His white colleague, Matthews, respected the sincere Christianity of Mississippians and believed the Galloway congregation would respond "in terms of faith rather than in terms of traditional social mores."[1]

The two bishops seriously underestimated Mississippians' preferences for tradition. Unknown to them, only the day before, a Methodist official of the Jackson area had promised "that if anyone, up to and including his own bishop, should come to any of their churches with a 'nigra,' he would be turned away." As a bright and beautiful Easter morning dawned, worshippers in newly purchased finery streamed into Galloway's sanctuary. As they ascended the wide steps leading to the massive, eight-columned portico, Golden and Matthews noticed that the crowd seemed animated by something other than eagerness to celebrate the resurrection. Three policemen stood vigil. Bystanders, kept at a distance only with some effort, shouted epithets. One especially vocal onlooker remarked on the bishops' "probable ancestry and ultimate destination." When halted, the bishops introduced themselves and asked to enter for worship. The greeters—though courteous, by the bishops' own accounting—replied that the two were not welcome. The bishops asked to see the pastor, and as they waited, a few members offered appreciation for their efforts. When it became clear the service had started and

the pastor had not appeared, Golden and Matthews left a prepared statement and departed to worship at a nearby black Methodist church.[2]

A similar ordeal unfolded just a few blocks away at Capitol Street
Methodist Church that same Easter Sunday. Seven seminary professors,
all ordained Methodist ministers from out of state, came to worship
with two black laymen. As soon as the party set foot on church property,
four usher-guards met them. When the ministers' spokesman requested
admission to worship, the usher replied that the church would "admit
no Negroes." When the spokesman asked him to justify this policy, the
usher answered, "No questions, and no answers. If you don't leave at
once, I'll have the police arrest you." True to the officer's word, when the
group lingered a bit longer, Jackson police arrested the nine for trespass-
ing and for disturbing public worship. At their cursory trial the following Monday, each received a $500 fine and six months in jail.[3]

Violent convulsions wracked the Magnolia State in 1963 and 1964—
the tragic murder of Medgar Evers, the jailing of hundreds of activists,
the epidemic burning of black churches, the disappearance and death of
civil rights workers—and these horrors easily obscure the concomitant
crisis in Mississippi's white faith communities. Yet beginning in June
1963, black activists literally took the movement to the church doors.
Their campaign set off turmoil in Jackson's white congregations, raising
the stakes in the battle over black equality and sending reverberations
all the way to the top ranks of the denominations, across the nation,
and around the world.

Almost overnight, the ordinarily unremarkable act of going to
church acquired new meaning. Accustomed to celebrating their all-
white world in placid quiescence, Jackson's houses of worship devolved
into confused and fractious bastions of intrigue, as conflicting interpretations of the Christian faith clashed outside the doors and tension rose
within. For most white Mississippians, the visits only confirmed the
crass opportunism of the freedom struggle and the apostate character
of their denominations; the moral theater played out on these church
steps worked no conversion on their racial attitudes. In fact, activists regarded many of Jackson's congregations as so impenetrable that
they abandoned their efforts outside some sanctuaries quite early in
the saga. At houses of worship where the visitors persisted, Mississippi
Christians displayed both the strength and the significance of religious

resistance to black equality by ceremoniously rejecting black worshippers and their supporters for the better part of a year.

At a few Jackson congregations, a small minority of moderates hoped that the graphic message of the campaign would result in a change of policy. Absent such changes, the activists and their allies aspired to elicit intervention from the highest echelons of their denominations. This drama on church doorsteps made 1964 a decisive moment for white American religion. Though the major Protestant denominations had endorsed the idea of black equality, they lumbered slowly toward realizing such principles in their own ranks. Denominational leaders often capitulated to their segregationist constituencies, pursuing "voluntary" and gradual approaches to desegregation and softening their language on the legitimacy of civil rights activity. Now events outside Jackson sanctuaries begged for more forceful action. Nationally, Methodists and Presbyterians responded with ringing and very public embraces of the black freedom struggle, though Methodists failed to approve immediate elimination of segregation in their administrative structures. Throughout the denomination, many Southern Baptists wanted to offer similarly strong endorsements of the civil rights quest, but their Deep South constituency hamstrung these efforts. The events of 1964 sealed American religion's embrace of the idea—though not always the actual reality—of racial equality as a Christian principle, even as white Mississippians continued to reject the notion that God championed the poor and oppressed in their state.

"Interfering with Divine Worship": The Church Visit Campaign

In June 1963, the church visit campaign unleashed its potent symbolism in a white Mississippi that already reeled from civil rights initiatives. The cloud of Ole Miss remained in the atmosphere, and dust from "Born of Conviction" continued to swirl. In early May, Mississippians watched their Alabama neighbors squirm under national scrutiny when police turned fire hoses and attack dogs on protesting black youth in Birmingham. Following quickly on the heels of those storms, Jackson activists expanded a boycott with direct-action efforts that sent movement fervor skyrocketing and swelled the activists' ranks. When Mayor Allen Thompson rejected a set of modest demands, demonstrators

held sit-ins at the Capitol Street Woolworth Store and picketed outside. White thugs beat the lunch-counter group, while local authorities
arrested the pickets, who included national NAACP leader Roy Wilkins
and Mississippi Field Secretary Medgar Evers. When the first mass
march of the Jackson movement accompanied these efforts, police and
state troopers carried 450 of the participants to a makeshift jail at the
state fairgrounds.[4] White Jacksonians had good cause to believe that the
travail of Birmingham had come to them.

A small group of Jackson's white clergymen worked behind the
scenes to facilitate negotiations between black activists and white city
officials. Reverend Ed King, a white Mississippi native and controversial Methodist minister who worked as chaplain at the historically black
Tougaloo College and served on the local NAACP strategy committee,
arranged two interracial ministers' meetings. Both interracial and inter-
denominational, the meetings included several leaders of Mississippi's
Catholic and Protestant communities, as well as prominent Jackson
pastors. Almost all those who attended had reputations for racial moderation. Though the fact of the meetings themselves seemed a sign of
progress, they produced little substance. The white ministers could not
even choose a press representative willing to appear with the black ministers' spokesman, Dr. S. Leon Whitney. To avoid notice, they slipped
out a side door while Whitney met the assembled news corps.[5]

Since the ministers' meetings had failed, Ed King pursued a different strategy. He hoped that moderates in the community's white
churches would respond to an even more direct plea. Believing that the
path to opening Mississippi lay through the churches, he and Medgar
Evers brought integrated teams to worship at downtown Jackson services on Sunday, June 9, just nine days after the mass march. That first
Sunday, twenty-two local blacks—mostly college students from Tougaloo—sought admission to two Methodist, two Baptist, and one Catholic
sanctuary. At Galloway Memorial, this effort precipitated the dramatic
resignation of Dr. Selah, detailed in chapter 6. At First Baptist, Governor Ross Barnett arrived for Sunday school just in time to witness the
deacons' chairman refusing admission to an integrated party of four.[6]

The June 9 church visitations touched white Jacksonians' nerves,
already raw from two weeks of racial demonstrations and national media
attention. But the city's travail mushroomed the following Tuesday, June

11, when a gunman murdered the NAACP's Medgar Evers. Dismayed African Americans poured into the streets, and the funeral procession of 5,000 that marched that Saturday threatened to turn disorderly. Only the pleading of movement leaders, black ministers, and Justice Department official John Doar averted expanded violence. After Evers' funeral, the Jackson movement suffered serious setbacks, as local leaders struggled against machinations from national civil rights organizations and the Kennedy administration.[7] It lived on, however, in the church visit campaign. Even as Medgar Evers' body traveled by train for burial at Arlington National Cemetery the following Sunday morning, eighteen black students sought to worship at three Jackson churches.[8]

That Sunday initiated a campaign that endured ten months, and downtown Jackson's once serene Sabbaths turned tumultuous. The activist worshippers spared no denomination, calling that summer on thirteen sanctuaries—Baptist, Methodist, Presbyterian, Catholic, Episcopalian, Disciples of Christ, Pentecostal, and Lutheran—in Jackson and its suburbs. Though nearly all of the churches rejected the visitors, the Catholic sanctuaries and St. Andrew's Episcopal Church consistently admitted them. When refused entry, activists sought to remain outside as long as possible to engage ushers and others in dialogue about the moral wrong of segregation. A police presence always lurked nearby, and activists expected arrests, though none materialized at first.[9]

A kind of panic rippled through white Mississippi churches, as congregations that had not previously done so rushed to forestall confusion about policy.[10] Though nothing suggested the visitations would extend beyond Jackson, Presbyterian churches in Holly Springs, Starkville, Meridian, Hazlehurst, Canton, and Hattiesburg all adopted whites-only worship policies.[11] The Hazlehurst resolution "agreed to deny admission to Negroes" and further provided that "should any such visitors actually enter the church during a service, the pastor is to bring the service to an immediate conclusion."[12] Perhaps alone among Mississippi churches, a Methodist congregation in Tupelo voted to admit black worshippers if they came.[13]

Appearances of white solidarity on the doorsteps to the contrary, deep divisions beset the Jackson churches. Few congregations maintained their closed-door policies with complete unanimity, and the visits precipitated extraordinary tension. In some, moderate members felt deeply chagrined by the behavior of their white coreligionists, while staunch segregationists resorted to wrangling and intrigue. Courageous pastors like Dr. Roy Hulan at First Christian Church suffered for their stand on open worship. The Sunday after Medgar Evers' murder, Dr. Hulan's sermon advanced the notion of collective guilt for the tragedy, even as the ushers rejected two black visitors without his knowledge. When he preached even more urgently about the Christian faith's implications for race relations on the following Sunday, a move to oust him quickly developed. Though Hulan had served First Christian for nine years with great success, the congregation dismissed him in August by a vote of 172–92.[14]

The turmoil at one of Jackson's well-known "liberal" churches, Fondren Presbyterian, displayed itself in a confusingly contradictory policy. The pastor, Dr. Moody McDill, promised to resign if the church turned away black worshippers. After months of deliberation, the Session settled on a resolution that declared the church open to all. However, the convoluted statement instructed ushers to encourage individuals who wanted to "create controversy" to go elsewhere, while permitting them to be seated in the balcony if they insisted on staying.[15] At Capitol Street Methodist, Dr. Roy Clark and other moderates stringently objected to the closed-door policy, and Clark asked Bishop Franklin to find another appointment for him. At St. Andrew's Episcopal Church, the rector insisted on admitting the activist worshippers, but ushers usually directed them to the back row, and segregationists in the congregation kept up constant pressure to reverse policy.[16]

Mississippi's segregationist machinery reached in to manipulate events at Trinity Lutheran. The church council voted to admit activists who sought entry, but some members voiced strong objections. One parishioner appointed himself a sanctuary guard and turned away a white minister of the same denomination and four black companions. Another very active segregationist, Fritz Schluetter, launched a campaign to reverse the council's decision, turning for help to the Mississippi State Sovereignty Commission.[17] Director Erle Johnston responded with a letter for circulation among the congregation. The missive argued that no "Negroes . . . sincerely wish to join you for prayer and worship. It is far more likely they are trying to prove a point or to make martyrs of themselves with the assistance of a few liberal members of your congregation."[18] But Johnston went further than supplying an argument for continued segregation. He passed to local newspaper editors the names and printed statements of one of the "liberal members," claiming that the man was "operating a one-man campaign to integrate Trinity Lutheran Church." As to how the editors might use this information, Johnston suggested: "Here is a case of a Jackson citizen openly encouraging integration and it might make good material for a column."[19] Johnston went still further, striving to heighten pressure on Trinity's pastor and his wife by informing the superintendent of Jackson's school system, where the pastor's wife taught, that "Rev. Wade H. Koons . . . has openly advocated integration of the races. . . . We have information, unverified, that [Mrs. Koons] is indoctrinating some of the students with beliefs contrary to ours." Johnston advised the superintendent that "[this] is for your information and whatever action you care to take."[20] When the matter of admitting the black worshippers came up for a vote again at Trinity Lutheran, the church council did a complete about-face, choosing a racially exclusive policy by well over the necessary two-thirds margin.[21] The congregation then quickly drove Reverend Koons from the pulpit.[22] Thus within a matter of months, the church visit campaign precipitated the departure of at least six ministers from their pulpits in Jackson alone. In addition to the exits of Bill Selah, his associate, Jerry Furr, Roy Hulan, Wade Koons, and Roy Clark, Dr. Spencer Murray left North Park Presbyterian Church in September.[23]

The church visitations set off anxiety and tension among Jackson whites, but in early October these ordeals acquired an added dimension. On World Wide Communion Sunday, when Jackson sanctuaries sported posters featuring hands of various colors reaching for cups from a communion tray, police began arresting the visitors. As the police presence expanded, white families on their way to worship passed by officers with a full complement of billy clubs, wagons, barking dogs, and noisy walkie-talkies.[24] That first Sunday, police arrested three young women—two black students from Tougaloo College and their white friend from the Chicago area—as they tried to attend Capitol Street Methodist Church. The judge meted out sentences of six months imprisonment and $1,000 fines a piece, the stiffest ever imposed for violation of Mississippi's statute against "interfering with divine worship." Ironically, though the girls had been arrested while trying to visit a Methodist church, two national agencies of that denomination paid their appeal bonds.[25]

From the start, the church visits riveted public attention, but the arrests of the three girls increased national fascination with the spectacle. Network news shows reported the incident, national papers carried stories about it, and ministers commented on the affair from their pulpits. The campaign provoked particular interest from the Chicago area, as the region's Methodist bishop called the girls' arrests and convictions "a tragedy which belittles American democracy and Christian witness around the world" and is "totally contrary to Methodist discipline and the law established by our governing body."[26] Galvanized by white Mississippians' temerity, a flood of ministers and other sympathetic white Christians from the Windy City poured into Jackson to join the church visit campaign. In subsequent months, with rhythmic regularity, waves of integrated parties from other parts of the country crashed against Jackson church doors, ready to land inside the sanctuary or go to jail. By the end of 1963, local police had arrested thirty-one people, many of them white ministers from out of state.[27]

As these visits continued Sunday after Sunday and into 1964, countless mini-dramas unfolded outside Jackson sanctuaries. When not arrested, demonstrators often simply remained on the church steps, kneeling in prayer. Loathe to physically eject the visitors, the First Pentecostal Church simply locked the doors.[28] Once, a member of Galloway Methodist brought a black student to Sunday school. The two made it past the "color guard," but police came into the Sunday school class and interrupted the lesson to arrest them, citing the white man for "disturbing public worship"—in this case, by attending Sunday school at his own church.[29] Neither did white Mississippians always accurately judge the racial origins of visiting worshippers. On one occasion, ushers at Galloway Memorial Methodist turned away a Panamanian student who came to hear a missionary speak about her own country; on another, men at St. Luke's Methodist dismissed a female Fulbright scholar from India from the sanctuary after handling her roughly.[30]

Mississippi whites often met the condemnation of outsiders with an utter lack of contrition and a brazen reassertion of their commitments to segregated worship. In this spirit, Methodist women's groups in Jackson withheld funds from the two national Methodist agencies that helped pay the fines of the arrested girls. Their own local group, they claimed, did not "condone any illegal or unlawful acts committed under

Figure 7.1 Tougaloo College students and northern ministers turned away from Capitol Street Methodist Church, October 27, 1963. ©Matt Herron/Take Stock/The Image Works.

the banner of Christianity."[31] The Citizens' Councils answered the threat of mixed-race worship by offering meetings for laymen who wanted to keep their churches segregated.[32] As national press agencies tried to document the campaign, segregationist leaders grasped the poor public relations in images of white deacons and ushers turning away well-dressed and polite young blacks from worship services. Thus, they labored prodigiously to prevent photographers from catching such confrontations on film and even tore film from cameras. In one instance, police arrested Matt Herron, a photographer on assignment from *Life*. Ultimately, Herron did capture photographs of the church visit campaign, but only by renting a motel room across from Capitol Street Methodist Church and shooting with a telephoto lens through a crack in the door.[33]

White Mississippians resorted to a cache of familiar arguments to justify the exclusion of black worshippers. Resolutions on worship policy claimed that the visitors "are not seeking religious instruction or to worship, but have other motives."[34] Pastors who agreed with the closed-door policies insisted on the compatibility of segregation and the Christian faith.[35] Even though the state's African Americans had worked with Mississippi native Ed King to initiate the project, critics blamed it on "the riffraff that comes from the North for the purpose of causing trouble."[36] The *Jackson Clarion-Ledger* reminded its readers that Christians' priorities lay in evangelism, not ameliorating social ills.[37] For his part, Selah's temporary replacement at Galloway urged parishioners that "any problems, all problems, can be solved in the prayer room."[38]

Activists performed their theater on Jackson church doorsteps for national audiences, as newspapers in New York, Chicago, Pittsburgh, Norfolk, Atlanta, and New Orleans reported these incidents. News of this Christian intransigence even traveled around the world, evoking a flood of censure from American missionaries abroad. Working in places as diverse as the Congo, Rhodesia, Brazil, Costa Rica, Mexico, Korea, Taiwan, and Japan, 202 Presbyterian missionaries published an open letter, admonishing that the Jackson ordeals seriously undermined their work: when "[a] picture of Negroes being turned away from a white church is front-page news around the world . . . non-Christians [develop] serious doubts about the validity of the gospel." The missionaries recommended reversing this obstacle to the church's work by opening "the doors and fellowship of all churches to any person who comes to worship."[39] A Methodist missionary in Japan scolded the Galloway congregation for the shame they brought to global missionary work: "If Negroes and white men can't worship God in America, what right has a missionary to go to a foreign country to tell of . . . the worldwide community of love of those united in Christ?"[40]

Though the church visit campaign sparked similar efforts in other cities, nowhere did activists assault sanctuary doors as relentlessly nor endure rejection as consistently, as in Jackson. In the church visits, black activists sought more than simply to break the color barrier in yet another venue. A faith devoted to the racial hierarchy injected the life blood into segregation, and penetrating this heart would alter the entire body. More convincingly than any white supremacist sermon, the campaign demonstrated the religious underpinnings of black inferiority—a relationship often obscured in the daily and routine operation of southern life. Americans who had hoped that the South's strong religious commitments might mitigate white supremacy were given to understand that southern religion, by and large, sanctified black suffering rather than ameliorated it. Those who turned away black worshippers viscerally understood the importance of this religious foundation and fought to preserve it.

In a sense, the black activists and segregationists who clashed outside Jackson's sanctuaries brought into public confrontation competing visions of the faith: a southern Christianity, in which a commitment to the racial hierarchy occupied a central place, and an emerging American version, in which an embrace of human equality was rapidly becoming a given. Commitments to racial justice had heretofore seemed incidental, rather than essential, to American Christianity. America's leading denominations had offered verbal, if mostly untested, support for the idea of black equality, but the debacle in Jackson churches involved them in the struggle as never before. Mississippi churches, they felt, had betrayed their faith and embarrassed all Christians before the nation and the world. Now, the activity on Jackson doorsteps forced the denominations to confront the process of desegregation within the church and to openly embrace civil rights protest as a legitimate cause. National religious responses to the Jackson church visit campaign gave the Christian commitment to racial justice a new, axiomatic quality.

White Mississippians and the Methodist General Conference: "The Shame of Both of Us"

Bill Selah's precipitous departure from Galloway Memorial Methodist Church in June of 1963 left a congregation in free fall. Its members held a wide range of outlooks on the racial crisis, but hard-line segregationists wielded primary power in church affairs. Many parishioners feared that the Methodist Church would force them to integrate. These folks kept alive the sense of drama and intrigue by constantly attacking the denominational hierarchy, subjecting every utterance to a litmus test of do-or-die segregation, and, above all, clinging to the "closed-door" policy. Others members believed strongly in the moral imperative of a church that welcomed all as equals, but this minority—having witnessed the vituperation heaped upon the twenty-eight "Born of Conviction" signers and hearing constantly the shrill and censorious voice of the segregationists—remained almost utterly silent. The bulk of Galloway members probably sat somewhere between these two poles, torn by conflicting loyalties and confused by the voices asking for assent.

Although the activist worship parties visited many Jackson churches, these incidents especially unhinged Galloway's already agitated congregation. The steady decline in membership initiated in the last months of Selah's tenure accelerated during the pastorate of his successor, Dr. W. J. Cunningham. Cunningham observed that, ironically, some members left because they believed the church would soon integrate, while others stopped coming because they thought it would never accept black worshippers. Though Cunningham advocated for an open door and did press the issue in committees and with individuals, the official board of about 200 members governing the church stood fast. Thus, while Galloway's ushers—sometimes literally—formed a physical barricade across the door of the church and police wagons carted away the activists, the congregation inside shriveled. Some left for churches with firmer commitments to segregation, such as First Baptist and First Presbyterian. Others joined less embattled Methodist congregations. A few just stopped going to church altogether. Within months, Mississippi Methodism's grand flagship church cast only an emaciated shadow of its former self.[41]

In November 1963, the Methodist Council of Bishops aimed an ecclesiastical arrow directly at Galloway and other Methodist churches in Jackson. The bishops' strongly worded statement declared that "The Methodist church is an inclusive church. We decry, on legal as well as on Christian grounds, the denial to any person of any color or race the right to membership or the right to worship in any Methodist Church. Further, to move to arrest any persons attempting to worship is to us an outrage. We call upon all Methodist institutions where such has not been done, to bring their racial policies and practices in line with the Christian principle of racial inclusiveness to which we are committed."[42]

If this high-level disapprobation failed adequately to shame Galloway, the vise-grip on the congregation tightened when the two bishops presented themselves on Easter Sunday. That a Jackson Methodist church would turn away its own bishops seemed to take racial commitments to new heights. To many Americans, it now appeared beyond all doubt that Mississippi Christians missed the main point of religion. In a sermon to his congregation at Christ Church, New York, Dr. Harold Bosley referred to the incident as "a step that cannot be tolerated" and "a sin against the God who we see in Jesus Christ." Bosley went on to describe the weekly rejection of worshippers from the Jackson churches as the "shame of both of us" and called for the perpetrators to be "firmly disciplined by the Methodist Church."[43]

From his editorial desk at the *Advocate*, Sam Ashmore strove to highlight the message implicit in the bishops' visit and to bring moral clarity to Jackson's troubled congregations. In deep anguish over the "travail of Mississippi Methodism," Ashmore described seeing the rejection of the bishops as akin to "witnessing the crucifixion of Jesus Christ." Ashmore asked whether "two Methodist bishops should be told to leave a Methodist church" and if such a policy were "consistent with Christ's teaching that 'whosoever will may come.'" Ashmore believed that "most Mississippi Methodists deplore what is happening in our beloved church and many are praying that truth and righteousness may prevail, that Methodism may rise from its agony and travail to new heights."[44]

Ashmore's optimism about the sentiments of his readership to the contrary, Mississippians directed a flood of anger at the bishops. Tension over the church visits pulsed through the entire state. A lawyer from the Delta resented the two bishops as "hypocritical Pharisees." "Horrified and concerned that a Bishop of the Methodist Church would lend his influence and presence to such an effort," one pastor thought the two had set out only to "ridicule and criticize earnest, sincere Christians that are striving to live up to Christian standards." From Pickens, a woman expressed sympathy for "the two beleaguered Jackson churches." A church leader from Hollandale "deplore[d] the way such brainwashed Methodists are trying to lead the people astray." A Methodist from Magee corrected the editor's anguish over the condition of the church: "there is nothing wrong with Methodism in Mississippi today." A layman from Neshoba County thought Ashmore misread his constituency. "You are going to find that a vast majority believe in segregation of the races, believing that God originally separated the races of the world, in His wisdom knowing it was best for all concerned." Another vowed that devotion to white supremacy would trump local church loyalties: "The day that my church is intergrated [*sic*] then that is the day that I will try to find another place to worship."[45]

For his part, Mississippi's own bishop, Marvin Franklin, remained silent, as he had during the Meredith affair and throughout the Born of Conviction episode. After Galloway and Capitol Street turned away Methodist leaders that Easter Sunday, his weekly column mentioned nothing about the extraordinary events at two of the largest churches under his care, nor did he acknowledge the affront to his two bishop colleagues. He failed to affirm the official policy of the Methodist Church or to embrace the Council of Bishops' statement, and he offered no guidance for parishioners who sought to pick their way through the morass of competing voices. Instead, he gushed at the thrill of performing an Easter-day baptism with actual water from the Jordan River.[46]

Even before the Jackson incident, Methodism's 1964 General Conference promised to pivot on issues of race. The publicity around Galloway's rejection of the bishops—only weeks before the conference convened in late April—raised the ante and set the stage for high drama. For over a decade, Methodism had trudged indecisively toward abolishing the denomination's all-black Central Jurisdiction. However, in early 1964, a committee of black Methodists pressed for immediate elimination of the segregated unit. Such a move would deprive open-ended gradualism and "voluntarism" of its evasive power; for this very reason, progressive leaders endorsed the proposal, while segregationists opposed it.

Many Mississippians predicted that "race-mixers" would use the conference to "force racial integration of the churches in the South," and some ninety-two Mississippi congregations and individuals sent entreaties asking the General Conference not to alter the current administrative system in the church.[47] Knowing that the church visit campaign and its implicit message would serve as a centerpiece of discussions at the conference, a group from Jackson produced "His Name in Vain," a booklet that aimed to discredit the activist worshippers and to defend racially exclusive religious practices. Featuring pieces by Seth Granberry, the new pastor of Capitol Street Methodist, John Satterfield, and two laymen, the booklet described the activists who staged the church-visit campaign as ill-informed, self-righteous hypocrites who only wanted to use *"[God's] name and [God's] church* as a pawn in power politics [emphasis in the original]." A piece by Granberry condemned the Council of Bishops' statement as a "harmful and self-defeating" pronouncement that "cut across the long-endorsed customs of our people." Granberry also affirmed opposition to "all demonstrations and publicized 'marches' which move into any of our churches, attempting to break by force (or by what its proponents hold to be moral compulsion) the long-established attitudes of our people."[48]

The gathering of 50,000 Methodists in Pittsburg offered much that made the Mississippi delegation writhe. Celebrating Methodism's vast size and global diversity, the opening ceremony highlighted the contradictions in sending missionaries to Africans while denying church admission to their descendants in America. A processional delegation sporting the flags of forty nations opened the conference. The worship service that followed featured an invocation in Mozambique's Xitswa dialect, Bible readings in Hindi, a prayer in German, and an offertory petition in Spanish.[49] Bishop Gerald Kennedy offered an unequivocal episcopal address: "Prejudice against any person because of color or social status is a sin. . . . Every bishop and every district superintendent is bound by the discipline of the Church to oppose segregation and discrimination."[50] Other speakers—from the governor of Pennsylvania to a missionary from Malaysia—attacked segregation in the church with urgency; one even recommended excommunicating congregations or officials who turned away worshippers.[51]

Progressive Methodists staged several events that presented the Magnolia State as the epicenter of all the church's social ills. To much fanfare, five veterans of the Mississippi church visits attended Pittsburgh's First

Methodist Church on the conference's first Sunday. A press release presented this integrated group of worshippers as "symbols of the problem which Methodism faces at this general conference." On one occasion, about 125 pickets marched around the arena protesting the gradualism of the plan to abolish the Central Jurisdiction as a capitulation to segregationists; the same group held a prayer vigil that night.[52] Two days later, some 1,000 people protested segregation in Methodist churches by "kneeling-in" at the entrance to the arena.[53] A midnight "Rally for Freedom," organized in part by Ed King, featured veteran civil rights activist James Lawson and eleven Methodist bishops, including the two who had been turned away from Galloway. Aaron Henry, president of Mississippi's NAACP, offered the rally's closing speech.[54]

When it came to translating this copious symbolism into action, however, this Methodist General Conference choked a bit. On the one hand, it seemed to declare itself firmly in league with the chaos-makers on Jackson church doorsteps. It approved without debate a statement reiterating the Council of Bishops' censure of closed churches, and it countenanced the work of black activists in two separate moves: one that endorsed orderly demonstrations for civil rights and another that appropriated funds for those jailed or arrested in civil rights incidents.[55] Yet in other important respects, the General Conference appeared equivocal and accommodating to segregationists. The delegates refused to endorse any plan that would abandon voluntarism in the process of desegregation. A proposal to immediately eliminate the Central Jurisdiction failed to overcome resistance from the Southeastern Jurisdiction; moderates at the conference seemed more inclined to support their white coreligionists than to side with their black brethren and their progressive allies.[56]

Though neither segregationists nor progressives could claim total victory at the General Conference, to many Mississippians the proceedings confirmed their denomination's capitulation to every principle they abhorred. Within two weeks of the Mississippi delegation's return, MAMML's board of directors drafted a resolution that condemned the General Conference for its statements on race relations and civil disobedience. Describing his experience at the General Conference, John Satterfield highlighted Mississippi's status as a pariah: someone had distributed a magazine "devoted exclusively to derogatory and libelous statements concerning Mississippi in general and the Jackson Methodist Churches, in particular," and college students with placards containing "derogatory references to Mississippi" picketed the conference. Importantly, the MAMML board urged Methodists "to consider working toward the withdrawal of the Southeastern Jurisdictional Conference from The Methodist Church."[57]

Yet, if the events of 1964 ignited conservative religious defiance and further alienated conservative Methodists from their denomination, these same events also bolstered the courage and conviction of moderates. In mid-April—just after the rejection of the bishops from Galloway—a group of Methodists announced the formation of the Fellowship of Loyal Churchmen (FLC), with officers that included laymen from Jackson, Vicksburg, Philadelphia, and Biloxi. The FLC aimed to "help create a climate in our Conference in which churchmen with differing views can serve our church effectively." Although the group announced other goals that included "providing moral and financial support of ministers who face threat or political hindrance or who are forced out of their pulpits," it also offered a trenchant critique of the MAMML as "a small number of Methodists in the Mississippi Conference [who] have opposed the policies or positions of institutions, agencies, and boards and have urged members to withhold financial support. We deplore the actions of this minority among our Mississippi Methodists."[58] The *Advocate* also reasserted its commitments to a path that did not include segregationist defiance. The paper printed significant portions of the General Conference's statements on race, editorializing that "change must come to the Methodist Church. You could see it, you could feel it, you could know it, in no uncertain terms as the work of the General Conference went forward."[59] Though the statements of the newly formed FLC and of the *Advocate* appear extraordinarily mild, given the pressure that threatened to sever Mississippi Methodism from the denomination entirely, such affirmations set important tethers to the national church. Though these were extraordinarily small and thin lines, Mississippi desperately needed such connections outside itself.

For progressives and a few moderates outside Mississippi, the church visit campaign called attention to the church's complicity in segregation. In some respects it helped provoke the denominations to issue more decisive support for the goals and methods of black activists. However, the moral message in these episodes failed to convert those already committed to segregation and, perhaps more importantly, failed even to convince enough moderates to break their solidarity with their white southern brethren and act definitively to immediately eliminate racial barriers in the church.

At its outset, the church visit campaign offered fodder for caricaturing white Mississippians as hypocritical, petty buffoons. But as the church visits ended in April 1964 and Mississippi's notorious summer rampage unfolded in the ensuing months, the rejection of the black worshippers acquired a new meaning. As an ironic interpretive backdrop, the vignettes outside these sanctuaries deeply implicated Mississippi's religion in the orgy of violence against people and property that followed. Though respectable Jacksonians desperately wanted to parse the differences between their "desire to continue worshipping as an all-white congregation" and savagery against black citizens, many observers understood them as all of a piece.

Mississippi Baptists and the SBC: "In the Bottom of My Heart, I Am Thoroughly Ashamed of You"

Mississippi Baptists suffered fewer direct consequences from the church visits than Methodists. Southern Baptists had no bishops charged with supporting national church policies or disciplining ministers under their charge. Cherished commitments to liberty of conscience and local church autonomy meant that Baptists technically had almost no enforceable national church policies at all. Furthermore, no Southern Baptist ministers journeyed to Mississippi to join black activists in the assault on church doors. In fact, because they regarded Southern Baptist churches as more firmly closed than those of almost any other denomination, activists stopped visiting Jackson's white Baptist sanctuaries after less than two months. Nonetheless, the church visit campaign set the stage for a confrontation between denominational progressives and Mississippi Baptists, who defended their approach to religion and race as vigorously as ever. And when brutality and mayhem in the summer of 1964 flung their state onto the front pages of every major newspaper, only white Mississippians failed to grasp that this brazen savagery issued from the same deep source as the rejection of blacks from downtown churches. Their racial troubles prompted no reflective reevaluation of their Christianity among the state's Southern Baptists, its largest and most representative white faith community. Rather, members of this communion most often recommended only more of the same kind of religion that had nurtured white supremacy for decades.

In view of Methodists' stunning achievements only weeks before, the SBC annual meeting in May 1964 carried special opportunities and heightened expectations with regard to race relations. Given the more progressive instincts of the Christian Life Commission (CLC), Deep South segregationists always reserved special concern for what this agency might say at the convention. Each year, conservatives routinely perused the agency's report—which always circulated in advance of its presentation—for content that might make trouble for them at home. At this year's meeting in Atlantic City, New Jersey they found much that disturbed them. The report—as agency director Foy Valentine intended to present it—condemned segregation, affirmed that civil rights protests sought "redress of legitimate grievances," called for support of the impending Civil Rights Act, and, in a move that seemed directly calculated to shame the Jackson churches, gave explicit praise to those Baptist congregations who had adopted "open door" policies.[60]

Leaders from the Deep South feared the implications of these provisions. The reference to civil rights protests cast a positive light on incidents widely abhorred by white Mississippians: freedom rides, lunchcounter sit-ins, the Meredith incident, and voter-registration drives. Mississippians further resented the implied endorsement of the demonstrations on their church doorsteps and the inherent condemnation of their desire to maintain all-white congregations. In sum, this report accepted the legitimacy of black agitation, censured the South for racially exclusive worship, and embraced the end of legal segregation. By approving this report, the SBC would place itself publicly at odds with the political interests of most white Mississippians and with the policies and practices of most Baptists in the state. By now well experienced with the reactions progressive statements provoked from their churches, Mississippi's Baptist leaders feared the consequences if the SBC issued these pronouncements about race.

A group of messengers from Louisiana, Alabama, and Mississippi, including Douglas Hudgins, Chester Quarles, and Joe Odle, gathered at the convention headquarters hotel the night before the CLC was to present its report. The group invited Foy Valentine to join them, and for several hours the Deep South leaders urged Valentine to make changes in the report. Valentine refused, explaining the reasoning behind each of the statements and adding that some had pressed him to make even stronger recommendations.[61]

The ad hoc meeting broke up shortly after midnight. The next day however, when Valentine offered his report before the thousands of Baptist messengers, Dr. James Middleton of Louisiana brought a substitute recommendation that considerably softened Valentine's language and intent. The substitute made no statement at all about civil rights legislation. Instead of commending churches that had adopted open-door policies, Middleton's rather innocuous resolution claimed that "the final solution to these [race relations] problems must come on the local level, with Christians and churches acting under the direction of the Holy Spirit and in the spirit of Jesus Christ."[62] A fiery two-hour argument on the convention floor ensued, and when the vote was called, the softer substitute motion narrowly prevailed.[63] This outcome stunned and frustrated more progressive Baptists who had hoped to approve the original version. Southern Seminary professor Dr. Ed McDowell confronted Middleton, his former student: "You have just stood here before God and all this Convention and denied everything that I and all the other professors at Southern Seminary tried to teach you; and I want you to know that in the bottom of my heart, I am thoroughly ashamed of you."[64]

As Baptists returned home, debate about the appropriate response to the racial crisis continued, with convention events as a focal point. Frustration over the discarded progressive statement poured from every corner of Southern Baptists' domains. Individual pastors wrote convention executives about their profound disillusionment with their fellow Baptists.[65] The editors of Baptist papers from Georgia, Maryland, Virginia, and North Carolina joined the chorus that cast shame on the Deep South mavericks.[66] Yet, the charges lobbed by their coreligionists formed only part of a tidal wave of calumny that broadsided the Mississippians. Articles in secular papers like the *Raleigh News and Observer* added further weight.[67] Even Wake Forest College President Dr. Harold Tribble wrote to ask Chester Quarles, his former student, about "reports that you led in a movement . . . to water down a recommended statement concerning race relations." Tribble scolded: "Is this the mood of our Baptist leaders in Mississippi, or can we look for some kind of positive leadership that will inspire our people in all parts of the Convention and on the mission fields?"[68]

As news about the convention incident circulated, the Mississippians waxed defensive. Joe Odle had no intention of letting the accusations against him and his fellow Mississippians go unanswered, and he personally rebutted the accusations of progressives outside the state: "Mississippi and Alabama pastors . . . are not 'racists' as they have been charged, neither is there any 'hate' in their hearts toward the Negro race." Chester Quarles launched an even more sweeping rejoinder. Answering Dr. Tribble with a five-page defense, Quarles reminded him about the uniqueness of Mississippi's racial problems, Baptist commitments to the right to differences of opinion, the necessity of local solutions to local problems and, perhaps most emphatically, the extensive nature of Mississippi Baptists' outreach among its black population as evidenced by the Department of Negro Work. Like Odle, Quarles very much wanted to answer charges that Mississippi's race trouble indicated a failure of true religion: "when our own Baptist brethren cast such words as 'unchristian attitudes' and 'unchristian actions' and write in anger about the 'Alabama-Mississippi level of race relations,' [it] does not help. It hurts."[69]

Odle and Quarles defended themselves in private correspondence, but other Mississippi Baptists stepped up to publicly defend their Christianity. In the pages of the *Baptist Record*, W. Levon Moore, pastor of Pontotoc's First Baptist Church, rejected the characterization of Mississippi pastors as "weak, spineless, prejudiced, unchristian, and generally afraid of their congregations." Moore argued that civil rights concerns occupied a place "secondary to . . . redemption from sin through Jesus Christ." Like Moore, Joe Odle depicted racial issues as "a distraction," arguing that Baptists needed to get back "to our main Baptist business[:] Bible teaching and preaching, evangelism, missions, church development, and Christian living." A. A. Roebuck of Hazelhurst complained that "Christians, churches, and denominations have allowed themselves to become embroiled in various social, ideological and economic arguments and disputes. [The Apostle] Paul . . . did not question God's wisdom in making different races, different birds, different seasons." Like Odle and Moore, Roebuck concluded that spiritual needs trumped all others: "The race problem is [difficult], but the sin problem is greatest. . . . The Hearts of men should be changed, not the color of their skin."[70]

Mississippi's rank and file church members also bolstered their leaders' defenses in aggressive attacks on the argument for racial equality and it sources. In Jackson County, Baptists expressly endorsed the substitute resolution adopted in Atlantic City, castigating the CLC for its "integrationist policy of promoting a philosophy foreign to the thought and the conviction of the vast majority of this Association."[71] In Pike County, where bombs and arson destroyed black homes, businesses, and churches in a frenzy that brought the number of such incidents to twenty-five between May and October, Baptists demanded the abolition of the CLC because it "promot[ed] in these troublous times a spirit of disunity and discord."[72] Congregations in Grenada, Moss Point, and Durant cancelled all contributions to the CLC, and three churches near Hattiesburg severed their relationship with the SBC.[73] Mississippi Baptists also assaulted the racial message in SBC literature. The Salem Baptist church condemned its "liberalistic trend."[74] The Hazlehurst Association announced that "the cause of Christianity is being undermined . . . through Baptist agencies [and] our denominational leaders are more interested in social reforms than support of the Gospel of Christ."[75]

These defenses coincided with a visible escalation of civil rights activity and race-related violence in Mississippi. Indeed, Baptist messengers returned home from the Atlantic City convention just as college students and other workers flooded the state; Quarles answered Harold Tribble only eleven days before three civil rights workers disappeared from Neshoba County, and while thugs bombed civil rights headquarters and shot into the windows of workers' homes and offices, Joe Odle urged Baptists to reject the "distraction" of race issues. As Mississippi's Baptist layfolk castigated the CLC, black churches burned in a frenzy that claimed fifty-four sanctuaries by the end of September. Indeed, as the state witnessed its worst moments of the racial crisis, Baptists not only insisted that their religion bore no relation to the turmoil; they leaned ever-harder on the theology that enabled white supremacy to thrive.

The palpable hostility to the SBC and its agencies raised the possibility of an en masse defection, a fear Quarles expressed repeatedly to denominational leaders. In September, he offered this stark assessment of Mississippi Baptists' mood: "At the present time, it would not be a very great effort to lead the majority of the churches of the Mississippi Baptist Convention out of the Southern Baptist Convention."[76] Exasperated from working to quell discontent, Quarles admitted he felt tempted to give up his post and "look for a good quarter-time church with a bird dog and shotgun."[77] Quarles and other leaders blamed the turbulent nature of Baptist life in Mississippi, not on the state's atmosphere of defiance and its militant efforts to create conformity, but on the progressive actions of the SBC.

The burning of the black churches provided a point of entry for some white Mississippi Baptists who wanted to speak out against violence. However, they strove to satisfy this goal safely within Mississippi's system of segregation and largely without threatening it. Joe Odle used his position as editor of the *Baptist Record* to set the trend in motion. In "Smoke Over Mississippi," Odle expressed sorrow over the church burnings and condemned the criminal violence in Mississippi. At the same time, he hedged his bets with segregationists by condemning the civil rights activity of outsiders with equal fervor. "Mississippians of both races are deeply distressed by the tragic events . . . They see the futility of the efforts of outside groups, however well meaning they may be, in securing solutions in the conflict, since they know that the final solutions must come from Mississippians themselves." Mississippi Baptists widely applauded the editorial—as they had the Department of Negro Work—as evidence of Baptist goodwill toward African Americans. In reality, however, the editorial represented a new departure only in that it condemned violence. In all other respects, it merely reaffirmed what Mississippi Baptists and segregationists of all faiths had maintained, repeating Mississippi's favorite rhetorical claims for denying the legitimacy of both federal intervention and black activism: that outside efforts to bring about racial justice hurt more than they helped and that only Mississippi could solve its racial problems. The course of civil rights events would prove both these assertions naïvely misguided.[78]

A few county Baptist associations joined Odle's call against violence.[79] In October, the Mississippi Baptist Convention Board passed a resolution that condemned violence and anarchy, and messengers to the state convention one month later approved a law-and-order resolution that they had rejected the two preceding years. The pronouncements marked the first time official bodies representing Mississippi Baptists had registered opposition to such behavior. The announcements, however, represented no change of heart on the merits of black equality. Tellingly, like Odle's editorial, in the same breath that they disowned violence, these statements condemned civil rights activity. Indeed, the Mississippi convention resolution also rejected federal intervention, spurned "the actions of outside groups," and censured the Christian Life Commission for taking "liberal positions not in accord with the thinking of many Southern Baptists."[80]

That fall, religious leaders from almost every denomination and faith in Mississippi joined to rebuild the black churches that had burned. Choosing as their chairman W. P. Davis, the white director of the DNW, the interfaith and interracial group drew great attention from both inside and outside Mississippi. Contributions poured in from as far away as California. College students contributed labor, businesses donated free materials, and an architectural firm in Jackson even drew up the plans at no charge.[81] Named "Beauty for Ashes," the program especially made Mississippi Baptists proud, since it was launched under their auspices and the committee represented the first integrated group to meet in the Baptist Building in Jackson. Just as apparently remarkable as its interracial character, the group included a large cross-section of faith traditions, with representatives from Mississippi's Protestant, Catholic, and Jewish bodies. When *Time* magazine ran an article about the project, along with a picture of W. P. Davis, the African American Baptist Dr. S. Leon Whitney, and Catholic Bishop Richard Gerow surveying the ashes of a burned church, Baptists felt they had contributed to the healing of Mississippi's image. Yet however commendable, "Beauty for Ashes" represented more work in the tradition of "Smoke Over Mississippi" and the DNW. It presented no real challenge to traditions of segregation, and left the racially divided character of Mississippi's religious landscape unaltered.[82] In fact, a Baptist woman from Starkville encouraged the rebuilding effort as a reward for the state's black citizens who had not participated in civil rights activity, but had "remained calm and loyal to their communities and white friends." "Mississippi Negroes," she thought, "have stood their ground against the evil elements seeking to inflame them."[83] Thus, white Mississippi Baptists displayed a moral revulsion "to the use of violence in the defense of white supremacy, not to white supremacy itself," as the historian Charles Payne has observed of many white Americans.[84] Indeed, Mississippi Baptists rejected segregationist violence, even as they insisted on preserving a rigid racial hierarchy.

* * *

The church visit campaign and the national and local spectacles it created complicate our understanding of the relationship between moral suasion and civil rights victories. On the one hand, the church visit campaign moved America's largest Protestant bodies—and those most well-represented in the South—to unambiguously declare segregation and other forms of racial oppression out of keeping with the tenets of Christianity. Faced with vivid displays of the holy symbiosis between southern religion and white supremacy, national religious leaders and America's leading Protestant bodies deprived the idea of white supremacy of support in the strongest of terms. Even for Southern Baptists, who failed to reach the standard of other denominations in this regard, these institutional responses amounted to a turning point. Given American religion's long-standing embrace of white supremacy in many different forms and its fuzzy equivocation on the subject of racial equality during the civil rights era, this strong stance signified a different direction.

On the other hand, ringing endorsements of human and racial equality at the national level made little difference in local churches and in ordinary lives. If white Americans more explicitly embraced the idea of racial equality in 1964 and afterward, they seemed less enthusiastic about the reality of it, as demonstrated by Methodists' refusal to mandate an immediate end to the Central Jurisdiction. Serious obstacles to actual racial equality in the church remained. As the next chapter will demonstrate, denominational endorsements of racial justice could easily become uncoupled from the kind of action needed to make this justice a reality. Though Americans outside the South sanctioned racial equality as a Christian ideal, they proved little better equipped than Mississippians to make meaningful connections between their Christian faith and the structures of everyday life.

Finally, the civil rights theater outside Jackson sanctuaries seems to have availed little on the Christian consciences of segregationists, and the alternative gospel advanced by activists appeared unable to work any conversions on their racial attitudes. Many Mississippians answered the shame heaped upon them only with defiance and a recitation of the myths that had undergirded white supremacy for years. While the integrated church visits did serve as a line in the sand for many moderates, the campaign appears primarily to have nurtured and brought to the fore a moderation that already existed. While Mississippians said less and less publicly about the Christian mandate for segregation in the years after 1964, little in their behavior suggests they ceased to believe in it.

8

"Warped and Distorted Reflections"

Mississippi and the North

Writing for the *Christian Century* after 1964's turbulent summer, Richard Marius described Mississippi as an ironic paradox, both "embarrassing and enraging." The one-time Baptist-preacher-turned-historian observed, "It can be worth your life these days to work for civil rights in Mississippi—and yet Mississippi is probably the most devoutly religious state in the nation." Underscoring Christians' utter complicity in the horrifying episodes that riveted the nation's attention, he "wonder[ed] how the church there can stand its own shame and cowardice."[1]

By the time Marius penned these words, his readers recognized Hattiesburg, Canton, Clarksdale, McComb, and Jackson as sites of sustained civil rights activity, aided by mostly white clergy from the North. As in the church visit campaign, the clerical presence in these initiatives added a visibly religious subtext to African Americans' quest for full human rights. Ministerial activism suggested that the weight of Christian teaching, ethics, and morality lay with the demands of black citizens, not with their white oppressors. This gospel, advanced across regional lines, conflicted sharply with the faith of most Mississippians.[2]

Northern ministers converted few in the state to their understanding of Christianity, much as the church visit campaign had failed to alter the convictions of white Mississippians. Instead, these clerics' presence provoked an overt display of the holy symbiosis between white religion and white supremacy. Though Marius wondered how Mississippi believers tolerated their own disgraceful conduct, few claimed to feel any chagrin. Indeed, these communities met the religious challenge to white supremacy with brazen and near-unanimous resistance, demonstrating how patently absurd they regarded the notion that real Christianity demanded an end to white supremacy.

In Canton and Hattiesburg especially, local spiritual leaders and congregations conferred an ideological and moral imprimatur on community resistance. In Canton, segregationists demanded this support even from those who preferred not to give it. The solid front of resistance could not afford, and would not permit, any Christian response except an utter rebuke of Madison County blacks and their allies. Canton whites required all community religious bodies to participate in rituals of exclusion that disallowed not only black demands, but also the alternative gospel espoused by outside activists. Meanwhile, in Hattiesburg, lay and professional religious leaders needed no coercion to articulate the religious underpinnings of the racial hierarchy. As scores of northern clergy joined black citizens in a months-long vigil at the Forrest County Courthouse, local whites answered the Christian claims in their efforts with a religious message of their own. Advancing a theological rather than a racial justification for rejecting the activism of these northern ministers, they advocated a role for the church and for believers limited strictly to the ecclesiastical and denied a Christian foundation for civil rights activism.

Readers of the *Christian Century* outside Mississippi followed these events with interest, and many no doubt shared Richard Marius' incredulity at their coreligionists' behavior. However, probably few in his left-leaning Christian audience pondered the claim with which he ultimately softened his critique. Suggesting that the state was less an anomaly within the nation than it appeared, Marius concluded that "in deepest reality the problems of the church in Mississippi are but warped and distorted reflections of the problems of the church in American society." Progressive believers probably preferred to hone in on the apparently yawning chasm between conditions in Mississippi and those in the rest of the country, rather than to believe that America shared the South's racial dilemma.[3] This same notion that a more progressive and liberal North issued the call for equality to a resistant and callous white South persists in both popular and scholarly historical accounts. The northern clerical presence in civil rights initiatives offers an image that bolsters this impression. Yet a closer examination reveals much about the affinity between northern whites' religious and racial convictions and those of Mississippians. The northern ministers who went south appear not to have fully represented the sentiments of their home communities; they served, rather, as spokesmen for only one religious perspective. Their parishioners at home often expressed a strong racial solidarity with Mississippi whites, as they prioritized white communities' rights to self-determination over commitments to equal treatment for black Americans.

Canton: No Hospitality

As the church visit campaign continued to unhinge congregations in Jackson, blacks in nearby Canton initiated a project that included a boycott of local businesses, a voter registration drive, mass meetings, and citizenship schools. As movement activity blossomed in 1964, Canton whites fought back, arresting local activists, stalling voter registration, intimidating black citizens, and bombing homes and churches. The phalanx of people and institutions committed to white resistance included the town's religious leaders and its houses of worship.[4]

Thus, as northern ministers and faith-inspired college students amplified the efforts of resident blacks, whites in the town offered a near-unanimous rejection of the religious message implicit in their efforts. At the Baptist church, a group that included the pastor elucidated for the visiting ministers the wrongs of their mission to Mississippi.[5] One minister informed his activist coreligionists that the love of Jesus, not the clerical presence at the courthouse, would solve the state's racial woes.[6] City officials seemed to take special delight in dealing harshly with the northern clergy. Sheriff Jack Cauthen informed Presbyterian minister Bob Beech that Cantonians did not "count you as ministers . . . to us you're just outside agitators."[7] The pastor at the local Methodist church met the activists at the door to announce that they were unwelcome; on a subsequent attempt, thugs beat two young men after deacons turned them away.[8] On still another visit, men from the same church rushed down the steps to shove a white visitor against his car with such force it broke a window, and ushers told two young women who made it inside the church to leave. On return to their car, they found the tires slashed.[9]

Among Protestant congregations in the city, only the First Presbyterian Church refused to honor the ban on Christian hospitality. Guided by their cerebral and theologically liberal—by Mississippi standards—pastor, Richard T. Harbison, the congregation made it a policy to welcome three white northern Presbyterian students who regularly came

to worship that summer. Harbison also received the northern ministers into his study, and used his influence and connections to arrange
release from jail for arrested colleagues.[10]

Yet the openness that Harbison strove to nurture exacted a toll on
congregational unity. Citizens' Council leaders and members also
worshipped at First Presbyterian, and in their eyes, the congregation's
policies constituted a serious breach in the wall of white solidarity.
Attendance dropped, and many members received the young workers
coolly; sometimes few but Harbison and his wife even spoke to them.
The young activists suffered for their audacity—one Sunday morning,
someone poured sugar into the oil reservoir of their car. Undaunted,
they continued to come to church. When a liberal-minded parishioner
invited them for a Sunday dinner, pressure from Citizens' Council leaders compelled her to rescind the invitation.[11]

A small contingent of parishioners with Citizens' Council ties visited
Harbison at his home one Saturday morning to insist that the church
join other Canton congregations in utterly spurning the white civil
rights activists. The leader among them explained, "To us, the community and the church are one and the same. And what goes for the community has got to go for the church." When Harbison arrived to lead
worship the next day, he learned how diligently these Citizens' Councilors had worked behind the scenes. In contradiction to the Session's
stated policy, ushers had turned the civil rights workers away from
services. Many of the members appeared visibly wrought, while others
seemed impervious to the distress. A member of the previous day's delegation moved about with copies of a resolution that recommended the
church deny access to "all persons, without distinction of race or color,
actively associated or affiliated with . . . so-called civil-rights groups
currently operating in Mississippi." The Session, meeting just before the
morning's service, defeated the exclusionary proposal by a vote of six to
three. But since the three workers had been rejected that day, Harbison
called off the worship service.[12]

The Session's vote to continue admitting the workers proved only
temporary. While Harbison vacationed the next week, the group met
and again put the resolution to bar the civil rights workers to a vote.
This time, in the absence of the progressive pastor, it passed unanimously, and the First Presbyterian Church joined the rest of Canton

in its policy of "no hospitality." Harbison resigned the Canton charge immediately upon his return.[13]

Less than two years after leaving Mississippi, Richard Harbison offered his own incisive explanation for his church's capitulation: "The church . . . was a break in the solid dike of massive resistance which was the official policy of state and community, and it could not be abided." Indeed, the architects of resistance needed all elements on board. While Mississippi religion usually proved an enthusiastic supporter of massive resistance of its own initiative, when faith tried to forge a different path, white supremacists quickly brought it into line.[14] Harbison and the moderates in his congregation displayed a minority sentiment among Mississippi Presbyterians. In other towns visited by northern clergy, Presbyterians needed no persuasion to close ranks in resistance. They willingly offered themselves as apologists for the theology that under-pinned white supremacy and delegitimzed ministerial activism

Hattiesburg: "Deliver Us from Such Mission Work"

When black activists launched a voter-registration campaign in Hat-tiesburg in January 1964—practically simultaneously with the Canton drive—their allies also included scores of white ministers from north-ern and midwestern communities. These ministers came to offer moral support, encouragement, and protection for blacks in a county where efforts to exclude them had achieved legendary status. The ministers hoped that the mere fact of their presence would speak to the almost universally religious white citizens of Hattiesburg, pricking their con-sciences to recognize the immorality of segregation and inspiring them to let Christian compassion dictate new racial arrangements. The white citizens of Hattiesburg, however, heard no such message. Already well-practiced in the Christian defense of segregation, their conservative understanding of the Gospel equipped them to render a complete, and even mocking, denial of the ministers' legitimacy.[15]

In Hattiesburg as well as other Mississippi towns, Presbyterians dom-inated among the northern ministerial activists, and they presented special problems for Mississippians of the same faith tradition. Though the northern clerics technically represented a different denomination—the United Presbyterian Church in the U.S.A. (UPCUSA), or Northern

Presbyterian Church—public perception, history, tradition, and inter-faith cooperation connected them to their Mississippi coreligionists. For their part, Hattiesburg-area Presbyterians represented only a fraction of the community's Christian citizens, numbering but 1,300 in four con-gregations in a city of about 23,000 whites. In spite of their small num-bers, however, members of this tradition dominated among the town's political and business elite. In 1964, Presbyterians occupied the posts of city commissioner, district attorney, city attorney, and circuit judge. They directed Hattiesburg's two largest banks, served on the city's library board and its chamber of commerce, presided over large local busi-nesses, and held office in civic organizations like the Civitans and Rotary Clubs. Significantly, the executive editor of the *Hattiesburg American* and two of its reporters worshipped at Presbyterian churches.[16]

The fundamentalist approach that characterized much of Mississippi Presbyterian theology seemed especially concentrated in the Meridian Presbytery, the administrative home of the Hattiesburg churches. This brand of Presbyterian conservatism not only hewed to a literal interpre-tation of the Bible; it also relied heavily on foundational Presbyterian texts, including a version of the Westminster Confession unrevised since its adoption by the then-newly formed Southern denomination in the nineteenth century.[17] Mississippi ministers rigorously tested the theol-ogy of applicants for ordination—especially those from liberal seminar-ies. Such interrogations vetted candidates on the Virgin Birth, miracles, reunion with the "northern" church, and racial integration. Mississippi Presbyteries often rejected suspected liberals, sometimes even over the objections of the congregations that called them.[18] Enhancing the ortho-dox character of Mississippi Presbyterianism, a well-established "pipe-line" funneled to Mississippi pulpits the graduates of Westminster Semi-nary, an institution outside Philadelphia founded in 1929 in the wake of the fundamentalist-modernist controversy by the arch-conservative J. Gresham Machen. The pastor of Hattiesburg's historic First Presbyterian Church, Reverend William Stanway, a Minnesotan by birth, had come to Mississippi via just this pipeline. Since his arrival in Hattiesburg in 1959, Stanway had held the conservative Presbyterian banner high, leading a drive to expunge "liberal" doctrine from denominational publications.[19] Ed Jussely, who served Hattiesburg's much smaller Bay Street Presbyte-rian Church, stood very close to Stanway on theological issues.[20]

In addition to embracing a staunch theological conservatism, members of the Meridian Presbytery had worked as assiduously as any in the state to restrain their denomination as a religious voice for racial change. In 1954, when Southern Presbyterians' General Assembly endorsed the *Brown* decision, the Meridian Presbytery led efforts to censure that body. Members of Hattiesburg's Bay Street Church had even suggested strong language that "reprove[d] and condemn[ed]" the Assembly.[21] Ultimately, the Meridian Presbytery—independently of the Mississippi Synod— specifically asked the denomination to "refrain from publishing articles pro or con regarding the abolition of segregation of the races."[22]

Bolstering its status as a bastion of theological and racial conservatism, Hattiesburg had its own home-grown defender of these principles who had achieved minor national celebrity. The civic-minded business leader L. E. Faulkner, for thirty-seven years by turns an elder, deacon, and Sunday school superintendent at the city's First Presbyterian Church, had written voluminously in defense of segregation and other beliefs dear to conservative Presbyterians. In particular, Faulkner harped constantly on the inappropriateness of the Southern Presbyterian Church's efforts in "the social and political sphere." Emphasizing the church's need to stay focused strictly on spiritual affairs, Faulkner garnered acclaim and recognition for his work from ultra-conservatives nationwide during the 1950s. Though he died in 1961, his writings, published in the *Hattiesburg American* and widely distributed in pamphlet form, had imbued local citizens with a firm conviction that commitments to a truly biblical Christianity required rejection of all forms of the social gospel.[23]

Conservative theology did not coexist with white supremacy by accident, for the fundamentalism that dominated Presbyterian theology in Hattiesburg served an important role in preserving racial arrangements. This particular brand of conservatism adhered strictly to a doctrine, often called the spirituality of the church, that restricted religious bodies to "that which is ecclesiastical." Coming into wide use among southern Presbyterians in the nineteenth-century, this doctrine had gained currency in the thought of divines like James Henley Thornwell (1812–1862), who depicted slavery as a political question and therefore outside the purview of the church. An early twentieth-century proponent of this idea, J. Gresham Machen, had adhered to it so firmly that he broke with many other fundamentalists in arguing that the church could not even support temperance legislation.[24] Proponents of the spirituality of the church often cited both the Westminster Confession of Faith, which required religious bodies "not to intermeddle with civil affairs," and the Book of Church Order, which claimed such institutions had no "jurisdiction in political or civil affairs." This doctrine thus helped adherents frame their opposition to civil rights efforts as high-minded theological commitments to the church's true mission.

By 1964, Hattiesburg whites had already clashed significantly with federal authorities over black voting rights. Forrest County blacks numbered about 12,000, but only about twenty-five of the 7,000 blacks of voting age had registered to vote before 1959. When Theron Lynd assumed the county registrar's post that year, he refused to allow black citizens even to apply for registration. Lynd went on to deny the United States Justice Department access to his files in 1961, and the department responded with a lawsuit to obtain them. Pursuant to the suit, Lynd permitted blacks to apply for registration, but he failed all those who attempted to take the test on Mississippi's constitution. In addition, he subjected African Americans to a range of frustrating obstructionist tactics. His ludicrous questions mocked the entire process, and even candidates like David Roberson, a student working on a Master's of Science at Cornell, failed them. In a final decision, the U.S. Supreme Court upheld a lower court's judgment that ordered Lynd to cease his discriminatory practices and promised contempt proceedings if he did not comply.[25]

Handed down the first week of January 1964, this ruling emboldened a Hattiesburg black community that had heretofore staged no large mass meetings or organized marches. Though NAACP leader Vernon Dahmer had invited SNCC workers into the community in 1962, the nucleus of local activists had managed to persuade only about 150 blacks to go to the courthouse to register by the end of 1963. But now local activists determined to test Lynd's promise to comply with the Supreme Court's order. Their new and highly visible campaign included key leaders and civil rights veterans like Charles Evers, John Lewis, James Forman, Fannie Lou Hamer, Robert Moses, the comedian Dick Gregory, and scores of white ministers.[26]

On a late January morning, by turns foggy, misty, and rainy, about 200 Forrest County blacks lined up at the courthouse to await admittance to

Figure 8.1 White ministers in the picket lines at the Forrest County Courthouse during the early months of 1964. By permission of the Moncrief Photograph Collection, Mississippi Department of Archives and History.

Lynd's office. Walking a picket line in front of the courthouse, fifty-one white ministers supported their mission, their presence visibly testifying to their belief that Christian morality lay with the black citizens seeking the vote. The preponderance of these ministers—thirty-two of them—belonged to the United Presbyterian Church; twelve Episcopalians, two Jewish rabbis, and a few from the Disciples of Christ, Unitarian, and Methodist faiths rounded out the delegation. Hailing from Illinois, New York, New Jersey, Missouri, and nine other states, the clergymen included leading denominational figures, university professors, ordinary pastors, and even the son-in-law of New York Governor Nelson Rockefeller. Most had been personally recruited for the project by staff members of the various religious agencies that worked with COFO. Sprinkled in the picket line with the ministers, black activists carried placards that read "one man, one vote."[27]

As in Canton, the activist clergy met a firm rejection from Hattiesburg whites. When synagogue leaders at B'nai Israel heard that two rabbis and several Protestant ministers from the picketing delegation planned to attend Friday evening prayers, they threatened to cancel the service. Though this threat did not materialize, only about fifteen people attended worship that night.[28] In keeping with their behavior throughout most of the civil rights years, the city's thirty-three Baptist congregations said nothing as the voter-registration drive commenced, concentrating instead on a cooperative spiritual rejuvenation program aimed to "provide the spark for a deep spiritual and moral awakening in the entire area" through simultaneous revivals over a two-week period.[29] Summing up local Christian sentiments, one citizen described the activist clergy as "excuses for Christian ministers, modern John Browns from the North, [who] could better serve their calling and the nation by spending their time trying to correct the morals of the northern Negroes than to be rambling to Hattiesburg for the main purpose of race agitation and trouble-mongering, imposing their political putridness on an already over-beleaguered state."[30]

Local apologists for Mississippi's racial status quo brandished familiar arguments to discredit the voter registration initiative. They denied that blacks encountered obstructions in registering to vote, characterized the campaign as the product of outside agitators, and highlighted racial unrest in the North.[31] More importantly however, white Hattiesburgians focused their criticism on the clergymen and the religious mandate implied in their presence. Since Presbyterians dominated among the visiting ministers, the city's elite of that tradition seized the opportunity to advance a theologically based rejection of civil rights work. They drew on their long preparation in the fundamentals of the faith to denounce the clerical activists. Leonard Lowrey, the Presbyterian elder and Sunday school superintendent at the helm of the *Hattiesburg American,* took the lead, oozing contempt for the ministers and their activism in his daily editorials. He began his critique with the familiar doctrine of the spirituality of the church: "We know of no Biblical warrant for ministers marching in picket lines." Lowry thought the clergymen seemed, inappropriately, "more interested in righting social and political wrongs, real or imagined, than in preaching the Gospel and saving sinners."[32] He urged fellow citizens to pray that the "misguided" ministers would go home and pursue "a ministry centered around Christ and the Bible."[33] Another Presbyterian on the staff of the *Hattiesburg American* condemned the ministers' activism as a product of misguided northern theology: "Many God-fearing people are being given cause to wonder just what is happening to the Presbyterian church in the North. What is the source of this sinister pattern of law defiance in the name of morality?"[34]

If Hattiesburg whites feared that the moral message in the ministers' presence might prick the racial conscience of onlookers, local Presbyterians assured them that their theology would not permit it. Just days after the campaign began, the four area Presbyterian churches released a strongly worded statement intended to disassociate themselves from their northern coreligionists. Reminding Hattiesburg residents that the Presbyterians among the picketers belonged to a different denomination, the statement highlighted local Presbyterians' lack of sympathy with the northern ministers and emphasized the doctrinal reasons southern Presbyterians opposed their work. Civil rights activities "are out of accord with the doctrinal standards and the historic position of the Presbyterian Church in the United States. . . . According to . . . the Word of God, we do not believe that it is the calling of ministers of the Gospel to be engaged in such coercive political pressure movements."[35]

In the second week of the campaign, a fresh group of white clergymen replaced the initial delegation of fifty-one, and the northern ministerial presence seemed firmly hunkered down in the city for the foreseeable future. Perhaps in an effort to stymie this ministerial witness that showed no sign of abating, the Hattiesburg police began to arrest the ministers. A large policeman positioned himself in the path of Reverend Roy Smith, a Disciples of Christ minister from Boulder, Colorado. When Smith tried to walk around him, the officer stepped in front of him and the two "bumped bellies." The officer arrested Smith for "assault with intent to do bodily harm to a police officer." The next day, after they encircled and squeezed a group of ministers into a small ring between a set of barricades, police arrested nine others, claiming that the ministers obstructed traffic in and out of the courthouse. The white ministers and their allies clearly believed that their arrests had been contrived, but local reporters maintained that the ministers had provoked arrest, seeking "the additional publicity which attends arrest and jail."[36] As she sentenced the nine to four-month jail terms, city Judge Mildred Norris admonished, "You ought to be shining examples of good citizenship, yet you have need to be taught the first principles of citizenship."[37]

Forrest County Christians, indeed, had no openness to a gospel message that included a demand for racial equality. Believing that they adhered to a pure and deeply spiritual gospel, they easily critiqued the northern clergy's efforts as the product of a wrong-headed and misguided Christianity. The moral suasion that white northern ministers hoped would trouble the consciences of Mississippi Christians elicited only an at-the-ready defense, demonstrating how effectively southerners' fundamentalist theology served their racial ideology. While the northern ministers might have anticipated such a reaction from Hattiesburg whites, a trans-regional white sympathy displayed in many northern communities no doubt surprised them more.

"Anywhere South of the Canadian Border": Hattiesburg in Illinois

Though many Americans regarded Mississippi as unique in its racial practices, these clerical forays provoked significant controversy in the pastors' communities of origin. Demonstrating the truth of Richard Marius' claim that "the problems of the church in Mississippi are but warped and distorted reflections of the problems of the church in American society," many of the white, largely middle-class constituents served by ministers from Ohio, Nebraska, and Illinois condemned the clergymen in ways that sounded much like Hattiesburg whites.

Some of the picketing ministers enjoyed firm support. Certainly their denomination had conferred its blessing. Northern Presbyterians' most recent General Assembly had endorsed civil disobedience as a legitimate means to achieve civil rights goals, and a denominational agency had issued the call for help with the Hattiesburg campaign.[38] Local churches and laymen also often applauded their ministers' participation. A Charleston, Illinois, church whose pastor joined the pickets affirmed that the congregation had a "moral obligation to stand [against] racial injustice."[39] The session of a Decatur church approved their pastor's southern sojourn by a vote of nineteen to three.[40] A layman from Lincoln, Nebraska, observed that "Most Lincolnites are proud of clergymen who back up their words with action. My own church took the unusual step of commending our minister publicly for his participation."[41]

These clear expressions of approval notwithstanding, deep cleavages about clerical activism wracked the ministers' home communities. A Homer, Illinois, church rejected the Presbyterian General Assembly's endorsement of civil disobedience "one hundred percent."[42] Some Illinois parishioners withdrew support from their churches, and congregational leaders received calls of complaint.[43] One of the picketing ministers admitted that he and his colleagues had "less than enthusiastic support from their own congregations."[44] Perhaps more tellingly, colorful and forceful expressions of an only thinly veiled white solidarity poured into city offices in Hattiesburg. An Illinois layman explained that "this movement has split our churches. Never in the history of the Presbyterian Church has there been such chaos. I think it is safe to say that the majority of the members of the Presbyterian Church is opposed to taking part in racial demonstrations. . . . We are ashamed of these rabble rousers. Our session went on record as being opposed to our pastor . . . taking part in these things."[45] A deacon from Decatur, Illinois, wired the Hattiesburg chief of police to inform him that the Decatur pastor among those arrested did "not represent the Presbyterian membership of Decatur," and that he would "be obliged" if the police would keep the minister in the Hattiesburg jail.[46] A woman from the same community wrote that "most of my friends and family feel it is a community problem and should be handled by that particular community."[47] Contrary to his fellow citizen from Lincoln, a Nebraskan wrote, "I would like to express my disapproval of [the pastors'] actions and would like to add that they do not represent the community of Lincoln."[48] From Ohio, a Presbyterian pastor confessed to Hattiesburg's mayor, "I am ashamed and disappointed with, especially, the thirty-one clergymen connected with my denomination, United Presbyterians, and ask you and the law-abiding citizens of your fair town to forgive them and overlook their uncalled-for actions. Please be reassured that the above group, by no means, fully represents our particular denomination . . . [although] it does appear, for the time-being, that the more 'radical' elements do have control. Many of us feel that the South should take care of her own particular problems, as she has been doing quite well during this splendid, gracious, history-making epoch."[49] Even Decatur Mayor Ellis Arnold expressed his concern that the local pastors who had gone to Hattiesburg were meddling inappropriately in someone else's affairs:

"We should be sure our own house is clean before pointing the finger at anyone else. . . . If I felt there was a need for Decatur or its citizens to enter into the Hattiesburg problem, I would be there. But I can't see that this need exists."[50] In perhaps the most striking example of Central Illinois Presbyterians' similarity to their southern coreligionists, when a white veteran of Operation Hattiesburg invited a black Forrest County minister to come north and deliver a guest sermon on a Sunday morning, the Illinois church's session objected, refusing to allow the black man in the pulpit.[51]

Students at Milikin University, a Presbyterian institution in Decatur, demonstrated similar divisions over the participation of two Milikin faculty members in the Hattiesburg project. The arrest of Emil Hattoon, a local pastor who also taught religion at the university, garnered intense interest. Upon his return, Hattoon's minor celebrity status grew. The local paper ran several articles in which he appeared a hip and earthy sort of minister. He played jazz clarinet as a hobby, spoke to reporters with his feet propped up on his desk, belonged to the NAACP, and casually referred to the police as "the fuzz." Yet, his image took a hit when the local paper revealed that Hattoon and his wife had not registered to vote since moving to Macon County eighteen months before.[52] When his fellow Hattiesburg veteran, friend, and dean of the chapel at Milikin, Robert Moore, arranged for Hattoon to speak at the university's regular weekly chapel service, more controversy erupted. Students' reaction to Hattoon's work in Hattiesburg revealed a deep ambivalence about their local ministers' engagement in civil rights work, as well as a significant strand of trans-regional white solidarity.[53]

Two students initiated the hoopla when they published a poem satirically depicting Hattoon and Moore as hypocrites and insincere do-gooders. In the op-ed piece that accompanied their verse, the students described Hattoon and Moore as offenders on par with Lee Harvey Oswald because they had chosen to break the law. As other students weighed in over the next six weeks, opinion seemed to run about one-to-one. A student offended by Hattoon's chapel address wanted to know "what action the Administration planned to take?" Another explained that he, too, was "opposed to the actions in Hattiesburg," because "until the South decides to end its prejudice, injustice, and hatred itself, through law, all the Emil Hattoons sitting in jail won't help." Others pointed out that, with a student body only 1 percent African American, Milikin could not boast of racial inclusiveness.[54]

Illinois Presbyterians' deep divisions about clerical involvement in civil rights activity culminated in a dramatic episode. A month into Operation Hattiesburg, eleven area ministers had gone to Forrest County, and more planned to participate. The Mattoon Presbytery called a meeting to allay Illinois parishioners' concerns about their ministers' activity, offering "an account of your church in the civil rights struggle" through the testimony of the local clergy who had participated. The Illinois Presbyterians invited Hattiesburg Presbyterians to send a written statement to the meeting. In their eagerness to secure a full and accurate hearing, the Hattiesburgians asked if they could state their case in person.[55] If northern ministers felt free to come south, parading their faith in an effort to publicly chastise Mississippi Christians, then Hattiesburg whites could justifiably take their own interpretation of the Gospel to their northern coreligionists.

Hattiesburg Presbyterians sent a delegation of able apologists, beginning with three pastors of local churches. Reverends William Stanway and Ed Jussely, already used to holding the line for segregation and conservative religion, were joined by Reverend Newton Cox of Hattiesburg's reputedly progressive Westminster Presbyterian Church. Cox had a more mixed theological pedigree than Stanway and Jussely, and his congregation had been founded in 1954 as an alternative to the archconservatism of First Presbyterian. But though he pastored Hattiesburg's reputedly "liberal" Presbyterian congregation, Cox always considered himself theologically conservative, and his congregation firmly rejected any association with the outside ministers.[56] In addition, the pastors brought along two prominent parishioners who made their living in the crafts of elocution and argument: *Hattiesburg American* editor Leonard Lowrey, who had already copiously denounced the ministers' project in print, and Frank Montague, a highly regarded local attorney, member of the Hattiesburg Chamber of Commerce, and an elder in Cox's congregation. The Hattiesburg delegation explained that they were going to Illinois "to state the position of the Hattiesburg Presbyterian churches and what they believe to be the historical position of Presbyterianism— that the church as an organization has no business taking part in political and sociological affairs." Before their departure, they asked townfolk to pray for them that "with God's help, [we] may present a convincing picture of the Christian church and its purpose as it has been understood down through the ages."[57]

Central Illinois Presbyterians clearly relished this face-off, with one observer claiming that nothing of this magnitude had visited the area since the Lincoln-Douglas debates. About 600 jammed the sanctuary and choir loft of Charleston's First Church.[58] Though the meeting purported to give an equal hearing to both sides of the debate, the Hattiesburg contingent dominated the proceedings, with the apparent consent of the moderator. The audience included ten local veterans of the Hattiesburg project, but only Reverend Robert Moore, who as dean of the chapel at Milikin enjoyed relative protection from the ire of disgruntled parishioners, offered testimony about his experience. Moore opened by insisting on the value of Presbyterian involvement in the civil rights struggle. After explaining the problems of discrimination at the clerk's office and the fear and intimidation that kept Forrest County blacks from registering, Moore concluded by describing civil rights activism as a ministerial duty: "In shepherding a Negro up the stairs of a courthouse we are as faithful to our ministry as in praying over the sick or dying. . . . We came in Christian conscience to proclaim liberty to the captives, to open the prison doors for those who are bound and to follow our Lord and Master who did the same."[59]

The Hattiesburg delegation dominated the remainder of the two-hour meeting. Reverend Stanway began by reading a five-page prepared statement from the Hattiesburg pastors. In keeping with the fundamentalist insistence on close adherence to primary texts, the statement included lengthy quotes from the Southern Presbyterian Church's founding documents, including the Westminster Confession of Faith. The pastors argued—as had conservatives in the Meridian Presbytery for years, as had Hattiesburg congregations' in their original joint rejection of the northern clergy, and as had Lowrey repeatedly in the *Hattiesburg American*—that the "provinces of Church and State are perfectly distinct" and that civil rights activity was not appropriate for the church and its ministers. "We find no justification in the Word of God nor in the Presbyterian standards for the invasion of our community by relays of ministers from various parts of the country intent upon participating in daily picket-lines at the Forrest County Court

House. [This demonstration is] a prostitution of the Church to political purposes."[60] Stanway then turned the pulpit over to Hattiesburg
attorney Frank Montague, who spoke at length, offering his "observa-
tions as a lifelong citizen of Hattiesburg." He vigorously contravened
the case laid out earlier by Reverend Moore, denying any discrimination at the voting registrar's office in Forrest County and rejecting the
claim that black citizens of Hattiesburg suffered reprisals when they
attempted to register.[61]

In a striking and strange addendum, white Illinois Presbyterians
further displayed their willingness to make common cause with white
Mississippians at the expense of black concerns. During a brief question and answer period, an Illinois minister stood to reveal the presence
in the audience of Reverend John Cameron, the black Hattiesburg pastor whose church served as a matrix of the voter-registration drive. The
minister hoped Cameron might address the discrepancies between the
two accounts of conditions for blacks in Hattiesburg. The moderator,
however, refused to let the black man speak, explaining that the Hattiesburg delegation had made exclusion of Cameron a condition of its
appearance in Illinois. Thus, by prearrangement, and in a rather artificial
way of marking off the white men's comments from the black man's, the
moderator adjourned the meeting with a benediction. He then invited
Cameron to take the floor and address the audience that remained.[62]

Subsequent evaluations of the meeting indicated that the Hattiesburg delegation had effectively communicated its point of view. Though
a writer for the *Christian Century* regarded the Charleston congregation as victim of a southern filibuster, the local paper characterized
the southern delegation's visit as a "rebuke" to the local ministers who
had participated in the demonstrations. For their part, the Hattiesburg
Presbyterians felt "encouraged by the warm and attentive reception" in
Central Illinois and thought that conversations with locals afterward
indicated that many "agreed wholeheartedly, or at least in large measure, with [our] statement as to the proper mission of the church." On
the other hand, they also thought "it was pretty obvious that among
most ministers of the United Presbyterian Church the 'social gospel'
has top priority and it appears that little is being said in sermons or
done in other activities to present Christ crucified as the only means of
salvation for a sin-wracked world."[63]

* * *

The stories of Canton, Hattiesburg, and Central Illinois challenge fundamental conceptions about the civil rights movement in America. Americans often prefer to regard that story as the triumph of morality—racists dropped their commitments to white supremacy because right required it. Convinced and convicted by the mandates of their faith, this narrative suggests, white Mississippians let the scales of prejudice fall from their eyes. However, the evidence from Hattiesburg and Canton points to the opposite conclusion. The faith-based message of equality for all won few converts. Changes eventually came to Mississippi and to other parts of America, but it seems something other than the demands of Christianity produced that transformation. As an agent of moral change, religion failed magnificently among its most ardent practitioners. Moreover, the specific theological commitments of Mississippians formed essential tools in the arsenal with which they deflected the religious critique of segregation. A gospel that demanded change in the social order stood little chance of converting a people long schooled to regard such a faith as dangerous heresy.

Finally, while the dramatic events of 1964 frequently appear in historical narratives as a confirmation of Mississippi's strange lack of synchronicity with the rest of the country, Illinois Presbyterians' behavior demonstrates a great sympathy for the resistant and recalcitrant Christians in the Magnolia State. Religiously speaking, white Mississippians seemed to have differed little from many of their conservative coreligionists outside the state. Civil rights events in northern cities that year, many also involving white clergy, would demonstrate that America's strong religious heritage had worked well to underpin white supremacy throughout the country, and religious commitments often did little to alter whites' perceptions of civil rights issues.

9

Race and the Restructuring of American Religion

In 1965, a white minister from Massachusetts called on Reverend Gwin Turner in his study at Bomar Avenue Baptist Church in Vicksburg. Turner talked some three hours with the northern cleric, who worked in black economic and political development with the National Council of Churches' (NCC) Delta Ministry. Reflecting later on their encounter, Turner sized up his colleague as "typical of the good-intentioned but misguided problem solvers now evident in the civil rights movement." To the Mississippian, the NCC minister displayed an "utter lack of understanding in things supernatural." He had rejected the essentials of Christian doctrine—the notion of a personal God, the resurrection of Jesus Christ, and the hope of an afterlife—and thus "had nothing left to preach except civil rights." Turner opposed the man's activism because it seemed to spring from just this misguided and dysfunctional spirituality. The Baptist pastor thought a better strategy for helping impoverished black Deltans would "deal with men's souls and lead men to be transformed from the inside out" through an experience of personal salvation.[1]

Five years later in another setting, Reverend Turner assumed leadership in a different fight. In a row with more moderate Baptists in 1970, he argued for the importance of literal biblical interpretation before a meeting of the Southern Baptist Convention in Denver. Turner contended that "a major factor in the decline of other denominations has been a persistent gnawing away of confidence in biblical infallibility." Since "not one great evangelistic pastor . . . accepts [a liberal approach to] the Word of God," Turner believed that embracing any other hermeneutic would cost Baptists their strong evangelistic emphasis, and thus their very soul.[2]

Though Turner's two struggles appear at first glance unrelated, his advocacy of a narrow hermeneutics grew directly out of his earlier opposition to black empowerment. The racial and religious turmoil that engulfed Vicksburg in 1965 ravaged wider territory by 1970. Traumatic unrest in America's cities revealed the pervasive reach of white supremacy, an assertive ideology known as Black Power displayed the impatience of movement activists, and southern whites fled from the public schools to avoid integration. Those same convulsions ignited the opening salvos in Southern Baptists' epic twentieth-century holy war. Fittingly, as a veteran saboteur of the civil rights movement, Gwin Turner wielded weapons he had honed in Mississippi in an auxiliary theater of the civil rights struggle.

In fact, many white Mississippians followed trajectories like Turner's. The advocates of segregation often morphed into champions of a restrictive emphasis on literal biblical interpretation, as contests over theology and denominational identity moved to center stage in every religious communion. Limited and narrow understandings of the Christian faith had sustained white supremacy, and religious assaults on the racial hierarchy struck at these very underpinnings. Indeed, faith-based efforts to meet the challenge of black equality raised the stakes in theological abstractions, and long-standing fissures in American Protestantism burst into open and irreparable chasms. Not surprisingly, in the late 1960s, the racial revolution produced extraordinary arguments about the meanings and implications of Christianity. In forcing a national reassessment of faith and its foundations, the civil rights movement represented both a profound moment of spiritual crisis and a prime opportunity for religious redefinition.

The racial paroxysms of the mid-twentieth century created a religious upheaval that revolved around the meanings and demands of the faith. Those eager to preserve segregation commonly claimed that integrationists advanced flawed conceptions of the Gospel that ensued from misguided readings of the Bible. True Bible believers, such apologists maintained, focused on soul winning, not civil rights activity. Conservatives who embraced this understanding continued to prefer a Christianity that located all morality in the individual and rendered social structures invisible. This conservative and restrictive insistence on evangelism, bolstered by biblical literalism, served as an effective weapon to discredit faith-based civil rights activity and to subvert the religious critique of segregation from within the Protestant traditions.

The Christian case for racial equality relied on a variety of approaches to the faith, but it seldom came from the advocates of exclusive evangelicalism and biblical literalism. When Gwin Turner and others insisted that the champions of black empowerment sprang from the more "liberal" elements within the American traditions, they identified real, not fabricated, connections. The enemies of white supremacy deployed spiritual truth drawn from broader biblical readings, a necessity in light of the Bible's silence on the specific subject of race-based segregation. While many such moderate believers esteemed the Bible highly, they made their case by reliance on doctrines like the brotherhood of man, the fatherhood of God, and the example of Jesus. Though many embraced a Gospel of individual salvation, they also grasped the truth that social structures shape individuals, and they did not limit their concept of redemption to souls alone.

Not surprisingly then, as they came to grips with the civil rights struggle, American Christians argued vociferously over the foundations, meanings, and implications of their faith, and their religious institutions fragmented and restructured. Members of Mississippi's most significant white faith traditions participated eagerly in these transfigurations. Mississippi Baptists contended for the fundamentalist position as the Southern Baptist Convention developed into a bastion of hard-line conservatism. Meanwhile, Southern Presbyterians, who lay astride the mainline/evangelical divide, disappeared from the religious landscape altogether. In a two-part move, the bulk of Mississippi Presbyterians quit the denomination in 1973, creating a new fundamentalist communion, the Presbyterian Church in America (PCA); the more moderate rump ultimately united with their northern coreligionists in 1983. For their part, Mississippi Methodists struggled to implement the demands of a racially inclusive church as they watched their denomination transform into an institution they hardly recognized.

The Southern Baptist Holy War, Mississippians, and the Racial Crisis

In the 1980s, a long struggle known alternatively as the Conservative Resurgence, the Controversy, and perhaps most vividly, the Southern Baptist Holy War, culminated in a radical alteration of America's largest Protestant communion. This contest placed the SBC firmly in the control of conservatives characterized by devotion to biblical infallibility and displaying little tolerance for other approaches to the faith. The transformation simultaneously obliterated the influence of moderate conservatives, moderates, and progressives who previously had played important roles in shaping denominational life. Interpreters of this conservative revolution, especially SBC insiders, generally place theology at the center of the struggle, and such concerns indeed dominated the rhetoric. Yet these theological differences alone do not adequately account for the fierce determination of fundamentalists to capture and define the SBC, for the champions of a variety of hermeneutic approaches had peacefully coexisted in the Southern Baptist Convention for decades. Only in response to progressive Baptists' attempts to engineer a far-reaching and meaningful response to America's racial crisis, efforts that culminated in 1968, did these disparities begin to appear insufferable. In championing inerrancy, conservatives hoped to preserve the SBC as a denomination committed to individualistic notions of social change through personal salvation, and staying this course meant reigning in its small socially conscious contingent who believed that America's racial, political, and economic arrangements needed salvation. The SBC's Holy War vividly illustrates how the civil rights challenge set off a deep and far-reaching argument over the essential meanings of Christianity.[3]

Though America had fixed its attention on the Magnolia State in 1964, pervasive black unrest revealed the national dimensions of racial oppression in the years immediately following. Riots rocked the Watts area of Los Angeles in 1965, and similar ravages visited Chicago, Omaha, and Cleveland the following year. 1967 brought the fiercest displays of all, as conflagrations precipitated by police brutality erupted that July in Detroit and Newark. African Americans struck out against inadequate housing, widespread poverty, and poor job opportunities. Americans watched incredulously as local police and thousands of national guardsmen moved in to quell days of rioting, looting, burning, and sniper fire in both cities. Combined death tolls amounted to over fifty, with hundreds more wounded, the vast majority of them African American. In addition, miles of property lay in ruins, demolished by fire, defaced by rioters, or damaged in conflicts with law enforcement. Though Detroit and Newark suffered the most far-reaching devastation, similar tumults visited Milwaukee, Wisconsin, Memphis, Tennessee, Durham, North Carolina, Cambridge, Maryland, and Cairo, Illinois, that same summer.[4] Americans had largely regarded race as a southern problem. They had believed the Civil Rights Act of 1964 and the Voting Rights Act of 1965 had laid the axe to the roots of injustice. Now they had to think again.

As 1968 dawned, a mood of reflection and self-evaluation enveloped America's religious communions. Moderate and progressive Baptists craved a faith that would confront systemic injustice and they hoped their denomination would proactively address spiraling racial turmoil. Christian Life Commission Executive Secretary Foy Valentine indicated his sense that "The threat of a racially explosive summer in the months ahead could be significantly lessened if we as God's people would do to our Negro brothers as we would have them do unto us." Drawing on understandings of Christianity that included strong and complex ethical dimensions, seminary professors, state-level leaders, pastors, and young people echoed the sentiments of agency heads like Valentine. A writer for the *Christian Century* noticed that this "new breed" of Baptist ministers believed that "salvation involves justice in society."[5]

In spite of such urgent national and denominational appeals, Mississippi Baptists resisted the notion that the billowing racial crisis demanded anything new of Christians. Pastor Bill Causey of Parkway Baptist Church in Jackson regarded progressives' calls as "so many voices shouting at us out of all this gathering storm."[6] At his editorial desk, Joe Odle of the *Baptist Record* felt a "barrage of pressure . . . to become more involved in the 'social action' programs of the day."[7] In this atmosphere, Mississippians offered their interpretation of Christian social responsibilities. Pastors, religious teachers, and layfolk responded to the plague of racial unrest by assuring one another that converting the lost remained their most important mission and, indeed, the best answer to the nation's problems. Pastor John Traylor of Calvary Baptist Church in Tupelo summoned a reminder from the great nineteenth-century evangelist D. L. Moody that "the world is a doomed ship which we cannot save." Traylor went on to admonish his coreligionists to "beware spending our time and resources in endeavoring to remake society according to the Christian ideals. Such will be possible only at the second coming of Christ."[8] The pastor of Hickory Ridge Baptist Church in Florence submitted that Baptists could only change the world by "chang[ing] the sinful nature of man into a spiritual nature like God."[9] Though allowing that social concern had a place in Christian ministry, Mississippi Baptists seemed to share a general consensus that they should "continue to major on evangelism."[10] As the debate unfolded, these Baptists bolstered their arguments by describing the misguided theology of those who emphasized programs of "social action." Traylor thought "certain ministers have lost confidence in the preaching of the Word of God." For his part, Odle regarded the call to greater social action with caution because "all too often social action is associated with liberalism in theology or even rejection of Christ and the Church altogether. Some of the most active social planners and activists of our day are atheistic or at least very liberal in their beliefs."[11]

1968 rendered dire predictions about racial discord prophetic. On April 4, the assassination of Martin Luther King, Jr., ripped into the nation's consciousness like a bolt of lightning and brought anticipated summer violence to premature realization. In the nine weeks between King's assassination and the SBC's annual meeting that convened on June 4, riots broke out in Washington, D.C., Baltimore, Chicago, Kansas City, New York City, and Louisville—in fact, in a total of 110 American cities. Some of them destroyed more life and property than had Newark and Detroit the preceding summer.

King died in Memphis, just over Mississippi's northern border. Yet Joe Odle of the *Baptist Record* distanced his readers from the ugly deed. As in his critiques of racial violence after the Meredith crisis in 1962 and the summer of 1964, he sidestepped any endorsement of black grievances or any notion of systemic injustice. Instead, he decried King's assassination as the work of a "godless, depraved, sin-sick individual," refusing to acknowledge collective complicity or to praise the black minister and his work. Calling the slain leader "controversial," Odle observed that "large numbers of people around the world considered Dr. King to be one of the greatest men of his generation," while others "looked upon him as a divisive figure who played into the hands of those who would destroy and divide the land." In bemoaning the national unrest precipitated by King's death, Odle recommended the same solution he and other Baptists had long advocated for racial ills: individual salvation. "The churches," he urged, "must move in with the message of the love of God and salvation in Jesus Christ."[12]

Odle's Mississippi constituency applauded this approach, though his failure to condemn King did not satisfy all. A pastor from Hattiesburg argued that King's ministry had brought "disobedience, rioting, burning property, murder, looting, etc." This minister affirmed Odle's recommendation of personal salvation as the best solution, for "no Christian has murder in his heart."[13] Another pastor who similarly denounced King believed that many of his colleagues shared this disdain.[14] When a lone layman suggested that white Mississippians *did* bear some responsibility for the leader's death, even his words indicated the prevalence of anti-King sentiment among Mississippi Baptists: "I fervently hope that the murderer of Martin Luther King was not a Mississippian, was not a member of my Sunday school class, or my church. But I know in my heart, he could have been."[15]

Mississippi Baptists' approach to race relations lay on a collision course with that of national leaders who regarded the chastened mood in the wake of King's assassination as a ripe opportunity to meaningfully address America's racial ills. Baptist progressives at the SBC offices in Nashville seized the moment to ask the Convention to reinvent itself as a critic of systemic injustice rather than a collaborator in it. Fourteen SBC officials worked feverishly to craft a startling 1,027-word statement that they hoped would address past shortcomings and mark a new day for Baptists as a force for social change. This "Statement on the Crisis in the Nation" acknowledged systemic injustice and frankly confessed collective Baptist guilt. In poetic and impassioned tones, it claimed that "the Christ we serve, the opportunity we face, and the crisis we confront compel us to action." The manifesto highlighted huge gaps between suburban affluence and deprivation in slums and ghettos, pointing to the millions trapped by "circumstance they cannot escape, injustice they cannot correct," and "heartless exploitation they cannot resist." Vowing to recognize the worth of every individual, to work for equality of opportunity, to welcome all people to Christian fellowship and worship, and to refuse participation in any movement that "fosters racism, violence, or mob action," the statement recommended the establishment of a Baptist task force to deal with these problems.[16] After working through multiple drafts, the authors aimed to present it to the SBC's executive committee just before the annual convention gathered in Houston. Executive committee endorsement would imbue the statement with considerable weight as it went before the Convention itself. And if the statement garnered Convention approval, it would represent an SBC response to the racial crisis radically different and much more far-reaching than any previous one. In order to endow the measure with the broadest possible backing, SBC President H. Franklin Paschall and Executive Secretary Porter Routh invited all heads of SBC agencies, editors of state Baptist papers, and state convention executive secretaries to sign it.[17] As an indication that the sense of urgency ran deep, of the seventy-four personnel asked to affix their names, seventy-one agreed to do so.[18]

The statement dramatically raised the stakes in the pending Convention meeting. Suddenly, the gathering that had promised only routine business seemed pregnant with explosive possibilities. Progressive Baptists could not contain their enthusiasm. C. R. Daley of Kentucky exulted, "Thank God . . . History will judge these as some of the most significant words ever uttered by Southern Baptists."[19] Many Baptists thought that more than a statement hung in the balance; they insisted, rather, that Southern Baptists stood on the threshold of an essential transfiguration. Foy Valentine believed the statement signaled that "Southern Baptist officialdom is moving away from its old racist origins. The culture here is finally being rejected in favor of Christ."[20] The expectant joy of progressives notwithstanding, the statement still faced the hurdles of executive committee approval and Convention adoption. At either stage, revisions could sabotage its strength; complete rejection would squander the transformative potential of the moment. Hopeful but realistic progressives recalled with frustration the 1964 SBC meeting, when messengers from the Deep South, with Mississippians among the leaders, had eviscerated a similarly bold initiative.

Perhaps predictably, no Mississippian signed the statement. Sharp debate between these conservatives and other leaders rang out before the Houston meeting even convened. Decrying the statement as a distraction, a Mississippi Baptist pastor complained, "Ever and anon we are urged to turn aside from the thing that has made Southern Baptists great and squander our energy, as well as our unity, in trying to correct imaginary inequities among our colored brethren."[21] While the state's leaders assessed the national mood and predicted that some version of the statement would pass, they downplayed the statement's significance before their reactionary constituents. The statement would, no doubt, undergo some revisions, and even so, explained Joe Odle, Baptist polity made the statement of little consequence in local congregations.[22]

The exciting and intrigue-filled SBC annual meeting materialized, perhaps even beyond some expectations. The very air in the Houston Convention Center seemed charged with the conviction that Southern Baptists could not ignore the upheaval beyond their sanctuaries, and this impulse seemed to flow from multiple directions. In a survey taken in the convention exhibit hall, 77.5 percent of attendees indicated their belief that "the elimination of all racial discrimination is a desirable goal of Christianity," and 64.5 percent said churches "should involve themselves more in social, political, and economic issues."[23] Sharing the concerns of the progressives, the Southern Baptist Sunday School Board offered a new educational curriculum intended to follow up on the "Statement on the Crisis in the Nation." Titled "We Hold These Truths," the material treated race in an open, unabashed, and often painful form. Though production of a new unit often took as long as a year, the board had dramatically accelerated the schedule to capture the momentum after King's death.[24] Further indicating that the craving to address the evils of the present world churned deep within Southern Baptist life, a group of students staged a silent vigil in the hallways. Concerns about race, poverty, and the war in Vietnam appeared on their placards with messages that asked, "Will this be the time for a relevant response of Southern Baptists to Social Issues?"[25]

In keeping with progressives' fears, the executive committee did, indeed, dilute the "Statement on the Crisis" before presenting it to the Convention, removing the pivotal confession of corporate guilt. On the convention floor, messengers recommended other redactions and alterations. Many messengers wanted to lay more responsibility at the feet of America's impoverished, preferring phrases like "circumstances they find it difficult to escape" over "circumstances they cannot escape." In this same vein, messengers added an admonition to black leaders to "encourage their followers to exercise Christian concern and respect for the person and property of others." But even these changes failed to satisfy some. One messenger introduced an amendment that admonished the Sunday School Board to "be more discriminating" in its race-related material. Others wanted to table the statement altogether, but both

Figure 9.1 Baptist College students plead with the SBC to offer a "relevant response to social issues" in 1968. Courtesy of the Southern Baptist Historical Library and Archives, Nashville, Tennessee.

motions went down in defeat.[26] Though these alterations disappointed progressives, all signs augured well for passage of the statement.

As messengers prepared to cast their votes on the statement, shocking news viscerally reaffirmed the nation's deep dysfunction. An assassin's bullet had felled Senator Robert Fitzgerald Kennedy in California, and Southern Baptists registered the meaning of their faith against this sobering backdrop: 5,687 voted to adopt the statement, and 2,119 voted against it. These ostensibly decisive numbers failed to capture the Convention's actual ambivalence, for even in this chastened mood, half the 15,000 attendees abstained from the vote entirely.[27]

Indeed, a pulse contrary to progressives' hopes demonstrated itself in the abstentions and in the Convention choice of a new president, a decision replete with meaning amid this pointed challenge to SBC identity. If the affirmation of the "Statement on the Crisis" indicated Southern Baptists' growing social concern and acceptance of a broader Christian mandate, the election of W. A. Criswell suggested an entirely different inclination. Criswell possessed impeccable credentials as a theological conservative and biblical literalist. Convention leaders, anticipating the trauma that the statement would occasion, appear to have hand-picked the Dallas pastor to allay the concerns of conservatives at this pivotal moment. Also affirming to conservatives, no Southern Baptist symbolized support for the racial hierarchy more than Criswell. In 1956, he had delivered a highly publicized segregationist sermon before the South Carolina legislature. In the intervening years, he remained a dogged civil rights opponent, steadily and vigorously defending school segregation.[28]

Yet Criswell and Convention leaders understood how desperately, in the aftermath of King's death and in the atmosphere of racial crisis, the SBC needed to shed its reputation as a supporter of racial oppression, even if altering the theological foundations that had supported it proved a more formidable task. Thus, leaders advised Criswell henceforth to carefully consider his public pronouncements about race, for his earlier statements seemed out of sync with the stirring words of the "Statement on the Crisis." Not coincidentally, Criswell made a well-known and dramatic about-face on segregation rather abruptly in the wake of his election. Before he even left the Houston meeting, he told reporters he "had changed." The very next Sunday at his church in Dallas, he preached on "The Church of the Open Door," a sermon that seemed to repudiate the congregation's earlier policy of excluding black worshippers. Now, Criswell claimed, First Baptist Church of Dallas would welcome "everybody."[29]

The convention proceedings left open a wide range of interpretations for those eager to assess the SBC. Some progressives read the entire affair as indication of a new day. Marse Grant of North Carolina's *Biblical Recorder* called it "a victory for moderation, tolerance, and understanding" and a defeat for "provincialism, racism, and prejudice."[30] *Home Missions* magazine best captured exactly what lay at stake when it suggested that the Convention stood at the crossroads of a new identity.[31]

However, Mississippi Baptists' interpretation of the Houston meeting jangled dissonantly against progressives' celebration of it, and the crossroads of a new identity quickly turned into a war over just that terrain. Joe Odle regarded the entire convention as a crystal-clear victory for conservatives: "Liberals among Southern Baptists found little in which to exult in the actions of this convention." For Odle, Baptists' choices to soften the "Statement on the Crisis" ensued from theology: "even though recognizing the need for more Christian action in the face of today's crisis . . . [Southern Baptists] are solidly dedicated to belief in the Bible as the authoritative Word of God, and to Jesus Christ as the divine Savior for lost men, and they refuse to move from that position." Odle clearly saw the statement as a flirtation with a heretical faith: "the churches will continue to give their first emphasis to preaching the Gospel, and simply will not follow those churches which have turned from Christ's gospel of salvation from sin, to a social gospel."[32]

Trouble for Baptist unity loomed. Odle identified "much more emphasis on social concerns than many Baptists like to see" coming from the various Baptist agencies. He saw growing resistance to this emphasis and thought "a serious conflict seems inevitable."[33] Indeed, Odle voiced objections that issued from many Mississippi congregations as they contended for their own versions of the faith against the vision of SBC progressives. A writer from Yazoo City thought the Houston statement had initiated a "stampede to disaster."[34] A Women's Missionary Union president from Indianola condemned official SBC material as "more Social Gospel," suitable for "any socialist group in the country." When *Newsweek* reported that the statement called for the integration of Southern Baptist churches, several Mississippi congregations panicked.[35] At the request of his board of deacons, the pastor of Amity Baptist Church in Woodland wrote Convention leaders to inform them that if they "continue[d] to be liberal" and "to support integration and try to get the churches to participate th[en] we are going to stop our support."[36] M. E. Carpenter of Brookhaven believed that the Sunday School Board "advocate[ed] all-out integration of Southern Baptist churches," and explained that such a plan had "destroyed the northern Baptist Convention and contributed to the riots in the northern, eastern, and western cities."[37] A layman from Hattiesburg urged "let's not wreck the work of the Home Mission Board by following the recommendation of a few thousand uninstructed delegates who voted [for] this recommendation at the Convention. External changes that last come only after the spiritual new birth changes the inner man."[38] From Carthage, a woman complained that "the local churches are being placed in the position of 'going along' with whatever you so-called leaders pass down." She thought these leaders' actions "were leading to a division in the SBC, and I mean not ideologically but literally." This writer linked these ominous trends to bad theology, to the notion that "the Bible is full of errors, that [the Virgin Birth and the bodily resurrection of Christ] are myths."[39]

Indeed, fundamentalists like these Mississippi Baptists sprang into action in the next two Convention meetings, demonstrating how the crisis manifesto had raised the stakes in the SBC's long-standing doctrinal fault lines. Onlookers thought the possibility of rupture loomed as a record number of messengers flocked to the 1969 meeting in New Orleans. Though black unrest continued, any urgency to address the nation's racial woes had evaporated. While several other denominations responded thoughtfully that year to the indictment of white religion in James Forman's *Black Manifesto*, Southern Baptists in New Orleans summarily dismissed it. With renewed conservative vigor, the Convention went on to spurn twelve recommendations from the Christian Life Commission. Further demonstrating a lack of sympathy for the social justice vision that flowed from SBC agencies, messengers rejected a new Training Union program that sat waiting on the docks for shipment. Though the measure cost the Sunday School Board a hefty sum, according to Joe Odle, this "groundswell of disapproval" indicated that Southern Baptists wanted "materials and programs that met, not only the needs, but also the desires of the rank and file of the churches." From all across the Convention, observers identified an anti-establishment impulse that percolated at Baptists' grassroots.[40]

If the SBC now seemed largely unconcerned about race, it displayed an acute obsession with biblical literalism. Roaring their approval of W. A. Criswell, the Convention reelected him president by a staggering vote of 7,482 to 450. Even more this year than in the previous one, Criswell's election signaled affirmation of the literalist hermeneutic, since he had just published a fundamentalist apology, *Why I Believe the Bible is Literally True*. Arguing for the divine inspiration of every word of Scripture, the book defended the biblical account of Jonah and the Whale and attacked evolution as a "big lie." Though a group of Southern Baptist pastors and seminary professors who championed "free and open analysis of the Bible" publicly opposed Criswell's book, Convention approval of the Dallas pastor suggested that such opposition lay outside the mainstream of Southern Baptist opinion.[41]

Mississippi Baptists participated eagerly in this conservative resurgence. The *Baptist Record* lauded Criswell as "one of our greatest scholars and preachers" and his book as "must reading." The paper went on to commend *Did Man Just Happen?*, Criswell's treatment of evolution in which he demonstrated the theory's "many flaws and weaknesses."[42] Odle praised the conservative actions of the Convention, doubling-down on the importance of simple belief in the Bible: "The Bible does not need to be defended, nor does [*sic*] its origins and makeup need to be fully understood by the average readers in order for it to have a message of God for the hearts."[43] Editorial reprints in the paper decried the "social gospel of socio-political involvement divorced from the blood atonement of Jesus Christ."[44] From Fulton, Mississippi, a Baptist layman who shared these assessments confessed, "For a long time now, I have been berating privately the convention Training Union and Sunday School writers for the very poor job they are doing. It seems to me they have turned all their thinking to social concerns instead of the Gospel of Jesus Christ. . . . It is certainly time that someone . . . told the bureaucrats in Nashville that Southern Baptists still believe what they are supposed to believe and have not gone after the fashionable error of the day, social concerns."[45] Others believed that the Convention had put "Liberals with their 'Anthropomorphic' gospel in their place."[46]

Though they seemed to have carried the day in 1969, conservatives remained vigilant. They fought these battles again in a newly organized fashion at the next Convention meeting, where Mississippians again played a significant role. Joe Odle addressed a conservative-organized conference called "Affirming the Bible" that convened just before the 1970 SBC meeting. In a lengthy message on "The Bible and Baptist leadership," Odle indicated that the extraordinary tension between rank-and-file Baptist layfolk and Convention leaders continued to rage and that the points of contention remained the same. "There is appearing in some of the literature, materials which are raising questions in the minds of a large segment of the Southern Baptist constituency. A rumbling is being heard that will not be silenced."[47] The thousands who attended this meeting defended conservative positions in the spirited annual convention that followed. Among their victories that year, conservatives won the withdrawal of a new volume of the Broadman Bible Commentary because its liberal hermeneutic "endangered [Baptists] as a people committed to the Bible." Gwin Turner, who as a pastor in Vicksburg in 1965 had decried the theology of northern clergymen working in the Delta Ministry, introduced the motion to halt publication of the commentary.[48] In addition to placing the SBC on the record for conservative biblical interpretation, convention messengers again strove to cripple the Christian Life Commission, though the intervention of skilled and seasoned denominational diplomats averted moves to dismantle it entirely.[49] The struggle to define Baptist identity had begun, and the battle lines that ultimately fragmented the SBC had been drawn.

As the racial crisis produced a mighty struggle over the meaning of American Christianity, the Southern Baptist Convention fleetingly embraced a faith that went beyond narrow spiritual and individual concerns to affirm a Christianity with implications for the present social and political order. Yet having stepped momentarily down a path of self-reinvention, the Convention's most conservative elements pulled it back, with Mississippians leading that call. Such theological resituating would prove an essential element in the ensuing decade, as firm commitments to biblical literalism often underpinned the positions of the religious right.

The struggle for the soul of the SBC required some fifteen more years to complete, and its origins in the civil rights struggle grew invisible as the fight came to focus on biblical inerrancy, polity, and politics. Even as the SBC's once-peaceful unity in diversity never fully returned after the 1968 "Statement on the Crisis in the Nation," the statement also marked the high-water expression of the SBC's racial progressivism. Though moderates and progressives continued to labor over ways to foster a socially conscious SBC, never again would conditions in America provide the perception of urgency that facilitated the passage of the statement. Never again would the largely conservative members of the SBC countenance such an effort to shift their focus from evangelism to a more socially conscious faith. And perhaps most importantly, never again would they accept the theological presuppositions that underpinned the notions of systemic injustice and corporate responsibility so evident in that statement.

"How Has the Gold Become Dim": Mississippi Presbyterians and the Birth of the PCA

Much in the same way that Mississippi Baptists felt out of sync with their progressive leaders, Presbyterians in the state also found themselves at odds with their denomination during the civil rights struggle.

But whereas Southern Baptist sought to redeem their communion and recapture it for the true believers, these Presbyterians found their denomination hopelessly apostate. Lacking sufficient influence to alter the Southern Presbyterian Church, they created an entirely new communion consecrated to fundamentalist ideals.

This move, executed in 1973, gutted the Southern Presbyterian presence in Mississippi, as a preponderance of communicants forsook the old denomination. The new institution, the Presbyterian Church in America (PCA), committed itself unabashedly to biblical inerrancy and narrowly evangelistic faith. In central and south Mississippi alone, eighty-four out of 150 congregations fled to the PCA, and Mississippi contributed more congregations to the new denomination than any other state. When the old communion reunited with its northern counterpart (UPCUSA) ten years later, a second mass exodus boosted the PCA presence even further.[50]

Like Baptist conservatives, nearly all the disaffected Presbyterians framed their struggle in theological terms and their more recent self-portrayals ignore or overtly reject any connections to the civil rights struggle.[51] Yet the new communion's birth in the racial travail reveals itself in several ways: in Mississippi Presbyterians' responses to the black freedom movement, in the anti-civil rights activity of leading PCA personnel, and significantly, in the denomination's rigid commitments to the theological ideals that had served the racial hierarchy. No religious upheaval so clearly demonstrates how ultra-conservative biblical interpretation and restrictive evangelical commitments underpinned segregation, and no institutional transformation so vividly displays how the civil rights challenge precipitated a struggle over the meanings and implications of the Christian faith.

Watershed moments in the civil rights struggle also mark the path in the creation of the PCA. Discord between fundamentalists and moderates had dogged the church for decades, but in 1964 Mississippi Presbyterians plotted their trajectory in radical defiance of denominational initiatives. That year, the Southern Presbyterian Church responded to rising racial turmoil with a sweeping embrace of black equality. Its General Assembly authorized use of denominational funds to support ministers who wished to participate in demonstrations, marches, or other civil rights initiatives. It reiterated an earlier condemnation of segregation, insisted that all churches adopt open worship policies, and ordered the dissolution of its sixteen remaining segregated presbyteries, five of which lay in Mississippi.[52] Southern Presbyterian progressives went still further, creating a denomination-wide Fellowship of Concern to work proactively for racial justice. The group immediately sent a letter to each member of the U.S. Senate, urging a "yes" vote on the impending Civil Rights Bill; 435 Southern Presbyterian ministers, educators, and laymen representing every southern state *except* Mississippi signed the letter.[53]

Mississippi Presbyterians rebelled against these initiatives. Jackson pastors B. I. Anderson and Dr. John Reed Miller argued against them because, in their view, "The heart of the gospel is not the treatment of others, but . . . 'Believe on the Lord Jesus Christ.'"[54] In Mississippi, the church all but declared war. Laymen professed grave fears about the apostate state of their denomination and flocked to a new conservative watch-dog group known as Concerned Presbyterians. A Jackson spokesman said the organization hoped "to rid our church of liberalism and get it back to the teachings of the Scriptures," adding that "since the last General Assembly, we have heard many Presbyterians talking about their local church 'pulling out' of the denomination. The feeling of these people is that the General Assembly has taken positions that Christians cannot support."[55] The Session of Alta Woods Presbyterian Church in Jackson expressly rejected the denomination's open-worship statement, declaring its intent "to continue the policy of not allowing all races, creeds, and colors entrance to the worship services of this church."[56]

Issues of race took center stage as Mississippians and denominational leaders subsequently grew more estranged. Hostilities erupted over a 1965 invitation to Martin Luther King, Jr., to speak at the Southern Presbyterian Retreat Center in Montreat, North Carolina. Representatives of congregations in Benton, Ackerman, Laurel, Grenada, and Jackson vilified their leaders for allowing the "creator of strife and unrest," "a known communist," and the "sponsor of the recent sex orgy enacted in Selma," to "desecrate" the place where so "many eloquent and consecrated" ministers had spoken.[57] Mississippians resisted when the General Assembly forced the white presbyteries in the Magnolia State to accept the administrative transfer of black churches. The move did not alter the racial composition of local congregations, but the St. Andrews Presbytery (northern Mississippi) received the black churches only in 1966.[58] Central Mississippi held onto its all-white status longer than any presbytery in the entire denomination; its seventy-three white churches forestalled the admission of three black congregations until 1968.[59] Even having accepted the churches, the Mississippi Synod refused to approve a recommendation for local congregations to "admit persons to membership without reference to race."[60]

Race and theology figured importantly when Mississippians rejected Southern Presbyterian Sunday school literature. Complaints about the material surfaced even in the 1950s, but the Covenant Life curriculum introduced in 1963 transformed that trickle into a flood. Conservative Mississippians wanted strict instruction in the foundations of the faith, but the Covenant Life series invited discussion, critical thought, and reflection, and it specifically aimed to challenge conservative racial assumptions.[61] Complaints about the literature indicated it did not play satisfactorily to Mississippians' beliefs in biblical inerrancy nor their evangelical inclinations: "never once does [Covenant Life] say or impl[y] that men are forever lost without Jesus Christ."[62] Some churches refused to adopt the curriculum, and two Mississippi pastors, Reverend Al Freundt and Reverend William Stanway, both open opponents of the civil rights movement, wrote alternative lessons.[63]

Hostility toward the denomination polarized Presbyterians in Mississippi, especially since some ministers and parishioners moderated their racial convictions over time, remained loyal to the church, and continued to participate in its programs. Segregationists labeled all ministers who did not adopt their own strident opposition to the denomination as "liberals," a damning appellation in Mississippi.[64] Moderates' support for the denomination appeared as aggressive warfare, and conservatives regarded themselves as victims of a coordinated and unjustified attack from these moderates and from an apostate General Assembly. They believed that if they failed to resist, "the sure alternative would be a 'Liberal take-over' of Mississippi Presbyterianism."[65]

The school integration crisis provided a final wedge. When a 1969 court order exhausted whites' strategies for avoiding integration, denominational loyalists and moderates worked to preserve the public schools.[66] Reverend Bill MacAtee in Columbia and Reverend Reginald

V. Parsons in Holly Springs worked in their communities to ease the transition.[67] One Jackson pastor urged his congregation to support public education and "not to merely accept or comply with what is lawful, but to stand with voice and hand for all that is constructive and positive."[68] Yet in spite of such admonitions, white Mississippians forsook the public schools for private church-sponsored academies, and their choices included Presbyterian "day schools" in Jackson, Clarksdale, Cleveland, Columbia, Columbus, Greenwood, Gulfport, Hattiesburg, and Laurel.[69] North Mississippians could find refuge in Memphis in the academy run by Second Presbyterian Church, while some churches, like Alta Woods Presbyterian Church in Jackson, did not establish schools but leased their spaces to groups that did.[70]

Fundamentalist Presbyterians began earnest work toward a separation that same year, bringing together conservatives to construct the administrative and financial groundwork for a new denomination. While preparatory rallies throughout the South drew an average of 300 attendees, one in Jackson boasted 900.[71] One historian has observed that the majority of congregations that joined the new denomination lay in black-majority areas where large numbers of whites had forsaken public schools.[72]

Many of the PCA's founding fathers had contributed eagerly and meaningfully to the fight against black equality. Perhaps most notably among such men, G. Aiken Taylor edited the *Southern Presbyterian Journal* as the voice of conservative disaffection. Taylor strove to undermine civil rights progress in the Magnolia State as it writhed in racial turmoil. He purposefully sought to sabotage the Delta Ministry, corresponding with Mississippi Sovereignty Commission head Erle Johnston in search of materials that might challenge the religious legitimacy of black Mississippians connected to civil rights activity. An important link in a web of anti-communist polemicists, Taylor stoked the fears of conservative Presbyterians and hammered the National Council of Churches with his editorial pen.[73]

Mississippian Morton H. Smith played a similar leading role in the formation of the PCA. Smith headed several committees that helped create the new denomination and served as its first stated clerk, occupying this post for sixteen years.[74] The very year of the PCA's founding, Smith published *How Has the Gold Become Dim*, a book-length apology for the breakaway that described the parent church's spiritual declension. Smith cited the denomination's opposition to segregation and its support for black equality and civil disobedience as damning evidence against it. He explicitly rejected the notion that segregation represented "a breach of Christian ethics," reminding his readers that God commanded "Israel to segregate itself from the Canaanites." Smith regarded both slavery and segregation as "legislated in the Bible," and argued that "it is debatable as to whether the Church should get into the matter of trying to change that particular cultural pattern, and branding one form of culture sinful as opposed to another."[75]

Other home-grown Mississippi segregationists who helped craft the PCA included Dr. Horace Villee of First Presbyterian Church in Columbus. Villee served as a "Contact Man" for Presbyterian Churchmen United, a predecessor organization of the PCA dedicated to fighting the proliferation of theological "liberalism."[76] He strenuously objected to Southern Presbyterians' initiatives on racial justice because they "destroy[ed] the segregation pattern that has worked so excellently in promoting racial harmony and good will."[77] Similarly, Mississippi pastor and seminary professor Reverend Al Fruendt, Jr., a defender of segregation and of Mississippi's strategies for preserving it, gave strong theological and organizational support to the breakaway movement.[78]

First Presbyterian Church in Jackson most vividly displays the ties that bound the defense of segregation to PCA leadership. This church adamantly rejected their denomination's endorsement of the *Brown* decision in 1954.[79] In subsequent years, the congregation and its pastor, Dr. John Reed Miller, relentlessly opposed every General Assembly initiative and every denominational agency that stood for racial equality.[80] Members of the Citizens' Councils occupied positions of leadership and responsibility in the congregation.[81] Like other downtown Jackson churches, First Presbyterian refused to seat black worshippers during the church visit campaign of 1963–1964, though black activists regarded it as so impenetrable that they quickly stopped wasting their efforts on it.[82] In 1965, as school segregation in Mississippi faltered under the guidelines imposed by the Civil Rights Act of 1964, First Presbyterian led the first wave of Mississippi churches to open private academies.[83] As it had provided spiritual leadership for the enemies of integration, so First Presbyterian guided the flocks who forsook their old denomination to join the PCA. Reed's successor in the pastorate, Dr. Donald Patterson, played a leading role in the PCA's predecessor organizations and chaired the steering committee that created the new denomination. Along with several of the church's ruling elders, Patterson helped write the new communion's foundational documents.[84]

But perhaps most significantly, this schism vividly illustrates how the racial crisis precipitated conflict over the meanings of Christianity. These Presbyterian dissidents understood their break with the parent denomination as a fight to preserve their faith in its purest form; indeed, they strove to return to the unadulterated theological foundations of their southern forefathers. These theological arguments did not serve merely as cloaks to hide the "real" issue of white supremacy. Rather, theology formed an essential foundation for their racial ideology. PCA apologists who railed against the corrupt theology of their coreligionists articulated a genuine, not an artificial, concern.

When the disaffected Presbyterians announced their new communion, they explained that "principle and conviction" led them to "reluctantly accept the necessity of separation" in order to preserve their own "purity of faith and practice." The parent church, they believed, accepted "deviations in doctrine and practice [that] resulted from accepting other sources of authority, and from making them coordinate or superior to the divine Word." Indeed, the Southern Presbyterian Church's failure to rely sufficiently and exclusively on the Bible caused it to lose "those views regarding the nature and mission of the Church, which we accept as both true and essential."[85] Among those essential concerns lost by Southern Presbyterians, the PCA architects identified two that they expected would define the primary commitments of their new communion: the spirituality of the church and the primary mission of evangelism. Simply put, the spirituality of the church insisted that as "a spiritual organism," the church could involve itself only in spiritual concerns, not political or social ones. Failure to appreciate its fundamentally spiritual nature had led the church away from its primary evangelistic mission and into the corrupt and secondary world of social amelioration. Importantly, these two principles enshrined as so essential to the new communion had served as primary arguments for conservative Presbyterians who condemned the Christian supporters of black equality.

The parent denomination which the PCA now forsook, the Presbyterian Church, U.S., had formed 112 years previously in a similar moment of racial crisis. Devoted to slavery and the success of the Confederacy, these schismatic forefathers had also framed their self-apology in theological terms, finding ample material in literal treatments of narrow Bible texts. They argued, with some justification, that the opponents of slavery had departed from faith in the Bible as the literal and inerrant Word of God. In the midst of these arguments, the Presbyterian divine James Henley Thornwell developed the doctrine of the spirituality of the church to bolster Southern Presbyterians' defense of slavery.[86] Now, in their twentieth-century quest to "return to purity of faith and practice," those who struggled to preserve their superiority over slavery's descendants clung tightly to precisely this doctrine, praising their slaveholding forefathers as the devoted champions of a pure and uncorrupted faith.[87] Far from distancing themselves from these historical antecedents, the PCA emphasized their spiritual ancestry, announcing the new communion on the anniversary of the old communion's birth. The new denomination's name, the Presbyterian Church in America, seemed ill-fitting for a church so thoroughly tied to the southern past.

Becoming United Methodists: "May God Have Mercy on Us All!"

Methodists faced an extraordinarily complicated struggle to define their faith as they confronted the theological implications of the civil rights movement. Just as in the SBC and the Presbyterian Church, efforts to address the civil rights challenge heightened the tension between the varied understandings of Christianity in the denomination. Many of these variations displayed themselves in Mississippi, though white Methodists there leaned overwhelmingly to the conservative theological end of the spectrum. A splinter movement devoted to white supremacy and biblical literalism took a small portion of Mississippi Methodists into a new communion in 1965, but perhaps the greater challenge confronted those who remained. Though intensely devoted to the church, these loyalists' strong segregationist preferences persisted, and their individualistic understandings of the faith made them an ill fit in a denomination replete with theological liberals, ecumenists, social justice advocates, peace activists, and black radicals. Some Mississippi Methodists who weathered the storms of these years look back on them as the time when the church "lost its way."[88]

Mississippi Methodism's hard-core segregationists defected much earlier than the Presbyterian dissidents. Threats to break away acquired new immediacy after the infamous General Conference of 1964 in Pittsburgh. In the minds of devoted segregationists, the celebration of racial equality at that gathering confirmed their incompatibility with an utterly apostate denomination. The leaders of the conservative Mississippi Association of Methodist Ministers and Laymen (MAMML) moved to realize their vision of a mass exodus. Working to form a new Methodist Church in the South, these leaders employed the talents of the professional Methodist red-baiter, Myers Lowman. Conducting him on a six-city speaking tour, MAMML leaders promised that Lowman would expose "the involvement of the Methodist Church in the current wave of left-wing agitation" and "disclose . . . the role of the churches in creating the present climate of racial unrest."[89]

Lowman's speaking tour warmed up segregationist Methodists for their grand departure. In early 1965, the MAMML garnered 7,500 signatures for a set of petitions that articulated grievances directly related to the church's promotion of racial equality; the group urged newly appointed Bishop Edward Pendergrass and his cabinet not to follow the stated policy of the national church in these matters. If Pendergrass failed to halt this progressive trend, the petitions threatened, MAMML's followers would withdraw from the church en masse, taking with them as many Methodist facilities and furnishings as possible under the provisions of the Church Property Bill.[90] In June of 1965, segregationist Methodists realized their threats. Conservative churchmen formed several new congregations throughout southern Mississippi, with two churches in Jackson under the auspices of their new organization, the Association of Independent Methodists (AIM). While only one small rural congregation withdrew from the conference intact, the new churches siphoned members from established congregations, and these immediately felt the departure in both money and morale. Galloway's weekly attendance and its monthly operating budget plummeted. Empty pews in the large sanctuary demoralized the much smaller congregation that continued to worship there.[91]

Far from cloaking its aims behind other concerns, the new denomination advertised its embrace of segregation, rejecting the claim that this practice violated Christian morality. Its "Resolution on Racial Integration" argued that "the Methodist Church confuse[s] the term 'discrimination' with 'segregation,' illogically maintaining that segregation is un-Christian." It went on to state, "Segregation is not discrimination . . . integration is not commanded by God nor taught by Jesus Christ." As the Independents unashamedly highlighted their commitments to segregation, they also underscored their esteem for narrowly evangelical Christianity, the Bible as the inspired Word of God, and conservative political ideology. They believed the Methodist Church embraced doctrines that "contradict or throw doubt upon the teachings of the Holy Bible," and it remained, in their view, insufficiently committed to free enterprise and democratic traditions.[92]

Though the schism distressed Methodists and their leaders, the Independents enjoyed only limited success. The new congregations struggled to find pastors, in part because even openly segregationist ministers wanted to retain the pensions, benefits, and salary they enjoyed in the secure and established Methodist Church. And though attendance dropped precipitously at Galloway and other churches, the erstwhile members did not all find their way to AIM fellowships. They simply drifted in and out of other congregations or stayed away from church altogether for a while.

Mississippi Methodists faced such formidable challenges after 1965 that the departure of the Independents—amounting to perhaps a few thousand among 185,000 white members—appeared but one wave in a floodtide of troubles that washed over them. Continuing vigorous support for the racial hierarchy revealed itself in a variety of ways. Mississippi Methodists quarreled with their national leaders over the operation of the Delta Ministry. Jackson's two most prestigious congregations, Galloway and Capitol Street Methodist, remained locked in internal struggles over the admission of black worshippers. Galloway finally reversed its exclusivist policy in 1966, a move that sent more members scurrying for the exits.[93] While moderate Methodist leaders urged support for public schools, parishioners packed their children off to private academies. Yet no challenge proved more difficult than the task of merging Mississippi's black Methodists into an administrative structure with its white members.

The General Conference of 1968 loomed for Methodists as a key juncture that would mark a major reorganization of the church. Plans called for Methodists to eliminate the segregated Central Jurisdiction as it simultaneously merged with a much smaller denomination, the Evangelical United Brethren (EUB). A new body—the United Methodist Church—would emerge from this transaction, free of racial distinctions and barriers. Yet as this moment of transfiguration approached, Mississippi's segregationists roused themselves to action. Under heavy lobbying, white Mississippi Methodists handily rejected the plan for the merger, objecting in particular to the dissolution of the Central Jurisdiction and a proposed target date of 1972 for merging white and black conferences.[94] Perhaps even more revealing of segregationists' intense fears about the coming changes, white supremacists unleashed a rash of violence on Mississippi Methodists identified with the movement. In late October 1967, arsonists burned a black Methodist church in Grenada served by an open movement activist. Less than three weeks later, a bomb severely damaged the parsonage of St. Paul's Church in Laurel, a congregation with active programs in voter registration, anti-poverty, and citizenship training. Just one week previously, the pastor had taken sixty-five local blacks to register to vote. About 300 black citizens in Laurel responded to the bombing by gathering at an AME church and marching to city hall in protest.[95] Four days later, a similar blast ripped off the front porch of the home of Robert Kochtitzky, a white member of Galloway in Jackson. Though not actually a civil rights worker, Kochtitzky was widely known as sympathetic to the movement.[96]

Against the backdrop of this violence and only one month after the death of Martin Luther King, Jr., Methodists convened in Dallas to consummate their much-anticipated union. Before 10,000 onlookers, two bishops in full regalia clasped hands across a table laden with symbolic paraphernalia and proclaimed the unity of the church. Most of the conference business focused on issues related to race. Among other proceedings, the conference established a Commission on Religion and Race and endowed it with $70,000 taken from a previously established $20 million fund for reconciliation.[97]

These celebrated measures did not satisfy many black Methodists. Objecting to inadequate representation on the governing bodies of the church, African American members picketed the auditorium on the first day of the two-week conference. Most important among their concerns, the sudden evaporation of the Central Jurisdiction did not completely solve the problem of segregation in the church. The smaller units, the all-black conferences, remained. At the insistence of white delegates from the Southeastern Jurisdiction who refused to accept any form of "coercion," the process for merging the white and black conferences remained ill-defined and vague. The assembled delegates approved 1972 only as a "target-date" for merger, rather than as an absolute deadline. Black Methodists objected to this capitulation to segregationist preferences with a bit of protest theater. Sitting in a silent vigil near the front of the auditorium during a communion service, they declined the elements when served and walked out.[98]

Though some southern white conferences merged quickly and smoothly with their former black counterparts, in Mississippi delay, stalling, and resistance characterized the process. Upon return from the General Conference, Mississippi's black conferences plunged into merger preparations, but the white conferences took few steps in that direction. Segregationists even spearheaded an unsuccessful effort to force the General Conference to abandon the non-binding "target date."[99] The all-white Mississippi Conference entered into no merger preparations, and the North Mississippi Conference waited to formulate a plan only in 1971, as the target date loomed.

While the planned merger would force no actual changes in the racial composition of individual congregations, it did require racial mixing in administration. District superintendents and bishops would preside without regard to race, and thus for the first time in nearly one hundred years, some administrators would supervise ministers and congregations of a different race. A white pastor might conceivably find himself reporting to a black superintendent and, on occasion, inviting him to share his pulpit. Furthermore, annual and district conferences (the yearly and quarterly gatherings of ministers and lay delegates from local churches) would lose their all-white character. In a very real sense, merger meant racial mixing—the very interaction white Mississippi Methodists had so consistently opposed—in at least some aspects of religious life.

Black ministers and members actually stood to lose quite a bit by the proposed plan. The 78,000 white Methodists in north Mississippi out-numbered the 14,000 black members by more than five to one.[100] The plan offered no guarantees that black members would occupy posts of authority, though it did recommend that the bishop appoint at least one black superintendent. Some black members expressed concern that in the newly merged conferences they would be "swallowed up" and lose "their sense of personal identity if black positions of leadership were threatened or removed." One minister objected that African Americans in the new structure might "wind up being water boys and trash boys again." Perhaps the most stirring appeal for passing the plan came from a pastor who argued that black Methodists would have a redemptive effect on their white coreligionists: "My college roommate was lynched, and if I were not a Christian I could hate every white man." "God," he argued, "can use black Christians to make the church what it ought to be." After a debate of only two hours, the all-black Upper Mississippi Conference voted yes to the merger by a healthy majority of 68 to 7.[101]

The merger proposal encountered an entirely different climate among white Methodists. A small group of moderates with a strong sense of loyalty to the church and a belief that faith demanded elimina-tion of racial barriers pushed the issue to the fore. This group included Dr. John Humphrey and Tupelo businessman Jack Reed. Writing in favor of merger, Reed praised the members of the black conferences and frankly acknowledged that "race is the basic issue here." In addition to ministers like Humphrey and laymen like Reed, the North Missis-sippi Council on Youth Ministries urged passage of the plan, explain-ing that "the Christian church should be a fellowship which excludes no persons, and [segregation] on the basis of race is a hindrance [to ministry.]"[102]

Yet, against this group of moderates, a large majority strenuously objected. William L. Sharp of Corinth cited a poll of "leading lay-men" that found 557 against merger, while only sixteen supported it. For his part, Sharp objected to the depiction of opponents of merger as "unchristian." Elaborating the history of the church, he argued that the system of separate jurisdictions had been beneficial, preserving the "dis-tinctive social, political, economic, and cultural views" of southerners. Surely, he thought, the revered southern bishops who had supported the creation of this system in 1939 defied characterization as "unchristian." Arguing that no authority of the church could force white Mississippi Methodists to merge with the black conferences, Sharp wondered whether "the zeal of a very small minority . . . to integrate the races has not benumbed their judgment and clouded their vision . . . I am unalterably opposed to merger in any shape, form, or fashion."[103]

Sharp's objections found confirmation in the words of George Yarborough. An ardent segregationist, Yarborough had both an extensive record of service to the church and a long career in state government behind him. Yarborough raised frank objections to the prospect of racial mixing in the church. "There is no such thing as a more or less, somewhat merger. . . . To merge means what it says—complete and all-encompassing." Yarborough objected to blacks seeking integration in order to end the stigma of second-class citizenship, though he apparently failed to realize how segregation created an artificially superior status for whites: "When we assemble for the purpose of worship, the attempt to enhance the social position of any participant by his physical presence is to bring matters of self-pride into what should be self-less."[104]

In spite of predictions that merger would fail, some leaders believed the measure had sufficient support from the clergy to assure passage. When the all-white North Mississippi Conference met to vote, Reverend Roy D. McAlilly presented the plan, emphasizing its biblical and theological implications and highlighting doctrines of brotherhood and church unity. Yet the discussion that followed abandoned theological matters altogether and concentrated instead on how best to quickly and easily defeat the measure. The vote that sent the proposal down in defeat revealed that lay delegates opposed it at higher rates than ministers. The clergy divided almost exactly in half, voting 104 in favor and one hundred against it, while the laity rejected it by a stunning 173 to twenty-four. A moderate Methodist who had watched the proceedings from the balcony of First Methodist Church in Columbus "could not believe the tragedy" she witnessed. A lifelong Mississippian, she had no illusions about why the plan had failed: "how few of us are willing to acknowledge and accept our black brothers. . . . May God have mercy on us all!"[105]

Roy Lawrence of the *Advocate* spoke as bluntly. Given the extraordinary paroxysms in Mississippi Methodism over the preceding decade and a half, his description of the meeting as "the most tumultuous and divisive in [the conference's] 102 years of existence" suggests a great deal. Disappointed that his coreligionists had ignored theological issues, Lawrence now believed the Conference would oppose merger, "regardless of the plan which had been proposed." Lawrence acknowledged that the "North Mississippi Conference has always had a reputation of being a conservative Conference," but he thought "the recent session pushed the Conference's record further to the right, and what we now seem to have is an ultra-conservative conference bordering on radical conservatism."[106]

White Mississippians' rejection of the plan frustrated the black Mississippians who had invested considerable energy in it. Members of the all-black Upper Mississippi Conference refused to enter again into negotiations about merger and requested that the United Methodist Board of Arbitration force white Methodists to merge.[107] Though a small group formed Mississippi Methodists for Merger to encourage the process along, most whites preferred to stall and delay. Indeed, it required looming action of the General Conference at the end of 1972 before white Mississippi Methodists accepted administrative merger with the black conference. Faced with a July 1, 1973, deadline, both white Mississippi Conferences accepted merger when the new bishop warned them that the General Conference would impose a plan from the outside if they did not voluntarily draft and adopt their own plan.[108]

Yet the debates over merger did not fully capture Mississippi Methodists' extraordinary distress in these years. In part, that anguish revealed itself in declining numbers. Between 1965 and 1977, white Mississippi Methodists lost nearly 14,500 members from their roles, with a drop of nearly 4,000 between 1971 and 1972 alone.[109] While these losses amount to less than 10 percent, they fail to account for those who began attending other churches without removing their names from the Methodist roles. According to the recollection of Vicksburg layman James Earl Price, former Methodists filled the pews in conservative churches of other affiliations: "We lost many churches, many ministers and many laymen. . . . I am reminded of the Methodist laymen we lost each time I attend a function . . . at another denomination. At almost every church I see someone, who in the past was a Methodist."[110]

Many white Methodists who stayed in the church did so in spite of an extraordinary sense of alienation. As a fifth-generation Mississippi

Methodist, Price stayed in the church, but felt painfully out of sync with the denomination's younger ministers and programs. In particular, he noticed a theological decline: the church "taught only social concerns . . . the literature became filled with social issues . . . it contained none of the old 'proclaim the Word' lessons. Some of it appeared to have little to do with the Methodists, the Bible, or the Christian religion."[111] Price believed that many Mississippi Methodists' sympathies lay with the like of Oral Roberts, Bob Jones, Jim Baker, Jimmy Swaggart, and Jerry Falwell, and this judgment accords well with statistics that show a rise in Mississippi's independent evangelical church membership, even as Methodist numbers continued to decline. Indeed, a friend of his agreed that the civil rights years "set the United Methodist church in Mississippi backward twenty-five years."[112]

* * *

Conservative Mississippi Methodists answered the theological challenge of the civil rights movement by reaffirming a "proclaim the Word" faith much like that of the state's Baptists and Presbyterians. Indeed, while black Americans waged a revolutionary fight to express their full humanity, many of Mississippi's white evangelicals defended the evangelistic faith they had known and practiced for decades. These holy wars do not represent perverse preoccupations oddly disconnected from the black freedom struggle; rather, they grew directly out of the racial revolution, for hanging onto white privilege required maintaining the religious ethos that supported it. Faced with the opportunity to reformulate their faith—to bring into it an understanding that the world and its systems might require redeeming, along with souls—white Mississippians chose to stay with a gospel that worked only on the hearts of individuals. Yet when recalling these internecine wars, many of Mississippi's Southern Baptists and Presbyterians place them in an historical vacuum, divorcing them completely from the black freedom struggle. In their view, conservatives' battles to defend and preserve a theological position grew only from pure devotion to those truths; the civil rights movement "had nothing to do with it."[113] For their part, Methodists often regard their church's focus on civil rights as a time of religious declension, a low point in the history of their church.

Institutionally and organizationally, none of these groups can claim that faith worked a racial conversion on them nor can they maintain that the moral imperative of black equality gripped them and made them into agents of change. If Presbyterians and Methodists who accepted their black coreligionists only with ecclesiastical coercion serve as a case in point, the evidence suggests that external compulsion, not an innate spiritual impulse, brought about racial change. Though some evangelical individuals certainly sympathized with the black freedom struggle, their examples stand as isolated and limited exceptions.

Ultimately, most evangelicals did make one religious adjustment as a result of the civil rights turmoil, adding "racism" to the catalogue of sins that the Christian should eschew. The addition, however, has little changed the basic individualistic orientation of this sort of evangelical faith. Very few conservative Christians believe the Gospel mandates alterations in the social and political order. Mississippi's white believers have rejected overt racism, like most Americans, even as they have clung to and defended the very theology that sustained the racial hierarchy and informed the defense of segregation.

Evangelicalism has become uncoupled from the racial hierarchy it once sustained, but it continues to structure moral visions—to identify evil, to define good, and to locate morality. For the most part, in this way of thinking, systems emerge only as the product of individual actions. Sin resides in people, not in the configuration of the society around them. The notion that the world might work in exactly the opposite way—that social, political, and economic arrangements might exert profound evil on individuals, limiting their destinies and proscribing their choices—hardly enters in. Vision so trained can hardly register the wickedness that ensues from social systems that hurt, disfigure, and profoundly disadvantage some, while reserving for others the best preparation, the choicest opportunities, and the smoothest pathways.

No understanding of the Christian faith, no interpretation of the Bible, lacks political implications. Mississippians' rejection of other gospels provided crucial groundwork for the political rise of the religious right. The politico-religious alliances that developed in the 1970s relied on these individualistic faith conceptions for their underpinnings in much the same way that white supremacy had relied on them for

support. As evangelicals rallied to action against the teaching of evolution, abortion, and expanded roles for women, they called on their
long-standing but freshly reaffirmed faith commitments to exclusive
evangelism, narrow biblical interpretation, and personal morality over
institutional and social justice. The theological battles waged in these
communions strengthened them for these fights, making certain that
the Christian faith would not serve as the foundation for an alteration
of society.

CONCLUSION

A Theology on the Wrong Side of History

The conservative religion of white Mississippians offered almost no help to the state's African Americans as they struggled to upend white domination. In fact, ideologically and institutionally, this faith served as a serious and persistent impediment to black activists' goals. Evangelicals fought mightily against black equality, proclaiming that God himself ordained segregation, blessing the forces of resistance, silencing the advocates of racial equality within their own faith traditions, and protecting segregation in their churches.

This story suggests much about moral suasion and its ineffectiveness in persuading a people to willingly relinquish power and privilege. In civil-rights-era Mississippi, such moral suasion proved largely fruitless. Whether advanced by white members of their own traditions or mounted by black activists themselves, whether made on paper in nationally distributed Sunday school material, missions magazines, and pamphlets or dramatized in the vivid theater of the church visit campaign, moral pleas proved too easily silenced, distorted, or dispatched. Few white Mississippians, it seems, experienced religious epiphanies about the immorality of segregation while the contest swirled in full force. Legal, economic, and legislative coercion forced the changes that ultimately came to Mississippi, and the scales of racial prejudice often fell from white eyes only well *after* African Americans appropriated their hard-won gains.

Yet, on the other hand, the opinions of a minority of white Christians quietly evolved, even while defiance roared on the surface of public life. Mississippi's religious moderates appear at every juncture in this story, demonstrating that faith helped some challenge the do-or-die methods and mentality required to preserve white supremacy, even if they only rarely went so far as to fully support the quest for equality. The moral force of faith helped coax and encourage a latent moderation in every community—though this moderation proved often limited in its convictions or powerless against the segregationist majority. These moderates did help tamp down extremism, diluted segregationist strength, and resisted segregationist conformity at various points. They encouraged compliance when change came and established networks of communication to ease the transition processes, all important work in civil-rights-era Mississippi. But they rarely jumped full-fledged into the fray to help black activists. Overt white religious support for destroying the racial hierarchy came largely from out-of-state practitioners of a faith quite different from the Christianity embraced by most Mississippians.

Mississippi Praying has argued that theology shaped evangelicals' responses to the demand for black equality. The literalist view of the Bible helped construe segregation as outside the purview of Christian concerns. On the other hand, moderates who began the civil rights years with flexible views of Scripture found a corresponding openness to the moral critique of segregation. As the civil rights challenge assumed national dimensions and the judgment on white supremacy expanded, the stakes in these theological divisions took on greater significance. When national denominational bodies responded to black unrest in ways that seemed to redefine their identities, Mississippians participated in far-reaching debates about the meanings and implications of Christianity. They occupied the vanguard of efforts to capture their traditions for the most conservative expressions of the faith. Though this study does *not* ascribe a special propensity for racism to conservative evangelicals nor argue that this theology fosters racism, it does demonstrate that certain ways of viewing sin, morality, and individual responsibility structure a people's thinking so as to obscure and discount collective and corporate responsibility.

Mississippi and America

Important questions remain about the relationship of American—not just southern—religion to white supremacy. Many aspects of this story seem to point toward a Mississippi hopelessly out of sync with the rest of the country, an image that certainly matches national perceptions in

1964 and the years immediately prior. The critique of segregation issuing from national religious leaders and denominational bodies, the
northern clerics who joined with black activists on the steps of Jackson
churches, and the ministers in the Hattiesburg picket line all seem to
suggest that a thoroughly egalitarian and racially innocent North issued
a clarion call for racial equality to a resistant and callous white South.

But in fact, such a dichotomy may be overdrawn. The objections
of some Illinois parishioners to their pastors' southern racial activism
indicate much about the religious limits on northern Americans' commitments to southern blacks and their struggle. Civil rights scholarship
increasingly depicts the movement as a national rather than uniquely
southern quest, but the impression remains in both scholarly and popular conceptions that northern Protestants embraced and supported
the movement, while their coreligionists in the South resisted it. If
structural and individual racism pervaded American life, it stands to
reason that religion played a role in maintaining the racial hierarchy
and resisting change in Detroit or Cleveland as well as in Jackson and
Birmingham.

In the spring of 1969, black activist James Forman delivered a searing
indictment of America's white religious institutions and their complicity in racial oppression. He interrupted worship services, confronted
denominational leaders at their headquarters, and invaded gatherings of national bodies to read his *Black Manifesto*, with its sweeping challenge and its demand for financial restitution. Though the vast
majority of his hearers dismissed these claims as ludicrous, Forman's
analysis of the church shared much in common with the assessment of
the roughly 300 black Methodists who had formed Black Methodists
for Church Renewal (BMCR) the year before. This coalition charged
that Methodism too often coddled the wealthy and privileged rather
than serving the poor and the oppressed. Though many white moderates and even liberals rejected these assessments outright, these black
Americans' argument about national church bodies resonates a great
deal with the theses that *Mississippi Praying* has advanced regarding
the faith in one Deep South state.[1]

As black activists probed the depths of America's racial problems
in the second half of the 1960s, they identified white supremacy as a
force so pervasive that it had infected America's entire culture, and they

described American religion as an eager accomplice in the evil that had oppressed them. Further scholarship will answer important questions about religion's relationship to the racial hierarchy in America, not just the South. How did local white Protestant churchgoers respond as black unrest and anti-poverty crusaders took the struggle into northern cities? To what extent did northern Protestants reject their ministers' activism and the "liberal" voices of their denominations when the challenge of black equality came to their own doorsteps? What role might such alienation have played in creating the larger conservative coalitions to which white Mississippians joined themselves in the 1970s? If we listen to the indictments of Forman, BMCR, and others, we may better appreciate how Mississippi does not deserve singular status as a place where religion served the interests of white supremacy.[2]

The Rise of the Religious Right

In the 1970s and 1980s, Mississippians worked prodigiously to promote personal morality and to create a climate conducive to it. Though this activity itself represented nothing new, their efforts in these later decades did differ from earlier ones in that they now dropped their previously professed caution about political activity. In 1982, the executive director of the Mississippi Baptist Convention's Christian Action Committee registered formally as a lobbyist, reflecting an essentially new philosophy among his coreligionists: "the church belongs in politics up to its eyeballs."[3] In further contrast to previous decades, these evangelicals championed a dramatically expanded range of issues. In the context of a wider culture that seemed increasingly threatening to their values because of its looser public sexual morality, changing roles for women, and important federal initiatives like the Supreme Court's 1973 *Roe v. Wade* decision, Mississippi evangelicals took leading roles in campaigns against abortion, homosexuality, and sexually explicit material in public media.

Yet perhaps most importantly, evangelicals' efforts in the 1970s and 1980s differed most from their political activities of earlier decades in that now they performed them in a dramatically altered national religious and political context. Before the black freedom struggle burst into public view, the nation's largest Protestant traditions—Methodist, Baptist, and Presbyterian—harbored rich theological diversity. In spite of occasional tension, institutional loyalties, common goals, and a shift-ing political climate helped communicants hang together in spite of their often dramatically different approaches to spiritual life. That reli-gious unity in diversity could not hold in the face of America's racial revolution. The once-fluid religious atmosphere evaporated during the 1970s as Southern Baptists reconfigured, Presbyterians fractured, and Methodists shriveled. To a significant extent, the racial crisis set these transformations in motion as it brought long-resident conflicts over questions of theology and its political implications to the fore. Missis-sippians played key roles in these developments.

These denominational changes formed an absolutely essential foun-dation for the rise of the religious right in American politics. The theo-logically diverse institutions of the mid-twentieth century would have made poor instruments for promoting the issues conservative evangeli-cals have championed since the 1970s, for these battles required lean and sharply focused soldiers. Only bodies stripped of their theological variety and flexibility could wield power in these campaigns. Evangel-icals no longer voice caution about political activity because, in their resurrected and monolithically conservative form, no challenge to their politics can arise to trouble unity within these bodies.

Mississippi evangelicals' responses to the racial crisis contributed importantly to this altered national religious context. Alienation from their national bodies during the racial crisis informed their efforts to reshape the national religious terrain. The denominations' relative pro-gressiveness on racial issues created extraordinary contention between Magnolia State evangelicals and denominational agencies, rendering these relationships tenuous and imperiled in the civil rights years. Yet, once they united with other similarly alienated conservatives outside the state to reshape the religious terrain—expunging the SBC's theolog-ically and socially progressive voices, creating a new Presbyterian com-munion devoted to biblical literalism, and forsaking the United Meth-odist Church in droves—Mississippians have happily thrived in bodies monolithically devoted to the theological premises they cherished all along. Mississippians' approval of these dramatic changes demonstrates itself in conservative evangelicalism's continued resonance there.

Significantly, however, theological diversity remains in Mississippi in the United Methodist Church, among the Presbyterians who stayed with the parent communion, and in the tiny contingent of Baptist moderates. The same theological divisions that had shaped evangelicals' responses to the quest for black equality continued to dictate their positions in the culture wars. While monolithically conservative groups championed the slate of issues identified with the religious right, the groups that survived the civil rights years with their theological elasticity intact have withheld their support from such endeavors. In the quite diverse Mississippi Methodist Conference, for example, arch-conservative Reverend Donald Wildmon rose to a position of national prominence in the late 1970s by working to limit access to pornography, monitoring the content of television and movies, and withholding funding from the National Endowment for the Arts. Yet Wildmon represented only one perspective in this communion, and he could not gain support for his Coalition for Better Television from his own home conference. And even as Mississippi provided national leadership for the struggle to limit abortion rights, the bishop of the Mississippi Methodist Conference supported "the legal option of abortion under proper medical attention" a statement that brought protesters out for a prayer vigil at the Methodist Building in Jackson.[4]

Reckoning with the Past: Religion and Race in Mississippi Today

An examination of Mississippi's current configurations of religion and race leads us to profitably ask how Mississippi has changed, how it has not changed, and how it reckons with its racial past. If the connection between Mississippians' conservative faith and their racial system once seemed strong, that relationship has since grown much more complicated. On the one hand, conservative religion continues to thrive and prevail in the Magnolia State. Southern Baptists there dwarf the nearest contenders even more decisively than they did in the mid-twentieth century, as their presence has mushroomed from the 480,000 members they claimed around 1960 to a whopping 907,000 as of 2010.[5] A miniscule nineteen Baptist congregations currently affiliate with the two associations favored by moderate Baptists—far less than in other states with smaller Baptist constituencies.[6] As for Presbyterians, the conservative PCA claims nearly three times the numbers of congregations in

Mississippi as its more moderate counterpart.[7] Conservative religion further expresses its continued vitality in the vigorous growth of independent, evangelical churches. The United Methodist Church (UMC), which successfully resisted conservative takeover but suffered devastating membership losses, is a shadow of its former self, with only two-thirds the congregations it had in 1954.[8]

The conservative traditions have not changed their gospel. Their message remains focused on the primacy of salvation and personal morality, and it continues to put the unencumbered individual—free from the constraints of social, political, or economic structures—at its center, supporting these tenets with very close, often literal readings of the Bible. The solution to all human problems, many Mississippians still believe, lies in changing individual souls, one at a time. First Presbyterian Church of Jackson, one of the most important congregations in the arch-conservative PCA from its founding to the present, announces on its website: "We believe that the only hope for the world is in the Spiritual regeneration of souls wrought by God through Jesus Christ."[9] Yet, as this study has demonstrated, racial change did not come to Mississippi by any such regeneration of souls. At least when applied to righting a perverse racial system, First Presbyterian's claim seems more a myth than a timeless spiritual truth.

Yet even as conservative religion thrives there, religious integration of a sort has come to the Magnolia State and to its once segregated communions. In a stunning demonstration, the SBC elected Reverend Fred Luter as the first black president in its history in 2012.[10] A few months later, Luter spoke from the pulpit of Jackson's First Baptist Church, the one-time spiritual home of Mississippi's most ardent architects of segregation and massive resistance.[11] The conservative Presbyterian Church in America, born in the midst of the racial crisis, also appears deliberately to have shed the trappings of its racial past. The PCA has an African American constituency and a coordinator for African American Ministries.[12] A few PCA churches have also rigorously disciplined neoconfederates in their pews for "the sin of racism."[13] In Mississippi, the PCA's outreach to African Americans outpaces Baptists'. An interracial congregation on the north side of Jackson worships under the leadership of an African American pastor, and the denomination even runs a student ministry on the campus of the historically black Jackson State

University.[14] Mission Mississippi, perhaps the most visible and innovative religious effort to bridge racial communities in the state, has arisen with the significant initiative of a white member of First Presbyterian Church, Jackson.[15] In the United Methodist Church, not only do black and white district superintendents supervise pastors and congregations of both races, but in 2012 the Mississippi Annual Conference welcomed an African American bishop, James E. Swanson.[16]

In keeping with these new racial realities, Mississippi's—and America's—white Christians now willingly and eagerly identify racial discrimination as a moral wrong. Racism has moved to a rather urgent spot at the top of the list of sins; everyone wants to avoid it and many exert themselves strenuously to demonstrate their freedom from it. Whereas their forbearers of not so long ago advanced the Christian underpinnings of segregation, today's evangelicals think differently. Yet since conservative evangelicals' theology has not changed, their understanding of racial problems as matters of individual sin remains essentially the same.

Still, the overt interracialism and fervent antiracism of these conservative communions challenge us to think about how these new racial attitudes and endeavors fit with a theology transported whole from the era of segregation. For no matter how vigorously evangelicals decry racism, the continued location of it in the individual—where they locate all social problems—hinders, rather than enhances, any understanding of the racial past and, as a consequence, the country's racial present. Focusing on racism as an individual sin for which practitioners must repent keeps the problem in *exactly* the same place segregationists located it during the Jim Crow era, while it also continues to pin responsibility for all their sufferings on blacks themselves. If America's troubled racial history owes to nothing more than people's personal peccadilloes, then correcting it lies in the simple matter of a "racial conversion." The scales of racism fall from one's eyes; one sees the light, decides no longer to be a racist, and goes about with a newly clear vision of reality. Yet if evangelicals grappled with their own civil rights history, they might confront the reality that such racial conversions rarely happened, and that change came in spite of their religion, not because of it.

Indeed, the easy repudiation of the sins of racist individuals requires little intellectual or emotional engagement with deep and complicated issues. More demands ensue from a confrontation with the difficult truths that America's race problems lie deeply embedded in its institutions and cultures and that they fundamentally concern the distribution of resources, power, and privilege. Such an encounter requires a complex morality and a willingness to probe the impact of corporate behaviors, institutional mentalities, and economic policies. Without a large-scale apprehension of where and how white supremacy operated historically and, by extension, where it may persist today, systems that privilege some while disadvantaging others continue their invisible and sinister work, though often in altered forms.

Through religion, in Mississippi as in the rest of the country, Americans continue to work out and articulate their ongoing visions of themselves, of what constitutes justice and equality, and of how they can negotiate between their personal virtue and their desires for power and privilege. Even as Mississippi and America have both changed a great deal, the deep, penetrating, and paradoxical relationship between religion and race remains with us still.

INTRODUCTION

1. Some of the best examples of this literature include Kevin Kruse, *White Flight: Atlanta and the Making of Modern Conservatism* (Princeton: Princeton University Press, 2005); Matthew D. Lassiter, *The Silent Majority: Suburban Politics in the Sunbelt South* (Princeton: Princeton University Press, 2006); George Lewis, *Massive Resistance: The White Response to the Civil Rights Movement* (London: Hodder Headline, 2006); and Clive Webb, ed., *Massive Resistance: Southern Opposition to the Second Reconstruction* (New York: Oxford University Press, 2005). The most important essays dealing with religion and white resistance are Paul Harvey, "Religion, Race, and the Right in the South, 1945–1990," in Glenn Feldman, ed., *Politics and Religion in the White South* (Lexington: University Press of Kentucky, 2005), 101–23; "God and Negroes and Jesus and Sin and Salvation: Racism, Racial Interchange, and Interracialism in Southern Religious History," in Beth Barton Schweiger and Donald G. Mathews, eds., *Religion in the American South: Protestants and Others in History and Culture* (Chapel Hill: University of North Carolina Press, 2004), 285–91; Jane Daily, "The Theology of Massive Resistance: Sex, Segregation, and the Sacred after *Brown*," in Webb, ed., *Massive Resistance,* 151–80; and David Chappell, "Disunity and Religious Institutions in the White South," in Webb, ed., *Massive Resistance,* 136–50. See also Paul Harvey, *Freedom's Coming: Religious Culture and the Shaping of the South from the Civil War through the Civil Rights Era* (Chapel Hill: University of North Carolina Press, 2005), ch. 4, and Randy J. Sparks, *Religion in Mississippi* (Jackson: University Press of Mississippi, 2001), ch. 10.

2. An important exception to this trend, Joseph Crespino, *In Search of Another Country: Mississippi and the Conservative Counterrevolution,* (Princeton: Princeton University Press, 2007), effectively includes religion in the analysis. An important work that places religion at the center of both blacks' and whites' understanding of the civil rights movement, though the interpretation clashes significantly with the one advanced here, is David Chappell, *A Stone of Hope: Prophetic Religion and the Death of Jim Crow* (Chapel Hill: University of North Carolina Press, 2005). Charles Marsh considers how religion shaped the responses of five people—black and white—who lived or worked in Mississippi

during the summer of 1964 in *God's Long Summer: Stories of Faith and Civil Rights* (Princeton: Princeton University Press, 1999). See also S. Jonathan Bass, *Blessed are the Peacemakers: Martin Luther King, Jr., Eight White Religious Leaders, and the "Letter from Birmingham Jail"* (Baton Rouge: Louisiana State University Press, 2001); J. Russell Hawkins, "Religion, Race, and Resistance: White Evangelicals and the Dilemma of Integration in South Carolina, 1950–1975" (Ph.D. diss., Rice University, 2010); Carter Dalton Lyon, "Lifting the Color Bar from the House of God: The 1963–1964 Church Visit Campaign to Challenge Segregated Sanctuaries in Jackson, Mississippi" (Ph.D. diss., University of Mississippi, 2010); Robert Patrick Rayner, "On Theological Grounds: Hattiesburg Presbyterians and the Civil Rights Movement" (M.A. thesis, University of Southern Mississippi, 2009).

3. Mark Newman, *Getting Right with God: Southern Baptists and Desegregation, 1945–1995* (Tuscaloosa: University of Alabama Press, 2001); Peter C. Murray, *Methodists and the Crucible of Race, 1930–1975* (Columbia: University of Missouri Press, 2004); Joel L. Alvis, *Religion and Race: Southern Presbyterians, 1946–1983* (Tuscaloosa: University of Alabama Press, 1994); Gardiner H. Shattuck, *Episcopalians and Race: Civil War to Civil Rights* (Lexington: University Press of Kentucky, 2000). See also Mark Newman's essays on most of the state Baptist conventions and desegregation, including "The Mississippi Baptist Convention and Desegregation, 1945–1980," *Journal of Mississippi History* 59, no. 1 (Spring 1997): 1–31.

4. Martin Luther King, Jr., "Letter from Birmingham Jail," in *Why We Can't Wait* (New York: New American Library, 1964), 64–84.

5. Samuel S. Hill, Jr., *Southern Churches in Crisis* (New York: Holt, Rinehart and Winston, 1966).

6. Chappell, *Stone of Hope.*

7. This distortion characterizes Chappell's *Stone of Hope*, which depicts religious support for segregation as "weak," in part because he finds so few of these segregationist polemics.

8. In addition to Hill, *Southern Churches in Crisis*, other works in this school include John Lee Eighmy, *Churches in Cultural Captivity: A History of the Social Attitudes of Southern Baptists* (Knoxville: University of Tennessee Press, 1972), and Kenneth K. Bailey, *Southern White Protestantism in the Twentieth Century* (New York: Harper and Row, 1964).

9. Paul Harvey offers a brief critique of the cultural captivity framework in "Religion, Race, and the Right in the South, 1945–1990."

10. Among the most important works in the extensive literature on the rise of the religious right are Daniel K. Williams, *God's Own Party: The Making of the Christian Right* (New York: Oxford University Press, 2010); Darren Dochuk, *From Bible Belt to Sunbelt: Plain Folk Religion, Grassroots Politics, and the Rise of Evangelical Conservatism* (New York: W. W. Norton and Company, 2011); J. Brooks Flippen, *Jimmy Carter, the Politics of Family, and the Rise of the Religious Right*

(Athens: University of Georgia Press, 2011); Lisa McGirr, *Suburban Warriors: The Origins of the New American Right* (Princeton: Princeton University Press, 2002); Angela Lahr, *Millennial Dreams and Apocalyptic Nightmares: The Cold War Origins of Political Evangelicalism* (New York: Oxford University Press, 2007); Will Martin, *With God on Our Side: The Rise of the Religious Right In America* (New York: Broadway Books, 1997).

11. For a profitable examination of the ways Mississippi has served in national narratives about the civil rights movement, see Joseph Crespino, "Civil Rights, the South, and the Nation in the Historical Imagination," in Matthew D. Lassiter and Joseph Crespino, eds., *The Myth of Southern Exceptionalism* (New York: Oxford University Press, 2010), 99–120.

12. Resolution on Racial Reconciliation on the 150th Anniversary of the Southern Baptist Convention, June 1995, http://www.sbc.net/resolutions/amResolution. asp?ID=899 (accessed October 11, 2010).

13. Michael O. Emerson and Christian Smith, *Divided by Faith: Evangelical Religion and the Problem of Race in America* (Oxford: Oxford University Press, 2001).

14. Richard C. Marius, "Ruleville: Reminiscence, Reflection," *Christian Century*, September 23, 1964.

CHAPTER 1

1. *Baptist Record (BR)*, October 4, November 1, 1956.

2. *Christian Century (CC)*, October 10, 1956.

3. Samuel S. Hill, *Southern Churches in Crisis* (Holt Rinehart, and Winston, 1966); John Lee Eighmy, *Churches in Cultural Captivity: A History of the Social Attitudes of Southern Baptists* (Knoxville: University of Tennessee Press, 1972); and Kenneth K. Bailey, *Southern White Protestantism in the Twentieth Century* (New York: Harper and Row, 1964). Other historians of southern religion who emphasize its long-standing individualistic orientation include John B. Boles, *The Great Revival: The Beginnings of the Bible Belt* (Lexington: University Press of Kentucky, 1996); and Charles Reagan Wilson, "Preachin' Prayin' and Singin' on the Public Square," in Charles Reagan Wilson and Mark Silk, eds., *Religion and Public Life in the South: In the Evangelical Mode* (New York: Rowman and Littlefield Publishers, Inc., 2005).

4. This was the assessment of Hill in *Southern Churches in Crisis* and also of Richard Marius, "Ruleville: Reminiscence, Reflection," *CC*, September 23, 1964.

5. The literature from many disciplines that explores the systemic or structural nature of racism is immense, and I cite only a few examples here. Greta de Jong, *Invisible Enemy: The African American Freedom Struggle after 1965* (Malden, MA: Wiley-Blackwell, 2010), offers a very good historical overview of structural racism, but the bulk of the analysis focuses on recent decades. Explanations of institutional racism can be found in the thought of black activists, such as Stokely Carmichael and Charles V. Hamilton, *Black Power: The Politics of Liberation in America* (New York: Random House, 1967), as well as in the literature

on whiteness and white privilege, for example, George Lipsitz, *The Possessive Investment in Whiteness: How White People Profit from Identity Politics,* rev. ed. (Philadelphia: Temple University Press, 2006), and Peggy MacIntosh, "White Privilege: Unpacking the Invisible Knapsack," in Paula S. Rothenberg, ed., *Race, Class and Gender in the United States: An Integrated Study,* 4ᵗʰ ed. (New York: St. Martin's Press, 1998).

6. Photographs and physical descriptions of many Mississippi churches can be found in Sherry Pace, *Historic Churches of Mississippi* (Jackson: University Press of Mississippi, 2007). County and City Data Book, *A Statistical Abstract Supplement* (Washington, DC: U.S. Government Printing Office, 1957). Eldie F. Hicks to Dr. A. C. Miller October 2, 1957, Christian Life Commission Papers. Box 1, Folder 3, Southern Baptist Historical Library and Archive (SBHLA), Nashville, TN. *BR,* May 26, 1955, January 3, 1957. Mackland Hubbell, interview with author, May 4, 2000. For a description and history of the Delta region of Mississippi, see James C. Cobb, *The Most Southern Place on Earth: The Mississippi Delta and the Roots of Regional Identity* (Oxford: Oxford University Press, 1994).

7. *BR,* September 27, 1956. Marius, "Ruleville: Reminiscence, Reflection."

8. As of the end of 1955, the Mississippi Baptist Convention Association claimed over 430,000 members; *BR,* March 22, 1956. Methodists claimed 183,749 members as of June 1954; *Mississippi Methodist Advocate (MMA),* January 5, 1955. Hill, *Southern Churches in Crisis,* 39. On Catholic membership, see Jack Winton Gunn, "Religion in the Twentieth Century," in Richard Aubrey McLemore, ed., *A History of Mississippi* (Hattiesburg: University and College Press of Mississippi, 1973), 477–91. On some of the "outsider" religious groups in Mississippi, see Randy J. Sparks, *Religion in Mississippi* (Jackson: University Press of Mississippi, 2001), 201–19, and Gunn, "Religion in the Twentieth Century," 490–91.

9. *BR,* November 8, 1956. Circulation figures for state Baptist papers from 1945–1970 are given in Mark Newman, *Getting Right with God: Southern Baptists and Desegregation, 1945-1995* (Tuscaloosa: University of Alabama Press, 2001), 211.

10. For personal incomes in Mississippi, see County and City Data Book, *A Statistical Abstract Supplement.* For a comparison of Mississippi Baptist giving with that of Baptists in other states, see *BR,* April 3, 1947. *BR,* January 31, 1957; March 22, 1956; *MMA,* April 6, 1960.

11. *BR,* October 11, 1956.

12. *BR,* September 30, 1954. See, for example, the listing of the one hundred Mississippi churches that gave the most to foreign missions in the preceding fiscal year, *BR,* June 14, 1956.

13. Hill, *Southern Churches in Crisis,* 23. Marius, "Ruleville: Reminiscence, Reflection." Charles Reagan Wilson offers a similar description of popular southern Protestantism in "Preachin' Prayin' and Singin' on the Public Square."

14. Marius, "Ruleville: Reminiscence, Reflection." *BR,* August 12, 1954.

15. For the classic study of fundamentalism, see George Marsden, *Fundamentalism and American Culture: The Shaping of Twentieth-Century Evangelicalism,*

1870–1925 (New York: Oxford University Press, 1980). For another work that explains the nuances within fundamentalism and their differences with other kinds of evangelicals, see Joel Carpenter, *Revive Us Again: The Reawakening of American Fundamentalism* (New York: Oxford University Press, 1999).

16. See, for example, the comments of native Mississippi Presbyterian Dr. Frank Caldwell in the *Charlotte Observer*, October 2, 1964.

17. *BR*, January 3, February 7, June 13, 1946.

18. R. Milton Winter, "Division and Reunion in the Presbyterian Church, U.S.: A Mississippi Retrospective," *Journal of Presbyterian History* 78, no. 1 (Spring 2000): 67–86. On Machen, see D. G. Hart, *Defending the Faith: J. Gresham Machen and the Crisis of Conservative Protestantism in Modern America* (Phillipsburg, NJ: P and R Publishing, 2003).

19. See, for example, the series of letters from 1957 and 1958 about the suitability of Reverends Richard Harbison and Robert L. Smith in Bertil Ivar Anderson Papers, Box 535, Folder 3, Presbyterian Church in America Historical Center, St. Louis, MO.

20. Hill, *Southern Churches in Crisis*, 33. Marius, "Ruleville: Reminiscence, Reflection." *BR*, November 20, July 17, 1947. On Mississippi's law against teaching evolution, see Sparks, *Religion in Mississippi*, 181–82, 250–51. David M. Nelson, *Conflicting Views on Segregation* (Greenwood, MS: Educational Fund of the Citizens' Council, 1954). Oral History with Will D. Campbell, Christian Preacher, June 8, 1976, The University of Southern Mississippi Center for Oral History and Cultural Heritage, University of Southern Mississippi Libraries (USMCO-HCH), Hattiesburg, MS, http://digilib.usm.edu/u?/coh,544 (accessed October 20, 2010).

21. David L. Chappell, *A Stone of Hope: Prophetic Religion and the Death of Jim Crow*. (Chapel Hill: University of North Carolina Press, 2004).

22. Grace Elizabeth Hale, *Making Whiteness: The Culture of Segregation in the South, 1890–1940* (New York: Pantheon Books, 1998).

23. The African Methodist Episcopal (AME) Church was organized in Philadelphia in the early nineteenth century, and the AME Zion church has its origins in New York during the same period; see Carol V. R. George, *Segregated Sabbaths: Richard Allen and the Rise of Independent Black Churches, 1760–1840* (New York: Oxford University Press, 1973). The National Baptist Convention began in 1880, but merged with several other black Baptist conventions in 1895 to become the National Baptist Convention of the USA. Some of the best literature on black churches and their formation in the years after the Civil War includes Evelyn Brooks Higginbotham, *Righteous Discontent: The Women's Movement in the Black Baptist Church, 1880–1920* (Cambridge: Harvard University Press, 1993); William E. Montgomery, *Under Their Own Vine and Fig Tree: The African American Church in the South, 1865–1900* (Baton Rouge: Louisiana State University Press, 1993); and Katharine L. Dvorak, *An African American Exodus: The Segregation of the Southern Churches* (Brooklyn: Carlson Publishing, 1991).

24. Joel Alvis, *Religion and Race: Southern Presbyterians, 1946–1983* (Tuscaloosa: University of Alabama Press, 1994), 13–45.

25. Thelma Stevens and A. Dudley Ward, *The Methodist Church and Race: A Guide to Understanding the Jurisdictional System and Race Relations* (Washington, DC: Woman's Division of Christian Service, the Methodist Church, 1962); Morris L. Davis, *The Methodist Unification: Christianity and the Politics of Race in the Jim Crow Era* (New York: New York University Press, 2008); Julius Del Pino, "Blacks in the United Methodist Church from Its Beginning to 1968," *Methodist History* 19, no. 1 (October 1980): 3–20; Peter C. Murray, *Methodists and the Crucible of Race, 1930–1975* (Columbia: University of Missouri Press, 2004).

26. Alvis, *Religion and Race*, 34–36, explores the hardships foisted upon black Presbyterians because of the segregated Snedecor Memorial Synod. For a similar description with regard to Methodism, see Del Pino, "Blacks in the United Methodist Church," and Murray, *Methodists and the Crucible of Race,* ch. 2.

27. Bulletin of Bay Street Presbyterian Church, Hattiesburg, MS, January 7, 1945, in Congregational Vertical Files, Presbyterian Historical Society (PHS), Philadelphia, PA.

28. Slaves who worshipped with their owners in the antebellum era also did so as "artificial" members of the family; see Dvorak, *An African American Exodus,* 174.

29. The biblical case for segregation receives sustained treatment in chapter 3.

30. On black Baptist membership, see Gunn, "Religion in the Twentieth Century," 480. By white Baptists' own calculations, in 1954 Mississippi's Southern Baptist membership stood at 417,000, while total black Baptist membership was 450,000. *BR*, September 16, 1954.

31. For membership statistics on black Methodists, see Murray, *Methodists and the Crucible of Race*, 45.

32. William P. Davis, *The Long Step*, typed copy in Department of Negro Work folder, Mississippi Baptist Historical Commission (MBHC), Clinton, MS. *Annual*, Mississippi Baptist Convention, 1963, 47.

33. Horace L. Villee to Rev. M. P. Calhoun, October 1, 1952, in Division of Christian Relations of the Presbyterian Church, US, (DCRPCUS), Box 1, Folder 1952 (collection unprocessed), PHS.

34. Mary Rosalind Healy, "Why I Believe in Social Separation of the Races of Mankind" (1960) in William D. Workman Papers, Box 32, Modern Political Collections, University of South Carolina Library, Columbia, SC. The author thanks Russell J. Hawkins for sharing this document from his research. Curtis J. Evans, *The Burden of Black Religion* (New York: Oxford University Press, 2008), argues that whites have historically attributed an innate, though often "primitive" and "emotional," spirituality to black Americans; however, Evans' study terminates in 1940.

35. Sunday school lesson outlines, in Archibald S. Coody Papers (ASCP), Box 24, Folder 1, Mississippi Department of Archives and History (MDAH), Jackson, MS.

36. Horace L. Villee to Rev. M. P. Calhoun, October 1, 1952, in DCRPCUS, Box 1, Folder 1952.

37. Sunday school lesson outlines, in ASCP, Box 24, Folder 1.

38. Gunnar Myrdal, *An American Dilemma: The Negro Problem and Modern Democracy* (New York: Harper and Brothers, 1944), 869.

39. Race Relations Sunday Survey, typescript copy, in DCRPCUS, Box 1, Folder 1954. Myrdal also reported that white preachers rarely addressed racial issues from the pulpit; see ch. 4.

40. Horace Villee to Rev. M. P. Calhoun, October 1, 1952, in DCRPCUS, Box 1, Folder 1952.

41. *MMA*, February 9, 1955.

42. *The Morning Star,* Greenwood, MS, February 10, 1953, Clipping in DCRPCUS, Box 1, Folder 1954.

43. See for example reports in *BR*, September 2, 16, and 23, 1954.

44. Neil McMillen, *Dark Journey: Black Mississippians in the Age of Jim Crow* (Urbana: University of Illinois Press, 1989), 246.

45. Sparks, *Religion in Mississippi*, 163–65. Paul Harvey, *Freedom's Coming: Religious Culture and the Shaping of the South from the Civil War through the Civil Rights Era* (Chapel Hill: University of North Carolina Press, 2005), argues that women's groups did the most effective interracial work in the South. See also John Patrick McDowell, *The Social Gospel in the South: The Woman's Home Mission Movement in the Methodist Episcopal Church, 1886–1939* (Baton Rouge: Louisiana State University Press, 1982). David Reimers, *White Protestants and the Negro* (New York: Oxford University Press, 1966), argues that white Protestants nationwide did little racially ameliorative work.

46. For a fuller description of the racial charter, see Peter Murray, *Methodism and the Crucible of Race*, 64. For rejection of it by women in the North Mississippi Conference, see *MMA*, June 15, 1955. The Women's Society of Christian Concern in the Mississippi Conference, however, affirmed the racial charter; *MMA*, February 15, 1956. See also Ray Branch, "Born of Conviction: Racial Conflict and Change in Mississippi Methodism, 1945–1983" (Ph.D. diss., Mississippi State University, 1984), 49.

47. This argument has been, in part, informed by Reinhold Niebuhr's writings on the difference between individual and collective morality. Niebuhr asserts that people are more immoral in groups than they are individually; see his *Moral Man and Immoral Society: A Study of Ethics and Politics*, repr. (Louisville: Westminster John Knox Press, 2002).

48. *Meridian Star*, May 22, 1954. *BR*, August 26, 1954.

49. *BR*, August (?) 1954. Chuck Westmoreland, "'To Preach Only the Bible': Billy Graham's 1952 Jackson Crusade and the Dilemma of Religion, Public Life, and Politics in the Modern South," an unpublished paper presented at the Southern Historical Association's Annual Meeting, Charlotte, NC, November 5, 2010, in possession of the author, who thanks Dr. Westmoreland for sharing his paper.

50. "Letters to the Editor," *CC*, November 25, 1964. Mary Rosalind Healy, "Why I Believe in Social Separation of the Races of Mankind."

51. Mary Rosalind Healy, "Why I Believe in Social Separation of the Races of Mankind."

52. *Madison County Herald*, February 27, 1964.

53. "An Address by John Satterfield," March 21, 1963, John Creighton Satterfield Subject File, MDAH.

54. "An Oral History with Dr. W. J. Cunningham," August 6, 1981, vol. 242, USMCO-HCH, p. 20, http://digilib.usm.edu/u?/coh,1492 (accessed December 7, 2010).

55. *Jackson Daily News*, February 20, 1949, quoted in Sparks, *Religion in Mississippi*, 196.

CHAPTER 2

1. See for example, *Baptist Record (BR)*, April 3, May 15, October 30, 1947. Mississippi Methodist Advocate (*MMA*), July 1, 1948.

2. *BR*, May 7, 1946.

3. *BR*, June 13, 1946.

4. *BR*, September 16, 1948.

5. For the debates that produced the pre–Civil War denominational schisms, see Donald G. Mathews, *Slavery and Methodism: A Chapter in American Morality, 1780–1845* (Princeton: Princeton University Press, 1965); John R. McKivigan and Mitchell Snay, eds., *Religion and the Antebellum Debate over Slavery* (Athens: University of Georgia Press, 1998); Mitchell Snay, *The Gospel of Disunion: Religion and Separatism in the Antebellum South* (Chapel Hill: University of North Carolina Press, 1997); C. C. Goen, *Broken Churches, Broken Nation* (Macon: Mercer University Press, 1997). On the role of southern religion after the war, see Charles R. Wilson, *Baptized in Blood: The Religion of the Lost Cause, 1865–1920*, 2nd ed. (Athens: University of Georgia Press, 2009), and Charles Reagan Wilson and Mark Silk, eds., *Religion and Public Life in the South: In the Evangelical Mode* (New York: AltaMira Press, 2005).

6. On Southern Baptist growth, see Nancy Tatom Ammerman, *Baptist Battles: Social Change and Religious Conflict in the Southern Baptist Convention* (New Brunswick: Rutgers University Press, 1990), 52, 58–59. *BR*, January 17, 1957.

7. *BR*, October 21, 1954, February 14, 1957.

8. For a treatment of the Methodist unification that deals mainly with the racial aspects, see Morris L. Davis, *The Methodist Unification: Christianity and the Politics of Race in the Jim Crow Era* (New York: New York University Press, 2008).

9. The Southern Presbyterian Church did grow significantly in this period, adding an average of one new church a week in the post-war period. Ernest Trice Thompson, *Presbyterians in the South, Vol. III 1890–1972* (Richmond: John Knox Press, 1973), 405.

10. Joel Alvis, *Religion and Race: Southern Presbyterians, 1946–1983* (Tuscaloosa: University of Alabama Press, 1994), explains the ways issues of theology and race

polarized the Presbyterian Church, U.S. See also *Southern Presbyterian Journal* (*SPJ*), August 4, 1954.

11. *BR*, May 15, 1947.

12. Biographical Sketch, Inventory to the Southern Baptist Convention, Sunday School Board Executive Office, James Lenox Sullivan Papers, Southern Baptist Historical Library and Archives (SBHLA), http://www.sbhla.org/downloads/795-354.pdf (accessed March 20, 2012). Biographical sketch, Henry M. Bullock Papers, Emory University Libraries, http://findingaids.library.emory.edu/documents/bullock186/ (accessed, March 20, 2012).

13. *BR*, October 10, 1957.

14. *SPJ*, February 7, March 13, April 10, 1952.

15. Alice G. Knotts, *Fellowship of Love: Methodist Women Changing American Racial Attitudes, 1920–1968* (Nashville: Kingswood Books, 1996), 104–107.

16. Biographical sketch, Francis Stuart Harmon Papers, Elmer L. Andersen Library, University of Minnesota, http://special.lib.umn.edu/findaid/html/ymca/yusa0020.phtml (accessed March 21, 2012).

17. *MMA*, May 4, 1960.

18. *New Orleans Christian Advocate* (*NOCA*), May 16, 1946.

19. *BR*, July 11, 1946.

20. *Commission,* Southern Baptist Commission, June 1945. Alan Scott Willis, *All According to God's Plan: Southern Baptist Missions and Race, 1945–1970* (Lexington: University Press of Kentucky, 2005), 68.

21. *World Outlook* (*WO*), May 1948, 5. *MMA,* December 2, 1959.

22. Thompson, *Presbyterians in the South*, 429. Also see charts in G. Thompson Brown and T. Donald Black, "Structures for a Changing Church," 62, and David Dawson, "Counting the Cost," 46, both in Caroline N. Becker and Scott W. Sunquiest, eds., *A History of Presbyterian Missions, 1944–2007* (Louisville, KY: Geneva Press, 2008).

23. Marjean Patterson, *Covered Foundations: A History of Mississippi Woman's Missionary Union* (no publication information available, 1978?), 147–51.

24. *WO,* September 1948. *MMA,* December 2, 1959.

25. *MMA,* December 2, 1959; *BR,* May 7, 1946. Letter from Congo missionaries, see *NOCA,* June 20, 1946

26. *BR,* January 23, 1947.

27. *MMA,* February 14, 1946.

28. *BR,* July 5, September 20, 1945

29. For the complexities of black Americans' struggles at war's end, see Stephen Tuck, *We Ain't What We Ought to Be: The Black Freedom Struggle from Emancipation to Obama* (Cambridge, MA: The Belknap Press of Harvard University Press, 2010), 206–38. On the labor activism of black workers in this era, see Robert Korstad, *Civil Rights Unionism: Tobacco Workers and the Struggle for Democracy in the Mid-Twentieth Century South* (Chapel Hill: University of North Carolina Press, 2003). On the *Morgan v. Commonwealth of Virginia* decision and the

incident that inspired it, see Raymond Arsenault, *Freedom Riders: 1961 and the Struggle for Racial Justice* (New York: Oxford University Press, 2006), 11–55.

30. For a good overview of Southern Baptist racial progressives, see Mark New-man, *Getting Right with God: Southern Baptists and Desegregation, 1945–1995* (Tuscaloosa: University of Alabama Press, 2001), 65–86. On Maston specifically, see Aaron Douglass Weaver, "The Impact of Social Progressive T. B. Maston upon Southern Baptist Life in the Twentieth Century," *The Big Daddy Weave: News and Commentary About All Things Baptists,* http://www.thebigdaddyweave. com/BDWFiles/Maston.pdf (accessed July 28, 2011). Ammerman, *Baptist Battles,* 65, n. 58.

31. Charles Marsh, *The Beloved Community: How Faith Shapes Social Justice, from the Civil Rights Movement to Today* (New York: Basic Books, 2005), 62–66.

32. *Annual,* Southern Baptist Convention (SBC), 1947, 340.

33. For example, Carlyle Marney, pastor of Emmanuel Baptist Church in Paducah, KY, adopted a racially progressive outlook. See Curtis Freeman, "'All the Sons of the Earth': Carlyle Marney and the Fight Against Prejudice," *Baptist History and Heritage* (Spring 2009), online at resulthttp://findarticles.com/p/articles/ mi_moNXG/is_2_44/ai_n48711386/?tag=content;col1.

34. On the work of these agencies, see Willis, *All According to God's Plan.*

35. Guy Bellamy, "Ten Commandments on Race Relations" (Atlanta: Home Missions Board, Southern Baptist Convention, n.d.).

36. *Commission,* June, 1945, 15.

37. *Annual,* SBC, 1947, 340–43.

38. *Annual,* SBC, 1947. *Quarterly Review,* October, November, December, 1947, 39–41.

39. Knotts, *Fellowship of Love,* 106. For more on Tilly, see Andrew M. Manis, "'City Mothers': Dorothy Tilly, Georgia Methodist Women, and Black Civil Rights," in Glenn Feldman, ed., *Politics and Religion in the White South* (Lexington: University Press of Kentucky, 2005), and Davis W. Houck and David E. Dixon, *Women and the Civil Rights Movement, 1954–1965* (Jackson: University of Mississippi Press, 2011), 98–111.

40. Knotts, *Fellowship of Love,* 139–42.

41. Knotts, *Fellowship of Love,* 136. See also Ellis Ray Branch, "Born of Conviction: Racial Conflict and Change in Mississippi Methodism, 1945–1983" (Ph.D. diss., Mississippi State University, 1984), 23.

42. *WO,* May 1948, 35; July 1948, 35.

43. *WO,* July 1949.

44. *NOCA,* August 22, 1946.

45. Henry Smith Leiper, *Blind Spots: Experiments in the Self-Cure of Race Prejudice* (New York: Friendship Press, 1944).

46. *WO,* May 1946, 3.

47. Central Jurisdiction membership from *WO,* June 1949. General Methodist membership from "United Methodist Membership as Compared to

the United States Population Census," General Commission on Archives and History, United Methodist Church, http://www.gcah.org/site/ pp.aspx?c=ghKJIoPHIoE&b=3828783 (accessed December 29, 2012).

48. Julius Del Pino, "Blacks in the United Methodist Church from Its Beginning to 1968," *Methodist History* 19, no. 1 (October 1980): 16–17.

49. Thompson, *Presbyterians in the South*, 442; Alvis, *Religion and Race*, 48.

50. Alvis, *Religion and Race*, 50–53.

51. Alvis, *Religion and Race*, 49.

52. Thompson, *Presbyterians in the South*, 421–22.

53. See, for example, *WO*, July 1945, July 1946, February 1948, February 1949; *Window*, March 1949, March 1950.

54. Thompson, *Presbyterians in the South*, 434–35.

55. *WO*, December 1949.

56. *WO*, June 1949.

57. *Commission*, July 1947.

58. *WO*, July 1949.

59. *WO*, September 1948.

60. *WO*, January 1946, 8–10.

61. Dr. W. J. Cunningham, "The Negro Question," October 27, 1943, sermon appended to "An Oral History with Dr. W. J. Cunningham," August 6, 1981, vol. 242, Center for Oral History and Cultural Heritage, The University of Southern Mississippi, University of Southern Mississippi Libraries, Hattiesburg, MS.

62. *NOCA*, August 21, 1946.

63. *MMA*, July 21, 1948.

64. *MMA*, June 9, 1949.

65. *NOCA*, February 21, 1946.

66. *BR*, May 2, 1946.

67. *BR*, May 2, 1946.

68. *BR*, September 26, 1946.

69. Jackson Daily News (*JDN*), June 4, 11, 25, 26, 1946.

70. *NOCA*, July 4, 1946; *BR*, July 4, 1946.

71. *NOCA*, July 18.

72. Victor M. Scanlan to Dr. Bob Shuler, May 23, 1951, in L. E. Faulkner Papers (LEFP), Box 51, Folder 9, McCain Library and Archives, University of Southern Mississippi, Hattiesburg, MS.

73. L. E. Faulkner bears no relation to the famous Mississippi author with the same last name. For examples of Faulkner's thought, see his pamphlet, "Reasons Why the Presbyterian Church in the United States Should Withdraw from the National Council of Churches of Christ in the U.S.A.," 1951, in LEFP, Box 37, Folder 16. See also Faulkner's articles in the *Hattiesburg American*, February 10, 17, 24, March 3, 10, 1951.

74. See Verne P. Kaub to Mr. L. E. Faulkner, April 17, 1951, LEFP, Box 37, Folder 16. *The Methodist Challenge*, June 1951.

CHAPTER 3

1. *Annual*, Southern Baptist Convention (SBC), 1954, 56; "Christian Life Commission Report to the Southern Baptist Convention Meeting in St. Louis 1954," Christian Life Commission Papers (CLCP), Box 1, Folder 11, Southern Baptist Historical Library and Archives (SBHLA), Nashville, TN. Also reported in *Jackson Clarion-Ledger* (*CL*), June 7, 1954, in Doug Hudgins Papers (DHP), First Baptist Church, Jackson, MS.

2. *Baptist Record* (*BR*), June 10, 1954.

3. See for example, John Lee Eighmy, *Churches in Cultural Captivity: A History of the Social Attitudes of Southern Baptists* (Knoxville: University of Tennessee Press, 1972), and Kenneth K. Bailey, *Southern White Protestantism in the Twentieth Century* (New York: Harper and Row, 1964). For a work that overstates white southern religious support for ending the racial hierarchy, see David L. Chappell, *A Stone of Hope: Prophetic Religion and the Death of Jim Crow* (Chapel Hill: University of North Carolina Press, 2004).

4. Black resistance to segregation has a history as old as the system itself, and the literature on it is immense. For two good recent overviews, see Emilye Crosby, *Civil Rights History from the Ground Up: Local Struggles, a National Movement* (Athens: University of Georgia Press, 2011), and Stephen Tuck, *We Ain't What We Ought to Be: The Black Freedom Struggle from Emancipation to Obama* (New York: Oxford University Press, 2010). For black activism in Mississippi, see Nan Elizabeth Woodruff, *American Congo: The African American Freedom Struggle in the Delta* (Chapel Hill: University of North Carolina Press, 2012); J. Todd Moye, *Let the People Decide: Black Freedom and White Resistance Movements in Sunflower County, Mississippi, 1945–1986* (Chapel Hill: University of North Carolina Press, 2004); Emilye Crosbye, *A Little Taste of Freedom: The Black Freedom Movement in Claiborne County, Mississippi* (Chapel Hill: University of North Carolina Press, 2005); John Dittmer, *Local People: The Struggle for Civil Rights in Mississippi* (Urbana and Chicago: University of Illinois Press, 1994); Charles M. Payne, *I've Got the Light of Freedom: The Organizing Tradition and the Mississippi Freedom Struggle* (Berkeley: University of California Press, 1995); Kenneth T. Andrews, *Freedom Is a Constant Struggle: The Mississippi Civil Rights Movement and Its Legacy* (Chicago: University of Chicago Press, 2004); Kay Mills, *This Little Light of Mine: The Life of Fannie Lou Hammer* (Lexington: University of Kentucky Press, 2007); and Neil R. McMillen, *Dark Journey: Black Mississippians in the Age of Jim Crow* (Urbana: University of Illinois Press, 1989).

5. Numan Bartley coined the term "massive resistance" in his 1969 classic, now published as a thirtieth anniversary edition, *The Rise of Massive Resistance: Race and Politics in the South During the 1950s* (Baton Rouge: Louisiana State University Press, 1999). Other early work on resistance to integration includes James Silver, *Mississippi: The Closed Society* (New York: Harcourt Brace and World, 1964), and Neil McMillen, *The Citizens' Councils: Organized Resistance to the Second Reconstruction, 1954–1964* (Champaign: University of Illinois Press, 1974). In recent

years, the literature on white resistance to racial equality has mushroomed. The best and most important work on massive resistance in Mississippi includes Joseph Crespino, *In Search of Another Country: Mississippi and the Conservative Counterrevolution* (Princeton: Princeton University Press, 2007); Charles W. Eagles, *The Price of Defiance: James Meredith and the Integration of Ole Miss* (Chapel Hill: The University of North Carolina Press, 2009); Yashuhiro Katagiri, *The Mississippi State Sovereignty Commission: Civil Rights and States Rights* (Jackson: University Press of Mississippi, 2007); Jenny Irons, *Reconstituting Whiteness: The Mississippi State Sovereignty Commission* (Nashville: Vanderbilt University Press, 2010); and Charles W. Eagles, "The Closing of Mississippi: Will Campbell, the $64,000 Question, and Religious Emphasis Week at the University of Mississippi," *Journal of Southern History* 67 (May 2001): 331–72. For two personal accounts from an architect of resistance, see Erle Johnston, *I Rolled with Ross: A Political Portrait* (Manchester: Moran Press, 1980), and *Mississippi's Defiant Years, 1953–1973: An Interpretive Documentary with Personal Experiences* (Lake Harbor Publishers, 1990). For general works on massive resistance, see Matthew D. Lassiter, *The Silent Majority: Suburban Politics in the Sunbelt South* (Princeton: Princeton University Press, 2007); Kevin Kruse, *White Flight: Atlanta and the Making of Modern Conservatism* (Princeton: Princeton University Press, 2007); George Lewis, *Massive Resistance: The White Response to the Civil Rights Movement* (Bloomsbury, USA: 2006); and Clive Webb, ed., *Massive Resistance: Southern Opposition to the Second Reconstruction* (New York: Oxford University Press, 2005). For an interpretation that emphasizes resistance before the *Brown* decision, see Jason Morgan Ward, *Defending White Democracy: The Making of a Segregationist Movement and the Remaking of Racial Politics, 1936–1965* (Chapel Hill: University of North Carolina Press, 2011).

6. *CL*, June 7, 1954, clipping in DHP.

7. *BR*, June 10, 1954.

8. *BR*, June 17, 1954. Copy of resolution also in CLCP, Box 1, Folder 8.

9. See letters in *BR*, June 24, July 1, July 8, September 2, 1954.

10. *BR*, June 24, 1954.

11. *BR*, October 21, 1954.

12. *BR*, July 8, 1954.

13. See for example *BR*, December 16, 1954. See also resolutions withholding funds in Executive Committee Records (ECR), Box 73, Folder 23, SBHLA.

14. *Hattiesburg American*, June 18, 1954.

15. *Meridian Star* (*MS*), June 14, 1954.

16. *MS*, June 9, 1954.

17. *MS*, June 7, 1954.

18. A good description of Baptist polity in this regard is found in Bill J. Leonard, *God's Last and Only Hope: The Fragmentation of the Southern Baptist Convention* (Grand Rapids: William B. Erdmans Publishing Co., 1990), 25–42.

19. See the description of interposition in Bartley, *The Rise of Massive Resistance*, 134.

20. *Mississippi Methodist Advocate* (*MMA*), June 9, July 1, July 28, August 11, 1954.

21. Peter C. Murray, *Methodists and the Crucible of Race, 1930–1975* (Columbia: University of Missouri Press, 2004), 70–72.

22. *MMA*, December 1, 1954.

23. *MMA*, April 27, 1955.

24. Ray Branch, "Born of Conviction: Racial Conflict and Change in Mississippi Methodism, 1945–1983," (Ph.D. diss., Mississippi State University, 1984), 43.

25. *MMA*, September 1, 1954.

26. *MMA*, June 15, 1955; February 15, 1956.

27. *MMA*, May 18, 1955.

28. *MMA*, June 22, 1955.

29. *MMA* July 21, 28, September 15, 1954; July 27, August 10, 1955.

30. *MMA*, December 22, 1954.

31. *MMA*, December 22, 1954; April 6, 1955. See also Branch, "Born of Conviction," 44–48.

32. "A Statement to Southern Christians," Minutes of the Ninety-fourth General Assembly of the Presbyterian Church in the United States, 194. These two statements are excerpted and explained in Dwyn Mecklin Mounger, "Racial Attitudes in the Presbyterian Church, U.S., 1944–1954" (Bachelor of Divinity Thesis, Princeton Theological Seminary, 1965), 152–57.

33. Mounger, "Racial Attitudes," 158–59.

34. Vote tally on "Statement to Southern Christians" given in Joel Alvis, *Religion and Race: Southern Presbyterians, 1963–1983* (Tuscaloosa: University of Alabama Press, 1994), 57. *Southern Presbyterian Journal* (*SPJ*), July 14, 1954.

35. *MS*, June 1954.

36. Handwritten note on Malcolm P. Calhoun to Dr. Marc C. Weering, September 28, 1954, in Malcolm P. Calhoun Papers (MPCP), Box 1, Folder unidentified (collection unprocessed), Presbyterian Historical Society (PHS), Philadelphia, PA.

37. Arthur M. Schneider to Rev. Malcolm P. Calhoun, September 30, 1954, in MPCP, Box 1, Folder unidentified.

38. *Minutes* of the Presbytery of Meridian, October 1954, 13.

39. *Minutes* of the General Assembly of the Presbyterian Church in the United States (GAPCUS), 1955, 36.

40. *Minutes*, GAPCUS, 1955, 39.

41. *Minutes* of the Presbyterian Church, U.S., Synod of Mississippi (PCUSSM), 1954, 446–47.

42. *Minutes*, PCUSSM, 1954, 448–49

43. *Minutes*, PCUSSM, 1954, 448–49.

44. Rev. G. T. Gillespie, "A Christian view on Segregation. An address made before the Synod of Mississippi of the Presbyterian Church, US, November 4, 1954," n.d., Citizens' Councils, Greenwood, MS.

45. *Southern Presbyterian Journal*, January, 1955; *Presbyterian Outlook*, March 14, 1955.

46. *MS,* June 14, 1954.
47. *MS,* June 7, 1954.
48. *MS,* June 10, 1954.
49. *BR,* July 22, 1954.
50. Resolution on Racial Relations, adopted by Copiah County Association, October 21, 1955, in CLCP, Box 3, Folder 9. Also in *Minutes* of Copiah Baptist Association, 1955, 24.
51. Stanley Smith to Dr. A. C. Miller, November 3, 1955, and November 14, 1955, in CLCP, Box 3, Folder 9.
52. The story of Cox and Minter's ouster from Providence Farm has been told in Will Campbell, *Providence* (Waco: Baylor University Press, 2002). I have drawn much of this brief sketch from Will Campbell to Al Kershaw, October 20, 1955, in Rev. Alvin L. Kershaw Papers, Series I, Folder 2, McCain Library and Archives, University of Southern Mississippi, Hattiesburg, MS.
53. Chester L. Quarles to Dr. Porter Routh, Dr. Merrill D. Moore, and Dr. Albert McClellan, November 10, 1955, in ECR, Box 73, Folder 23.

CHAPTER 4

1. Will Campbell to Editor, *Look* Magazine, June 4, 1957, in Will Campbell Papers (WCP), Box 54, Folder 22, McCain Library and Archives, University of Southern Mississippi (MLAUSM), Hattiesburg, MS.
2. Lillian Smith to Will Campbell, December 7, 1957, in WCP, Box 54, Folder 22.
3. Alexander F. Miller to Mr. Will D. Campbell, June 2 1958, in WCP, Box 54, Folder 22.
4. Will Campbell to Dr. Everett Tilson, August 22, 1957, in WCP, Box 54, Folder 22.
5. Paul Harvey has advanced this idea in several different venues: "God and Negroes and Jesus and Sin and Salvation: Racism, Racial Interchange, and Interracialism in Southern Religious History," in Beth Barton Schweiger and Donald G. Mathews, eds., *Religion in the American South: Protestants and Others in History and Culture* (Chapel Hill: University of North Carolina Press, 2004), 285–91; "Religion, Race, and the Right in the South, 1945–1990," in Glenn Feldman, ed., *Politics and Religion in the White South* (Lexington: University Press of Kentucky, 2005), 101–23; and *Freedom's Coming: Religious Culture and the Shaping of the South from the Civil War through the Civil Rights Era* (Chapel Hill: University of North Carolina Press, 2005). More recently, J. Russell Hawkins has offered a fulsome description of segregationist folk theology in "Religion, Race, and Resistance: White Evangelicals and the Dilemma of Integration in South Carolina, 1950–1975" (Ph.D. diss., Rice University, 2010). Joseph Crespino, *In Search of Another Country: Mississippi and the Conservative Counterrevolution* (Princeton: Princeton University Press, 2007), 63–70, offers a good description of segregationists' religious arguments, claiming that they advanced two fundamentally different and contradictory cases. On the one hand, they argued

that God had ordained the racial hierarchy, while on the other they depicted segregation and integration as political issues about which the church had no business speaking.

6. Harvey, *Freedom's Coming*, 229.

7. Contrary to the case made here, David Chappell, *A Stone of Hope: Prophetic Religion and the Death of Jim Crow* (Chapel Hill: University of North Carolina Press, 2005), argues that this mixing of religious and secular arguments indicated segregationists' understanding that biblical sanction for the institution was weak.

8. Rev. G. T. Gillespie, "A Christian View on Segregation. An address made before the Synod of Mississippi of the Presbyterian Church, US, November 4, 1954," n.d., Citizens' Councils, Greenwood, MS.

9. "Itta Bena Methodist Minister Explains Segregation in Sermon," *Morning Star*, Greenwood, MS, February 10, 1953, in Division of Christian Relations of the PCUS (DCRPCUS), Box 1, Folder unidentified (collection unprocessed), Presbyterian Historical Society (PHS), Philadelphia, PA.

10. *Jackson Daily News (JDN)*, March 18, 1958.

11. William W. Miller, "The Bible and Segregation: A Sermon" (no publication information available, 1956?).

12. D. B. Red, "A Corrupt Tree Bringeth Forth Evil Fruit," in William D. McCain Pamphlet Collection (WDMPC), Box 4, Folder 9, MLAUSM; D. B. Red, "Race Mixing A Religious Fraud," in WDMPC, Box 4, Folder 10.

13. Gillespie, "A Christian View on Segregation."

14. Erle Johnston, *Mississippi's Defiant Years: An Interpretive Documentary with Personal Experiences* (Lake Harbor Publishers, 1990), 25.

15. Erle Johnston, *I Rolled with Ross: A Political Portrait* (Manchester: Moran Press, 1980), 50.

16. Tommy Alewine, *Brandon News*, November 3, 1955, quoted in unidentified newspaper, Rev. Alvin L. Kershaw Papers (RALKP), Series II, Folder 12, MLAUSM.

17. Unidentified newspaper, March 4, 1959, clipping in Erle E. Johnston, Jr. Papers (EEJJP), Box 8, Folder 6, MLAUSM.

18. Diary entry, February 28, 1956, George Thomas Preer Papers (GTPP), Box 1, Folder 3, MLAUSM.

19. Elizabeth Sutherland, ed., *Letters from Mississippi* (New York: McGraw-Hill, 1965), 134.

20. Michael Jackson, *Paths toward a Clearing: Radical Empiricism and Ethnographic Inquiry* (Bloomington: Indiana University Press, 1989), 65, quoted in Robert Orsi, "Everyday Miracles: The Study of Lived Religion," in David D. Hall, ed., *Lived Religion in America: Toward a History of Practice* (Princeton: Princeton University Press, 1997), 8–9.

21. The best single treatment of the Kershaw incident is Charles Eagles, "The Closing of Mississippi Society: Will Campbell, the $64,000 Question, and Religious

Emphasis Week at the University of Mississippi," *Journal of Southern History* 67 (May 2001): 331–72.

22. *Time*, n.d., clipping in RALKP, Series II, Folder 11.

23. J. L. Rhymes to The Rev. Alvin L. Kershaw, September 9, 1955, in RALKP, Series I, Folder 4.

24. *Brandon News*, November 3, 1955, quoted in unidentified newspaper, in RALKP, Series II, Folder 12.

25. Margaret Lyons to Rev. Kershaw, n.d. (c. November 20, 1955), in RALKP, Series I, Folder 3.

26. G. Everard Godman, M.D., to Rev. Alvin Kershaw, November 13, 1955, in RALKP Series I, Folder 3.

27. Unsigned to Rev. Alvin Kershaw, November 10, 1955, in RALKP, Series I, Folder 2.

28. R. K. Daniel to Rev. Alvin Kershaw, November 4, 1955, in RALKP, Series I, Folder 2.

29. *JDN*, December 20, 1955, in RALKP, Series II, Folder 10.

30. Will Campbell to Al and Doris Kershaw, March 9, 1956, in RALKP, Series I, Folder 5.

31. *Memphis Commercial Appeal*, February 14, 1956, clipping in RALKP, Series II, Folder 11.

32. *Memphis Commercial Appeal*, February 14, 1956, clipping in RALKP, Series II, Folder 11.

33. Bulletin of St. Peter's Episcopal Church, November 13, 1955, Oxford, MS, in RALKP, Series II, Folder 17.

34. Emile Joffrion to The Reverend Alvin Kershaw, November 5, 1955, in RALKP, Series I, Folder 2; see also *Christian Century* (*CC*), May 9, 1956.

35. *New York Times*, February 21, 1956, clipping in RALKP, Series II, Folder 11.

36. Quotations from Charles Eagles, *The Price of Defiance: James Meredith and the Integration of Ole Miss* (Chapel Hill: University of North Carolina Press, 2009), 165–67, where this incident is described in detail.

37. This incident can be followed in the *JDN*, the *Clarion-Ledger* (*CL*), and the *State Times* (*ST*) during most of the month of March 1958.

38. *CL*, March 10, 1958.

39. *CL*, March 24, 1958.

40. *ST*, March 20, 1958.

41. *JDN*, March 14, 1958.

42. Indeed, other moderates—arguing both from a religious perspective and a non-religious one—expressed themselves during this affair. See especially letters in the *ST*, March 9, 13, 18, 1958. See also *MMA*, March 19, 26, 1958, and the editorial by Oliver Emmerich in *ST*, March 23, 1958.

43. *ST*, March 13, 1958, clipping in Ed King Collection (MUM00251), Box 2, Folder 3, Archives and Special Collections, J. D. Williams Library, University of Mississippi (JDWLUM), Oxford, MS.

44. *ST*, c. March 17, 1958.

45. *Hattiesburg American* (*HA*), February 15, 1955.

46. *HA*, February 23, 1955.

47. *JDN*, March 14, 1958.

48. Neil McMillen, *The Citizens' Council: Organized Resistance to the Second Reconstruction 1954–1964* (Champaign: University of Illinois Press, 1974), 37; and Numan Bartley, *The Rise of Massive Resistance: Race and Politics in the South During the 1950s*, 2nd ed. (Baton Rouge: Louisiana State University Press, 1999), 86.

49. *New Orleans States and Item*, April 15, 1959, clipping in WCP, Box 54, Folder 5.

50. *The Citizens' Council*, November, 1957.

51. *The Citizens' Council*, December, 1957.

52. *CC*, December 26, 1956.

53. Several ministers are on the "List of Recommended Speakers" in the Citizens' Council Collection, Box 1, Folder 10, JDWLUM.

54. On Citizens' Council identification of these Presbyterians, see Will Campbell to Al and Doris Kershaw, March 9, 1956, in RALKP, Series I, Box 34, Folder 5.

55. On Citizens' Council identification of these Baptists, see chapter 5.

56. On Citizens' Council membership of B. K. Hardin, see Carter Dalton Lyon, "Lifting the Color Bar from the House of God: The 1963–64 Church Visit Campaign to Challenge Segregation," (Ph.D. diss., University of Mississippi, 2010), 259, n. 533. Delmar Dennis, "The Unconquerable Land," pamphlet, 1964, in Citizens' Council Collection, Box 1, Folder 29, MLAUSM.

57. Will Campbell to Denominational Leaders, April 2, 1957, in WCP, Box 34, Folder 2.

58. David M. Nelson, *Conflicting Views on Segregation* (Greenwood, MS: Educational Fund of the Citizens' Council, 1954).

59. *The Citizens' Council*, April–August, 1957.

60. For samples of such articles, see *The Citizen*, April, May, December 1961, April, June, October, 1962, January, November, 1963.

61. *The Citizens' Council*, May 1958.

62. Will Campbell to Miss Sally Smith, January 11, 1957, in WCP, Box 7, Folder 12; Will Campbell to Reverend Ray Brewster, May 15, 1957, in WCP, Box 54, Folder 22.

63. Will Campbell to Reverend Ray Gibbons, May 12, 1964, in WCP, Box 54, Folder 22

64. Cornelius C. Tarplee to Rev Will D. Campbell, November 30, 1957, in WCP, Box 54, Folder 22.

65. Bartley, *The Rise of Massive Resistance*, 134, and John Dittmer, *Local People: The Struggle for Civil Rights in Mississippi* (Urbana and Chicago: University of Illinois Press, 1994), 37–38, 59, give good descriptions of these measures and Mississippi's strategies—legal and otherwise—for circumventing the High Court's decision.

66. *CC*, May 9, 1956.

67. *CC*, May 9, 1956.

68. *Delta-Democrat Times* (*DDT*), March 27, 28, 1956.

69. *DDT*, March 27, 28, 1956.
70. *MMA*, February 17, 1960.
71. *MMA*, February 10, 1960.
72. *MMA*, February 10, 1960.
73. *MMA,* February 3, 1960. Other expressions of opposition to the bill, some from entire congregations, are found in *JDN*, January 27, 28, February 3, 4, 12, 13, 15, 19, 23, 1960.
74. *JDN*, February 2, 1960.
75. *New Orleans Times Picayune,* March 2, 1960. For other expressions of support for the bill, including endorsement by individual congregations, see *JDN*, February 1, 3, 11, 23, 27, 1960.
76. *JDN*, March 1, 1960.
77. *JDN*, March 1, 1960.
78. *JDN*, April 1, 1960.

CHAPTER 5

1. *Baptist Record* (*BR*), November 18, 1954.
2. Mark Newman, "The Mississippi Baptists Convention and Desegregation, 1945–1980" *Journal of Mississippi History* 59, no. 1 (Spring 1997): 1–31.
3. John W. Cook to Rev. A. L. Goodrich, March 9, 1956, in Wilmer Clermont Fields Papers (WCFP), Box 71, Folder 5, Southern Baptist Historical Library and Archive (SBHLA), Nashville, TN.
4. Cecil Randall to Dr. W. C. Fields, October 16, 1956, in WCFP, Box 13, Folder 5.
5. Paul H. Leber to Dr. W. C. Fields, October 17, 1956, in WCFP, Box 13, Folder 5.
6. Joe T. Odle to Dr. Porter Routh, August 30, 1957, in Executive Committee Records (ECR), Box 21, Folder 20, SBHLA.
7. Recorded Report of a Portion of Citizens' Council Forum, T.V. Station WLBT, Jackson, Mississippi, Sunday, November 26, 1957, Chester Quarles Papers, Civil Rights Folder (#15), Mississippi Baptist Historical Commission (MBHC), Clinton, MS.
8. Resolution in ECR, Box 57, Folder 21; Doug Hudgins to Porter Routh, April 23, 1959, in ECR, Box 57, Folder 21.
9. D. B. Red to Editor of the *Baptist Record*, n.d. (c. 1958), in WCFP, Box 22, Folder 24. For a description of Red's segregationist pamphlets, see chapter 4.
10. Chas. C. Jones to Dr. A. L. Goodrich, March 5, 1956, in WCFP, Box 71, Folder 5.
11. Rev. Charles C. Jones to Dear Brother in Christ, "An Open Letter to Southern Baptists," n.d., in WCFP, Box 71, Folder 5.
12. Pamphlets and Promotional Materials, in Christian Life Commission Papers (CLCP), Box 5, Folder 6, SBHLA.
13. W. Douglas Hudgins to Dr. A. C. Miller, March 20, 1957, in CLCP, Box 1, Folder 3.
14. Resolution in ECR, Box 82, Folder 1.

15. William Watson to A. C. Miller, March 11, 1957, in CLCP, Box 1, Folder 3.

16. A. C. Miller, "The Christian Life Commission Gives Statement on Policies and Procedures," typed manuscript in CLCP, Box 1, Folder 3.

17. Corbett L. Patridge to Honorable Brooks Hays, June 11, 1957, in Brooks Hays Papers (BHP), Box 2, Folder 6, SBHLA.

18. W. Otis Seal to Dr. A. C. Miller, June 4, 1957, in CLCP, Box 11, Folder 9. Seal is listed on a "List of Recommended Speakers" for the Citizens' Council, Citizens' Council Collection, Box 1, Folder 10, Archives and Special Collections, J. D. Williams Library, University of Mississippi, Oxford, MS. See also "A Resolution" from Silver City Baptist Church, in ECR, Box 82, Folder 1, and A. J. McIlwain, M.D., to Dr. John W. Landrum, June 11, 1957, in BHP, Box 2, Folder 6.

19. G. W. Simmons to Dr. Porter Routh, April 3, 1958, in ECR, Box 88, Folder 2.

20. Vernon H. Broom to Dr. Leo Eddleman, September 13, 1963, in Southern Baptist Convention, Sunday School Board Executive Office, James Lenox Sullivan Papers (JLSP), Box 35, Folder 33, SBHLA.

21. "Resolution Concerning Church Literature adopted May 30, 1965, by the First Baptist Church, Moss, Mississippi," in JLSP, Box 35, Folder 33.

22. Broadsheet "Withdrawal of the book *The Long Bridge*," in WCFP, Box 71, Folder 5; see also Courts Redford to State Secretaries, WMU Secretaries and WMU Leaders, Editors of Baptist Papers, December 13, 1957, in WCFP, Box 71, Folder 5.

23. Joe Taylor to Mr. Philip B. Harris, September 9, 1963, and John Chamberlain to Mr. Philip B. Harris, August 22, 1963, in JLSP, Box 35, Folder 33.

24. Note attached to Adult Sunday School Quarterly, Southern Baptists Sunday School Series, July, August, September, 1963 in JLSP, Box 35, Folder 33.

25. *BR*, November 12, 1964.

26. For a good treatment of the Little Rock Crisis with an emphasis on the role of ministers, see Ernest Q. Campbell and Thomas F. Pettigrew, *Christians in Racial Crisis: A Study of Little Rock's Ministry* (Washington, DC: Public Affairs Press, 1959). There is a large literature on the Little Rock Crisis, including several memoirs and first-person accounts. For scholarly works, see John A Kirk, *Beyond Little Rock: The Origins and Legacies of the Central High Crisis* (Fayetteville: University of Arkansas Press, 2007), and Elizabeth Jacoway, *Turn Away Thy Son: Little Rock, the Crisis That Shocked the Nation* (New York: Free Press, 2007). Among memoirs and personal accounts, see Daisy Bates, *The Long Shadow of Little Rock: A Memoir* (New York: David McKay, 1962), and Melba Pattillo Beals, *Warriors Don't Cry: A Searing Memoir of the Battle to Integrate Little Rock's Central High* (New York: Washington Square Press, 1995). For examples of sympathy with white Arkansans in just one Mississippi newspaper, see coverage in the *Meridian Star*, September–October, 1957, especially editorials on September 8, 12, 22, 25, 29, October 10, 13, 20, 27, 30.

27. *BR*, November 7, 1957.

28. *Meridian Star*, October 10, 1957.

29. Transcript of Oral History Interview with Brooks Hays, August 15, 1977, 576, Brooks Hays Collection, Supplementary Papers (BHCSP), series 5, subseries 1, Box 1, Folder 3. Special Collections, University of Arkansas Libraries, Fayetteville, AR.

30. Hays claimed many personal friends among Mississippi's Baptist leaders, relationships that developed during the years he served as an attorney for the Department of Agriculture in a regional office that included the Magnolia State. Complicating things even further, in the run for SBC president, Hays had defeated the prominent Mississippi pastor Reverend Douglas Hudgins, whose downtown Jackson church always hosted the State Convention. Though Hudgins had won the post of first vice president, cancellation of Hay's invitation might have appeared the product of an unchristian resentment against Hays. Oral History Interview with Brooks Hays, 577.

31. Oral History Interview with Brooks Hays, 579–80.

32. Brother E. D. Estes to Hon. Brooks Hays, February 13, 1958, in BHP, Box 2, Folder 7.

33. Name obscured to Rep. Brooks Hays, June 13, 1958, in BHP, Box 2, Folder 8.

34. *The Citizens' Council*, December 1958. See also *Hattiesburg American*, November 12, 1957, and Roy V. Sims to Mr. L.U. Amason, November 14, 1958, in BHP, Box 2, Folder 8.

35. *Arkansas Gazette*, May 21, 1959; this clipping and others from unidentified newspapers in BHCSP, series 5, subseries 1, Box 1, Folder 1.

36. Material in WCFP, Box 22, Folder 24.

37. Chester L. Quarles to Dr. Albert McClellan, July 29, 1964, in ECR, Box 73, Folder 24.

38. See letters and other material in JLSP, Box 35, Folder 33.

39. Rev. Clyde Gordon, "A View of the Race Issue," n.d. (c. 1954–56), in WCFP, Box 71, Folder 0.

40. Will D. Campbell to The Rev. J. C. Herrin, March 5, 1962, in WCFP, Box 4, Folder 6.

41. Bradley Pope to Dr. Foy Valentine, December 5, 1962, in possession of author; Bradley Pope, "I Am an American," sermon preached at First Baptist Church, Shelby, Mississippi, June 30, 1963, in possession of author. Bradley Pope, interview with author, n.d. *BR*, November 5, 1964.

42. In some respects the portrait painted here corroborates the interpretation of Charles Marsh, *God's Long Summer: Stories of Faith and Civil Rights* (Princeton: Princeton University Press, 1997), ch. 3. However, Marsh presents Hudgins as apolitical, while I argue that he embraced and preached a specific political philosophy.

43. *20th Anniversary, William Douglas Hudgins, 1946–1966* in Douglas Hudgins Papers (DHP), First Baptist Church, Jackson, MS. Maurice Thompson, "To Bless Many Thousands," *The Beam*, September 26, 1966, in DHP. See also *BR*, July 17, 1962.

44. Clayton Sullivan, interview, quoted in Marsh, *God's Long Summer*, 96–97. "Meet Mister Baptist," unidentified Jackson newspaper, November 21, 1960, in DHP. *Jackson Daily News (JDN)*, March 7, 1958, April 2, 1961. *BR*, July 18, 1957.

45. W. Douglas Hudgins to Dr. Porter Routh, March 26, 1965, in ECR Box 57, Folder 22; *BR*, May 29, 1958.

46. W. Douglas Hudgins to Dr. A. C. Miller, March 20, 1957, in CLCP, Box 1, Folder 3.

47. A.C. Miller to Brooks Hays, September 29, 1955, in CLCP, Box 2, Folder 4.

48. Photo of ceremony in DHP.

49. John Dittmer, *Local People: The Struggle for Civil Rights in Mississippi* (Champaign: University of Illinois Press, 1994), 65. *Time* magazine concluded in 1967 that the *Daily News* published "unabashed prejudice," and the *Columbia Journalism Review* assessed the Jackson newspapers as "quite possibly the worst metropolitan newspapers in the United States," a charge that arose directly from their flagrantly prejudicial coverage of African Americans and civil rights activity. David R. Davies and Judy Smith, "Jimmy Ward and the Jackson *Daily News*," in David R. Davies, ed., *The Press and Race: Mississippi Journalists Confront the Movement* (Jackson: University Press of Mississippi, 2001), 85.

50. *JDN*, April 2, 1961, in DHP.

51. *JDN*, November 22, 1957.

52. Dr. W. Douglas Hudgins, "A Decade of Destiny: The 1960s," a sermon preached at the First Baptist Church, Jackson, MS, January 24, 1960, in DHP.

53. Hudgins, "One Nation Under God," delivered to the annual convention of the Mississippi Congress of Parents and Teachers, Jackson, MS, April 11, 1962, in DHP.

54. For an example of Hudgins' disdain for labor unions, see his Labor Day sermon, *JDN*, September 4, 1957.

55. Hudgins, "A Decade of Destiny."

56. Hudgins, "One Nation Under God."

57. Hudgins, "One Nation Under God."

58. Unidentified newspaper, n.d., and John Bell Williams to Dr. W. Douglass Hudgins, Jr., June 29, 1962, in DHP.

59. Hudgins, "A Decade of Destiny."

60. *Together*, June 1958, clipping in Department of Negro Work File (DNWF), MBHC.

61. This information is found in several places: Dr. W. P. Davis, *The Long Step: Mississippi Baptist Seminary, the great adventure in inter-racial religious education and missions* (typed manuscript); "Mississippi Baptist Seminary" (pamphlet); *Together*, June 1958; *BR*, September 13, 1973; "Sophia Sutton Mission Assembly" (pamphlet); *JDN*, February 5, 1956 (clipping); all in DNWF. See also Richard Aubrey McLemore, *A History of Mississippi Baptists* (Jackson: Mississippi Baptist Convention Board, 1971), and W. T. Moore, *His Heart Is Black* (Atlanta: Home Mission Board, SBC, 1978), 42–51.

62. Chester Quarles to Dr. W. Maxfield Garrott, February 9, 1965, in ECR, Box 73, Folder 24.

63. *Annual*, Mississippi Baptist Convention (MBC), 1962, 94– 95.

64. *Annual*, MBC, 1963, 47; 1958, 100

65. *Minutes* of the Attala County Baptist Association, 1958, 18.

66. Davis, *The Long Step*, 43.

67. Grace Elizabeth Hale, *Making Whiteness: The Culture of Segregation in the South, 1890–1940* (New York: Pantheon Books, 1998), 34.

68. Davis, *The Long Step*, 6, 43. An extensive literature documents the ways that whites perpetrated fears about the hypersexuality of blacks; in particular, the "myth of the black beast rapist" suggested that white women stood in special danger from the aggressive sexual onslaughts of black men. For a good point of entry into the literature on the myth of the "black beast rapist," see Jacquelyn Dowd Hall, *Revolt Against Chivalry: Jesse Daniel Ames and the Women's Campaign Against Lynching* (New York: Columbia University Press, 1979); George M. Fredrickson, *The Black Image in the White Mind: The Debate on Afro-American Character and Destiny, 1817–1914* (New York: Harper and Row, 1971), especially ch. 9; Joel A. Williamson, *The Crucible of Race: Black-White Relations in the American South Since Emancipation* (New York: Oxford University Press, 1984); Toni Morrison, ed., *Race-ing Justice, En-gendering Power: Essays on Anita Hill, Clarence Thomas and the Construction of Social Reality* (New York: Pantheon Books, 1992); and Stephen J. Whitfield, *A Death in the Delta: The Story of Emmett Till* (New York: The Free Press, 1988).

69. Davis, *The Long Step*, 116–18. For a detailed account of this demonstration and its significance in Mississippi's Civil Rights Movement, see Dittmer, *Local People*, 87–89.

70. Davis, *The Long Step*, 116–18.

71. Anne Washburn McWilliams, "Committee of Concern Gives Beauty for Ashes," draft copy in DNWF.

72. Moore, *His Heart Is Black*, 48.

73. Davis, *The Long Step*, 40, 55. The same incident is related in Moore, *His Heart Is Black*, 42–44. Interview with Dr. William Penn Davis, Mississippi Baptist Historical Commission Oral History Program, in DNWF.

74. Davis, *The Long Step*, 117; *Clarion Ledger*, November 17, 1972, clipping in DNWF.

75. See Davis, *The Long Step*, 87, 71, 110, and *The Baptist Student*, June 1968, in DNWF.

76. Typescript in DNWF.

CHAPTER 6

1. W. E. Lampton to James Silver, January 30, 1963, in James W. Silver Collection (JWSC), Box 23, Folder 9, Special Collections and Archives, J. D. Williams Library, The University of Mississippi (JDWLUM), Oxford, MS. See also *Jackson*

Daily News (*JDN*), January 8, 1963.

The "Born of Conviction" affair is mentioned briefly in many published works, but the most focused and best-researched account is Joe Reiff, "Conflicting Convictions in White Mississippi Methodism: The 1963 'Born of Conviction' Controversy," *Methodist History* 49, no. 3 (April 2011): 162–75. See also Carter Dalton Lyon, "Lifting the Color Bar from the House of God: The 1963–1964 Church Visit Campaign to Challenge Segregated Sanctuaries in Jackson, Mississippi" (Ph.D. diss., University of Mississippi, 2010).

2. *Mississippi Methodist Advocate* (*MMA*), January 2, 1963. *Jackson Clarion Ledger* (*CL*) January 8, 1963; Maxie Dunnam, interview with author, October 23, 1997.

3. James Rush to James Silver, January 17, 1963, in JWSC, Box 23, Folder 9. Methodist churches cannot technically fire their pastors, since ministers serve churches by the appointment of the bishop of the conference.

4. James B. Nicholson to James Silver, January 22, 1963, in JWSC, Box 23, Folder 9.

5. *MMA*, April 11, 1956.

6. *Scott County Times*, October 2, 1957.

7. *State Times* (*ST*), September 2, 1959.

8. For a discussion of Amendment IX and the movement toward dissolution of the Central Jurisdiction, see Peter C. Murray, *Methodists and the Crucible of Race, 1930–1975* (Columbia: University of Missouri Press, 2004).

9. *JDN*, June 12, 1957. See also *MMA*, June 26, 1957.

10. Hearings of the Southeastern Jurisdiction, October 24, 25, 1957, in Hearings on the Jurisdictional System, Interjurisdictional Commission Records, General Commission on Archives and History, United Methodist Church, Madison, NJ.

11. Neil McMillen, *The Citizens' Councils: Organized Resistance to the Second Reconstruction, 1954–1964* (Champaign: University of Illinois Press, 1974), 125-26, offers a good description of Evans and his career. Kochtitsky (also spelled Kochtitzky) subscribed to various publications, all perceived to have a leftist bent, for the Sovereignty Commission. See Sovereignty Commission Files 99-86-0-1-1-1-1 through 99-86-0-56-1-1-1, Mississippi Department of Archives and History (MDAH), http://mdah.state.ms.us/arrec/digital_archives/sovcom/.

12. *JDN*, February 24, 1960.

13. Among many examples, see resolutions in Bishops Office Papers (BOP), Box 1, Folders 2–7, 15–19, J. B. Cain Archives of Mississippi Methodism, (JBCAMM) Millsaps College, Jackson, MS. See, additionally, the protest lodged by Grace Methodist Church in Grenada, *JDN*, June 16, 1957, and the second resolution from Wesley Fellowship Class of Capitol Street Methodist Church, *JDN*, February 2, 1960. Editor of Methodist Publications Henry Morton Bullock agreed to meet with Mississippi Methodist about these publications at New Albany Methodist Church in the fall of 1957; see *Greenville Times*, September 12, 1957, and Ray Branch, "Born of Conviction: Racial Conflict and Change in Mississippi Methodism, 1945–1983," (Ph.D. diss., Mississippi State University, 1984), 61.

14. *Information Bulletin,* March 1961, Jack Troutman personal papers. The author thanks Dr. Joe Reiff of Emory and Henry College for sharing these materials from his research collection.

15. *Meridian Star,* September 1, 1957, and *MMA,* September 4, 1957.

16. *JDN,* August 4, 1959.

17. For examples of MAMML's anti-NCC impulse, see *Information Bulletin,* September 1960, August 1961. BOP, Box 1, Folders 2–7, 15–20 contain many resolutions from churches that demonstrate the animus against the NCC. On controversy about the NCC, see the *Advocate,* March 23, April 6, 20, 27, June 22, July 6, September 21, 1960, and October 1961.

18. *MMA,* April 11, 1956. On institutional commitments as spirituality, see Robert Wuthnow, *After Heaven: Spirituality in America Since the 1950s* (Berkeley and Los Angeles: University of California Press, 1998).

19. *MMA,* October 31, 1962.

20. *MMA,* July 24, 1963.

21. *MMA,* December 7, 1960.

22. Ashmore editorials in this vein are ubiquitous, but for examples see *MMA,* November 2, October 19, 1960, and January 23, 1964.

23. The Citizens' Councilor Louis Hollis, for example, praised the *Baptist Record,* hoping that "all Baptist laymen read it." See Recorded Report of a Portion of Citizens Council Forum, T.V. Station WLBT, Jackson, MS, Sunday, November 26, 1957, in Civil Rights Folder, Chester Quarles Papers, Mississippi Baptist Historical Commission, Clinton, MS.

24. Typed article (title obscured) by Malcolm H. Mabry, Jr., n.d., in BOP, Box 1, Folder 17.

25. Both of the following portraits of Selah resemble the one presented here, though neither attends to the question of Selah's theology: Joseph Crespino, "The Christian Conscience of Jim Crow: White Protestant Ministers and the Mississippi Citizens Councils, 1954–1964," *Mississippi Folklife* (Fall 1998): 41–42, and Lyon, "Lifting the Color Bar from the House of God."

26. *MMA,* September 4, 1963.

27. Dr. W. B. Selah, *Puddles and Sunsets,* an unpublished collection of sermons, in possession of author, iii and Annex B. No name to Dr. W. B. Selah, July 4, 1963 in William Bryan Selah Papers (WBSP), an unpublished collection of letters and newspaper clippings in possession of author.

28. *MMA,* April 3, 1958. Selah made a similar argument that same year when, along with the Mississippi moderate journalist Oliver Emmerich, he defended segregation at a Methodist sponsored conference on "human relations." See Paul Harvey, *Freedom's Coming: Religious Culture and the Shaping of the South from the Civil War through the Civil Rights Era* (Chapel Hill: University of North Carolina Press, 2005), 230.

29. *JDN,* June 12, 1957.

30. *JDN,* March 1, 1960.

31. *JDN*, May 30, 1950, and *CL*, September 10, 1946, both in W. B. Selah Subject File (WBSSF), MDAH.
32. *JDN*, July 19, 1946, in WBSSF.
33. From "Minutes of the Official Board," June 12, 1961 (typed manuscript), in W. J. Cunningham/Galloway Methodist Church Collection (WJC/GMCC), Folder 4, Small Manuscripts, JDWLUM.
34. *JDN*, July 19, 1946, in WBSSF.
35. *JDN*, February 6, 1948, in WBSSF.
36. The details of this controversy can be followed in *JDN*, *CL*, and *ST* during March and into early April 1958.
37. *MMA*, April 3, 1958.
38. Typed manuscript, "Millsaps College and Race Relations," in *Letters and Documents: Social Struggles—1960s*, a bound collection of materials in JBCAMM.
39. For a thorough treatment of the Freedom Rides, see Raymond Arsenault, *Freedom Riders: 1961 and the Struggle for Racial Justice* (New York: Oxford University Press, 2006).
40. Minutes of the Official Board, June 12, 1961 (typed manuscript), in WJC/GMCC, Folder 4.
41. Minutes of the Official Board, June 12, 1961 (typed manuscript), in WJC/GMCC, Folder 4.
42. Selah, *Puddles and Sunsets,* Annex A-1. For the Freedom Riders' ordeal in Mississippi and, specifically, Parchman Penitentiary, see Arsenault, *Freedom Riders*, chs. 7–9 and John Dittmer, *Local People: The Struggle for Civil Rights in Mississippi* (Urbana and Chicago: University of Illinois Press, 1994), ch. 5.
43. Selah, *Puddles and Sunsets*, Annex A-2.
44. Charles and Elsie Clark to Dr. W. B. Selah, n.d. (c. July 1963), in WBSP.
45. The most detailed narrative account of the integration of the University of Mississippi is Charles W. Eagles, *The Price of Defiance: James Meredith and the Integration of Ole Miss* (Chapel Hill: University of North Carolina Press, 2009).
46. Congressman Frank Smith, still in office but already defeated for reelection, did not support Barnett's calls for resistance. State Representatives Karl Wiesenburg and Joe Wroten were the lone holdouts against Barnett in the state legislature. See Dittmer, *Local People*, 138–42.
47. Typed manuscript in Russell H. Barrett Collection (MUM00024), Box 3, Folder 2, JDWLUM. The sermon was also printed in the October 8 edition of the *Memphis Commercial Appeal*.
48. *MMA*, October 17, 1962.
49. *MMA*, October 10, 1962.
50. O. Gerald Trigg to Dr. James W. Silver, February 26, 1963, in JWSC, Box 23, Folder 9.
51. "Guideposts," *Galloway News*, October 1962, in JWSC, Box 23, Folder 9. Also in *MMA*, October 24, 1962.
52. *MMA*, October 31, 1962.

53. Charles L. Stanford, Jr., "Love Disqualified," in Donald W. Shriver, Jr., *The Unsilent South: Prophetic Preaching in Racial Crisis* (Richmond: John Knox Press, 1965), 74.

54. Robert H. Walkup, "Not Race, But Grace," in Shriver, *Unsilent South*, 65–66.

55. Diary entry, October 7, 1962, in George Thomas Preer Papers (GTPP), Box 1, Folder 9, McCain Library and Archives, University of Southern Mississippi, Hattiesburg, MS.

56. *BR*, October 4, 11, 1962.

57. *New York Times*, October 5, 1962.

58. E. U. Parker, Jr., to Bishop Marvin A. Franklin, December 3, 1962, in BOP, Box 1, Folder 18.

59. Shriver, *Unsilent South*, 73.

60. Diary entry, October 7, 1962, in GTPP, Box 1, Folder 9.

61. J. H. Mitchell to Rev. K. I Tucker, October 22, 1962, in Sam E. and Anne Lewis Ashmore Papers (SEALAP), Box 1, Folder 7, JBCAMM.

62. *Minutes* of the Kemper County Baptist Association, 1962, 10; Minutes of the Sunflower Baptist Association, 1962, 13.

63. O. Gerald Trigg to Dr. James W. Silver, February 26, 1963, in JWSC, Box 23, Folder 9.

64. Albert H. Freundt, "Oxford Clergy Wrong in Calling for 'Repentance'!" *The Citizen*, October 1962.

65. Shriver, *Unsilent South*, 73.

66. *Annual*, Mississippi Baptist Convention, 1962, 59.

67. Mrs. M. G. Gray to Bishop Marvin A Franklin, October 1, 1962, in BOP, Box 1, Folder 19.

68. Reiff, "Conflicting Convictions," 162; Dunnam, interview with author.

69. *MMA*, January 2, 1963.

70. Some of the signers told of their experiences in letters to James Silver; see JWSC, Box 23, Folder 9. For letters or resolutions to the Bishop Marvin Franklin, see BOP, Box 1, Folders 7, 19.

71. Reiff, "Conflicting Convictions," contends that not every one of the twenty-eight who left Mississippi did so solely because of reactions against their stand on the race issue, though in most cases these concerns entered importantly in their decisions to leave.

72. Statements in BOP, Box 1, Folder 19. *JDN*, January 8, 1963, in JWSC, Box 23, Folder 9.

73. *CL*, January 7, 1963. Mrs. Nell M. Hearn to Bishop Marvin A. Franklin, February 14, 1963, and Maxie D. Dunnam to Bishop Marvin A. Franklin, January 31, 1962, in BOP, Box 1, Folder 19.

74. *The Denver Post*, June 30, 1963, clipping in JWSC, Box 23, Folder 9; *Christian Century*, November 20, 1963. See also *New York Times*, January 19, 1963.

75. *CL*, January 7, 1963.

76. *CL*, January 15, 1963. Copy of statement also in WJC/GMCC, Folder 4.

77. *CL*, January 15, 7, 1963.

78. Paul D. Hardin, Secretary, Millsaps College Faculty, to Bishop Marvin Franklin, January 25, 1963, in *Information Bulletin* (September 1963), Reverend Summer Walters private papers. The author thanks Dr. Joe Reiff of Emory and Henry College for sharing these materials from his research collection.

79. Dean M. Kelley to Bishop Marvin Franklin, February 20, 1963; Arthur M. O'Neil, Jr., to Bishop Marvin Franklin, January 16, 1963; William M. Justice to Bishop Marvin Franklin, March 21, 1963; James McKeown to Bishop Marvin Franklin, January 15, 1963; all in BOP, Box 1, Folder 19.

80. James S. Conner to Rep. Frank E. Smith, January 11, 1963, and Summer Walters to James Silver, June 18, 1963, both in JWSC; and Mark [unidentified] to Dr. W. B. Selah, June 10, 1963, in WBSP.

81. *JDN*, January 11, 1963; *The Citizen*, January 1963. The text also appeared in MAMML's *Information Bulletin*, January 1963.

82. *CL*, March 21, 22, 1963. Full text of address in John Creighton Satterfield Subject File, MDAH.

83. *CL*, March 21, 22, 1963.

84. Unidentified to Dr. J. D. Slay, March 8, 1963, in BOP, Box 1, Folder 19.

85. Selah, *Puddles and Sunsets*, Annex-1.

86. Selah, *Puddles and Sunsets*, Annex-1.

87. *Los Angeles Herald-Examiner, New York Times, Atlanta Constitution,* June 10, 1963, in WBSP. *CL*, June 10, 1963.

88. *Los Angeles Herald-Examiner,* June 10, 1963, *Great Falls Tribune,* June 10, 1963, *Rocky Mountain News,* June 10, 1963, in WBSP. Russell E. Clay to Dr. W. B. Selah, June 11, 1963; J. W. Brasher to Dr. W. B. Selah, June 10, 1963; Bill (name obscured) to Dr. W. B. Selah, June 11, 1963; Reverend Richard A. Thornburg to Rev. William B. Selah, June 10, 1963; Nat Griswold to Reverend W. B. Selah, June 10, 1963; George M. Curry to Dr. W. B. Selah, June 12, 1963; Newell S. Booth to Dr. W. B. Selah, June 26, 1963; Victor L. Rankin, to Rev. W. B. Selah, June 10, 1963; Jarrell McCracken to Rev. W. B. Selah, June 13, 1963; Rev. Charles E. Maier to Rev. W. B. Selah, June 11, 1963; Bishop Joseph B. Brunini to Dr. W. B. Selah, June 15, 1963; V. P. Crowe to Dr. W. B. Selah, June 12, 1963; Harley C. Shands to Dr. W. B. Selah, July 2, 1963; Charles and Elsie Clark to Dr. W. B. Selah, n.d.; and Paul E. Martin to Dr. William B. Selah, June 27, 1963; all in WBSP.

89. W. G. Wright, Jr., to Dr. W. B. Selah, June 17, 1963; Verna R. Wood to Dr. W. B. Selah, June 11, 1963; Jane Peters to Dr. W. B. Selah, June 10, 1963; all in WBSP.

CHAPTER 7

1. *Christian Century* (*CC*), April 15, 1964, 480. The story of the two bishops' visit is also told in the memoir of Galloway's pastor W. J. Cunnigham, *Agony at Galloway: One Church's Struggle with Social Change* (Jackson: University Press of Mississippi, 1980), and Peter C Murray, *Methodists and the Crucible of Race, 1930–1975* (Columbia: University of Missouri Press, 2004).

2. *CC* April 15, 1964, 480; April 22, 1964, 511–12.

3. *CC*, April 22, 1964, 511–12.

4. This description relies on John Dittmer's account in *Local People: The Struggle for Civil Rights in Mississippi* (Champaign: University of Illinois Press, 1994), 160–69.

5. These ministers' meetings are described in detail in Carter Dalton Lyon, "Lifting the Color Bar from the House of God: The 1963–64 Church Visit Campaign to Challenge Segregation," (Ph.D. diss., University of Mississippi, 2010); this is the most thorough existing treatment of the campaign. See also the account that focuses on Ed King's role in Charles Marsh, *God's Long Summer: Stories of Faith and Civil Rights* (Princeton: Princeton University Press, 1999), ch. 4. See also Autobiography of Edwin King, Ed King Manuscript (EKM), Small Manuscripts 78-3, Archives and Special Collections, J. D. Williams Library, The University of Mississippi (JDWLUM). According to Lyon, 83–92, white ministers who attended these meetings included Catholic Bishops Richard O. Gerow and Joseph B. Brunini, Episcopal Bishops Duncan Gray, Sr., and John Allin, Methodist Bishop Marvin Franklin, Rabbi Perry Nussbaum of Temple Beth Israel, Reverend Roy Hulan of First Christian Church, Dr. Moody McDill of Fondren Presbyterian Church, Dr. Roy Clark of Capitol Street Methodist Church, and Reverend Wade Koons of Trinity Lutheran Church. Dr. Chester Quarles and Dr. William P. Davis, both leaders of the Mississippi Baptist State Convention Association, attended the second meeting. Dr. Douglas Hudgins of First Baptist Church was invited to both meetings but did not attend. About twenty African American ministers also attended.

6. These events are described in several places: *Clarion Ledger* (*CL*), June 10, *Jackson Daily News* (*JDN*), June 11, and *CC*, November 27, 1963.

7. Dittmer, *Local People*, 165–67.

8. *CL*, June 17, 1963. Evers was interred at Arlington because he was a World War II veteran.

9. *CL*, June 10, 1963; Lyon, "Lifting the Color Bar," 105.

10. Many congregations had already established exclusionary worship policies in the spring of 1961, in anticipation of the arrival of the Freedom Riders.

11. Holly Springs resolution from Board of Deacons, First Presbyterian Church, Holly Springs, Mississippi, September 22, 1964, described in R. Milton Winter, "Division and Reunion in the Presbyterian Church, U.S.: A Mississippi Retrospective" *Journal of Presbyterian History* 78, no. 1 (Spring 2000): 71. Starkville and Meridian resolutions described in Donald Shriver, ed., *The Unsilent South: Prophetic Preaching in Racial Crisis* (Richmond: John Knox Press, 1965), 65, 73. Hazelhurst resolution in Minutes of the Session, Hazelhurst Presbyterian Church, June 5, 1963. Canton resolution in Minute Book No. B4 of First Presbyterian Church, Canton, Mississippi. Hattiesburg's Bay Street Church's resolution in Robert Patrick Rayner, "On Theological Grounds: Hattiesburg Presbyterians and the Civil Rights Movement" (M.A. thesis, University of Southern

Mississippi, 2009), 24–25. Including resolutions adopted by Jackson's First, Alta Woods, North Park and Central Presbyterian Churches, every Presbyterian Church in Mississippi whose records I have been able to check—either directly or through mention in other sources—passed a resolution in late May or June of 1963 to exclude black worshippers.

12. *Minutes* of the Session, June 5, 1963, Hazelhurst Presbyterian Church.

13. *CL*, June 24, 1963.

14. Story of Roy Hulan's ordeal told in great detail in Lyon, "Removing the Color Bar," 168–73.

15. Lyon, "Removing the Color Bar," 264.

16. Each of these stories told in greater detail in Lyon, "Removing the Color Bar."

17. Fred Patton to All Members of Trinity Lutheran Church, July 24, 26, 1963, in Sovereignty Commission Files (SCF), 3-79-0-1-2-1-1 and 3-79-0-1-1-1-1, Mississippi Department of Archives and History (MDAH), Jackson, MS, http://mdah. state.ms.us/arrec/digital_archives/sovcom/.

18. Erle Johnston to Mr. O. F. Schluetter, August 19, 1963, in SCF, 3-79-0-4-1-1-1.

19. Erle Johnston to Jimmy Ward, August 2, 1963 in SCF, 7-0-7-156-1-1-1, and Erle Johnston to Tom Ethridge, August 2, 1963, in SCF, 7-0-7-155-1-1-1.

20. Erle Johnston to Mr. Kirby Walker, September 20, 1963, in SCF, 3-79-0-7-1-1-1.

21. Erle Johnston, Jr., Memorandum, August 29, 1963, in SCF, 3-79-0-5-1-1-1.

22. *JDN*, January 27, 1964.

23. Joel L. Alvis, Jr., to The Reverend Brister H. Ware, May 15, 1984 and Murray Questionaire, n.d., in Joel Alvis Papers, Box 1, Presbyterian Historical Society (PHS).

24. *CC*, November 27, 1963. EKM, 36, JDWLUM.

25. *CC*, October 30, 1963. The agencies that paid their appeal bonds were the Board of Christian Social Concerns and the Woman's Division of Christian Services of the Methodist Church.

26. *CC*, November 27, 1963

27. Lyon, "Lifting the Color Bar," 365.

28. *CL*, June 24, 1963.

29. *CL*, October 21, 1963. The incident is told in detail in Marsh, *God's Long Summer*, 138–39.

30. *New York Times* (*NYT*), March 23, 1964, and *Mississippi Methodist Advocate* (*MMA*), April 1, 1964.

31. *JDN*, November 1, 1963; *Delta Democrat-Times*, October 31, 1963.

32. *CL*, September 22, 1963; *NYT*, November 3, 1963; January 5, 1964.

33. Email, Matt Herron to author, February 9, 2012.

34. *Minutes* of the Session, June 5, 1963, Hazelhurst Presbyterian Church.

35. Lyon, "Removing the Color Bar," 259, 398.

36. Presley J. Snow to Mississippi Methodist Advocate, April 10, 1964, in Dr. Sam E. and Anne Lewis Ashmore Papers (SEALAP), Box 1, Folder 7, J. B. Cain Archives of Mississippi Methodism (JBCAMM), Millsaps College, Jackson, MS.

37. *CL,* September 23, 1963.
38. *CL,* June 17, 1963.
39. *Presbyterian Outlook,* April 27, 1964, 5–6.
40. Sonja Hedlund to Friends in Christ, September 19, 1964, in Galloway Memorial/W. J. Cunningham Small Manuscripts, Folder 2, JDWLUM.
41. "An Oral History with Dr. W. J. Cunningham," August 6, 1981, vol. 242, Center for Oral History and Cultural Heritage, The University of Southern Mississippi, University of Southern Mississippi Libraries http://digilib.usm.edu/u?/coh,1492 (accessed December 7, 2010).
42. Resolution in Cunningham, *Agony at Galloway,* 27.
43. *NYT,* April 6, 1964.
44. *MMA,* April 8, 1964.
45. W. D. Womack, Jr., to Rev. Sam E. Ashmore, April 15, 1964; Floyd W. O'Dom to *Mississippi Methodist Advocate,* April 14, 1964; Mrs. Britton Hoover Maxwell to Sam E. Ashmore, April 9, 1964; Raymond F. Booth to the *Methodist Advocate,* April 18, 1964; Marvin R. Calder to Rev. Sam E. Ashmore, Editor, April 12, 1964; Presley J. Snow to *Mississippi Methodist Advocate,* April 10, 1964; Raymond F. Booth to the *Methodist Advocate,* April 18, 1964; all in SEALAP, Box 1, Folder 7.
46. *MMA,* April 1, 1964.
47. *MMA,* April 1, 1964, and *JDN,* April 16, 1964 memorials in *Daily Christian Advocate,* April–May, 1964.
48. "His Name in Vain," in Allen Eugene Cox Collection, Box 2, Folder 60, Special Collections, Mississippi State University, Starkville, MS.
49. *MMA,* May 20, 1964; *NYT,* May 4, 1964.
50. *MMA,* May 6, 1964.
51. Lyon, "Lifting the Color Bar," 439.
52. *NYT,* May 2, 1964.
53. *NYT,* May 4, 1964.
54. *JDN,* April 28, 1964; see also *Daily Christian Advocate,* May 1, 134.
55. *NYT,* May 4, 8, 1964. *Daily Christian Advocate,* April 27, 1964, 32; April 28, 1964, 60–61; April 30, 1964, 129–30; May 4, 1964, 307–38.
56. Lyon, "Lifting the Color Bar," 441–42, 448-49.
57. *Information Bulletin,* May 1964. The publication in question was probably the December 1963 issue of *Behold,* a Methodist magazine that had given extensive coverage to events surrounding the church visit ordeal.
58. *CL,* April 15, 1964.
59. *MMA,* April 1, May 20, 1964.
60. Foy Valentine, "Reflections on a Journey through the Racial Crisis," in *Proceedings of Southern Baptists and Race, a Conference Sponsored by the Christian Life Commission of the Southern Baptist Convention,* 11, in Christian Life Commission Papers (CLCP), Box 5, Folder 6, Southern Baptist Historical Library and Archive (SBHLA), Nashville, TN.
61. Valentine, "Reflections on a Journey through the Racial Crisis," 11.

62. Substitute motion quoted in Mark Newman, *Getting Right with God: Southern Baptists and Desegregation, 1945–1995* (Tuscaloosa: University of Alabama Press, 2001), 30.

63. *NYT,* May 22, 1964.

64. Valentine, "Reflections on a Journey through the Racial Crisis," 12.

65. See, for example, Robert J. Hearn to Dr. Porter Routh, June 15, 1964, Resolution of the Long Run Baptist Ministers' Conference, Louisville, Kentucky, June 24, 1964, and J. B. Halsell, III, to Dr. Porter Routh, June 25, 1964, in Executive Committee Records (ECR), Box 21, Folder 21, SBHLA.

66. *BR,* June 11, 1964.

67. *Raleigh News and Observer,* May 28, 1964.

68. Dr. Harold Tribble to Chester Quarles, June 1, 1964, in ECR, Box 73, Folder 24.

69. Joe Odle to Marse Grant, n.d., in ECR, Box 73, Folder 23, and Chester Quarles to Dr. Harold W. Tribble, June 10, 1964, ECR, Box 73, Folder 24.

70. *BR,* July 17, 31, August 13, 1964.

71. *Minutes* of the Jackson County Baptist Association, 1964, 37.

72. *Minutes* of the Pike County Baptist Association, 1964, 28.

73. Bob Leavell to Dr. Chester L. Quarles, September 1, 1964; Tolbert Bennett to Dr. Chester Quarles, July 14, 1964; Durell Makamson to Dr. Chester L. Quarles, July 9, 1964; Chester L. Quarles to Dr. Porter Routh, July 29, 1964; all in ECR, Box 73, Folder 24.

74. *BR,* August 6, 1964.

75. Chester L. Quarles to Dr. Albert McClellan, July 29, 1964, in ECR, Box 73, Folder 24.

76. Chester Quarles to Dr. Albert McClellan, July 29, 1964, in ECR, Box 73, Folder 24.

77. Chester Quarles to Porter Routh, September 22, 1964, in ECR, Box 73, Folder 23.

78. *BR,* August 6, 1964.

79. *Minutes* of the Alcorn Baptist Association, 1964, 29; *Minutes* of the Attala County Baptist Association, 1964, 28.

80. Mark Newman, "The Mississippi Baptist Convention and Desgregation, 1945–1980," *Journal of Mississippi History* 59, no. 1 (Spring 1997): 1–31.

81. Anne Washburn McWilliams, "Committee of Concern Gives Beauty for Ashes," draft copy in Department of Negro Work File, Mississippi Baptist Historical Commission (MBHC).

82. McWilliams, "Committee of Concern Gives Beauty for Ashes." *Time,* February, 1965.

83. *BR,* August 6, 1964.

84. Charles Payne, "The View from the Trenches," in Charles Payne and Steve Lawson, eds., *Debating the Civil Rights Movement, 1945–1968* (New York: Rowman and Littlefield, 1998), 132.

CHAPTER 8

1. Richard C. Marius, "Ruleville: Reminiscence, Reflection," *Christian Century*, September 23, 1964.

2. For secondary accounts of northern clerical activity in the South, see Michael Michael B. Friedland, *Lift Up Your Voice Like a Trumpet: White Clergy and the Civil Rights and Antiwar Movement, 1954–1973* (Chapel Hill: University of North Carolina Press, 1998); James Findlay, *Church People in the Struggle* (New York: Oxford University Press, 1993); and Mark Newman, *Divine Agitators: The Delta Ministry and Civil Rights in Mississippi* (Athens: University of Georgia Press, 2004).

3. Recent scholarship in civil rights studies has focused on the north and west. The best overview is Thomas J. Sugrue, *Sweet Land of Liberty: The Forgotten Struggle for Civil Rights in the North* (New York: Random House, 2008). For recent scholarly challenges to the notion of southern exceptionalism, see Matthew D. Lassiter and Joseph Crespino, eds., *The Myth of Southern Exceptionalism* (New York: Oxford University Press, 2010).

4. On the Canton campaign, see John Dittmer, *Local People: The Struggle for Civil Rights in Mississippi* (Champaign: University of Illinois Press, 1994), 187–88.

5. Edwin C. Johnson to Dr. Robert W. Spike, July 21, 1964, in United Presbyterian Church in the U.S.A Council on Church and Race Records, (UPCUSAC-CRR), Box 8, Folder 11, Presbyterian Historical Society (PHS), Philadelphia, PA.

6. Huber F. Klemme, "A Report of a Visit to Canton, Mississippi," February 26–29, 1964, UPCUSACCRR, Box 5, Folder 1.

7. Edwin C. Johnson to Dr. Robert W. Spike, July 21, 1964, in UPCUSACCRR, Box 8, Folder 11.

8. Elizabeth Sutherland, ed., *Letters from Mississippi* (New York: McGraw-Hill, 1965), 152; *New York Times (NYT)*, July 20, 1964.

9. Sutherland, ed., *Letters from Mississippi*, 152–53.

10. Richard T. Harbison, "The Church in Mississippi—1964," unpublished paper dated May 10, 1966, in possession of author; Richard T. Harbinson, interview with Bill Marshall, November 5, 1984, First Presbyterian Church Oral History Program, First Presbyterian Church, Lexington, KY.

11. Harbison, "The Church in Mississippi," 14; Harbison, Marshall interview.

12. Harbison, "The Church in Mississippi," 15; Harbison, Marshall interview; Resolution in Minute Book No. B4 of First Presbyterian Church, Canton, MS.

13. Harbison's vacation had included a visit with the pulpit committee at First Presbyterian Church, Lexington, Kentucky, and he had secured a call to that pulpit. Harbison, "The Church in Mississippi," 15; Harbison, Marshall interview.

14. Harbison, "The Church in Mississippi," 15.

15. A number of historical accounts briefly describe the Hattiesburg Minister's Project. See Newman, *Divine Agitators*, ch. 3; Findlay, *Church People in the Struggle*, 82–84; and Dittmer, *Local People*, 220. The most fulsome account of the reaction of local whites, however, is Robert P. Rayner, "On Theological

Grounds: Hattiesburg Presbyterians and the Civil Rights Movement" (M.A. the-sis, University of Southern Mississippi, 2009), which makes an argument about theology similar to the one advanced here.

16. Rayner, "On Theological Grounds," 10–12.

17. This version of the Westminster Confession excluded additional chapters on the Gospel and the Holy Spirit added in 1942, as well as broadened policy on divorce and remarriage enacted in 1959. See R. Milton Winter, "Division and Reunion in the Presbyterian Church, U.S.: A Mississippi Retrospective," *Journal of Presbyterian History* 78, no. 1 (Spring 2000): 67–86.

18. *The Presbyterian Outlook* 17 (June 1957). For examples of such interroga-tions, see material in Bertil Ivar Anderson Papers, Box 535, File 3, Pres-byterian Church in America Historical Center (PCAHC), St. Louis, MO. The case of Mac Hart is perhaps the most infamous example of a Missis-sippi minster failing his ordination exam because of his liberal theological views. The incident is explained in detail in Joel Alvis, *Religion and Race: Southern Presbyterians, 1946–1983* (Tuscaloosa: University of Alabama Press, 1994), 66–68.

19. Winter, "Division and Reunion," 76, 75.

20. Bill Stanway, interview with Robert Patrick Rayner, in Rayner, "On Theological Grounds," 48.

21. Arthur M. Schneider to Rev. Malcolm P. Calhoun, September 30, 1954, Division of Christian Relations, Presbyterian Church, U.S. (DCRPCUS), Box 1, Folder unidentified (collection unprocessed), PHS.

22. *Minutes* of the General Assembly, 1957, 36.

23. Faulkner's ideology is well represented in a series of articles he published in the *Hattiesburg American* on February 10, 17, 24, March 3, 10, 1951.

24. On James Henley Thornwell, see James Oscar Farmer, *The Metaphysical Confederacy: James Henley Thornwell and the Synthesis of Southern Values* (Macon, GA: Mercer University Press, 1985). On J. Gresham Machen, see D. G. Hart, *Defending the Faith: J. Gresham Machen and the Crisis of Conservative Protestantism in Modern America* (Phillipsburg, NJ: P and R Publishing, 2003).

25. This description of the Lynd case follows Dittmer, *Local People*, 179–80.

26. This description of the beginnings of the Hattiesburg movement follows Dit-tmer, *Local People*, 180–84; 219–21.

27. *Presbyterian Life* (*PL*), February 15, 1964, 30–33.

28. Rabbi Jerome Lipnick, "From Where I Stand," *Adath Jeshurun Clarion*, January 13, 1965, Civil Rights in Mississippi Digital Collection, University of South-ern Mississippi. http://digilib.usm.edu/cdm4/document.php?CISOROOT=/manu&CISOPTR=330&REC=2 (accessed September 23, 2010).

29. *Hattiesburg American* (*HA*), February 21, 1964.

30. *HA*, January 27, 1964.

31. *HA*, January 21, 25, February 10, 7, 1964.
32. *HA*, January 25, 1964.
33. *HA*, February 1, 1964.
34. *HA*, February 4, 1964.
35. *HA*, January 27, 1964.
36. Accounts of the arrests in *HA*, January 29, 1964; *Decatur Review* (hereafter *DR*), January 31; *Decatur Sunday Herald and Review*, February 16, 1964.
37. *Decatur Herald* (*DH*), February 4, 1964.
38. *HA*, February 3, 1964; *PL*, March 1, 1964.
39. *Minutes* of the Session, February 6, 1964, 278, First Presbyterian Church, Charleston, IL.
40. *DH*, February 2, 1964.
41. *HA*, February 15, 1964.
42. Jay Logan to Bob Beech, n.d. (1964), UPCUSACCRR, Box 8, Folder 17.
43. *Christian Century* (*CC*), March 11, 1964, 340–41.
44. *PL*, April 1, 1964, 27.
45. *HA*, February 22, 1964.
46. *HA*, February 4, 1964.
47. *HA*, February 8, 1964.
48. *HA*, January 24, 1964.
49. *HA*, February 15, 1964.
50. *DR*, February 4, 1964.
51. *PL*, April 1, 1964
52. *DR*, January 29, 30, 31, February 1; *DH*, February 1, 4, 5, 1964.
53. *DR*, February 5, 6, 9, 1964.
54. *The Decaturian*, February 7, 14, 21, 28, March 6, 13, 1964.
55. *DH*, February 11, 20, 1964; *HA*, February 22, 1964.
56. Cox himself did meet with the northern clergymen.
57. *HA*, February 22, 1964.
58. *PL*, April 1, 1964, 28.
59. Accounts of the meeting were given in the *HA*, February 24, 1964; *DH*, February 23, 24, 25, 1964; *Charleston Courier News* (*CCN*), February 24, 1964; *CC*, March 11, 1964; and *PL*, April 1, 1964.
60. *HA*, February 24, 1964; *DH*, February 23, 24, 25, 1964; *CCN*, February 24, 1964; *CC*, March 11, 1964; and *PL*, April 1, 1964.
61. *HA*, February 24, 1964; *DH*, February 23, 24, 25, 1964; *CCN*, February 24, 1964; *CC*, March 11, 1964; and *PL*, April 1, 1964.
62. *HA*, February 24, 1964; *DH*, February 23, 24, 25, 1964; *CCN*, February 24, 1964; *CC*, March 11, 1964; and *PL*, April 1, 1964. The account in *Presbyterian Life* estimated that two-thirds of the audience stayed to hear Cameron, while the *Charleston Courier News* thought "almost all" stayed.
63. *CC*, March 11, 1964; *CCN*, February 24; *HA*, February 24, 1964.

CHAPTER 9

1. *Baptist Record* (*BR*), April 29, 1965. A Delta Presbyterian minister described a similar encounter with an NCC minister in the *Presbyterian Journal* (*PJ*), August 26, 1964, 13.

2. Turner's comments in Jerry Sutton, *The Baptist Reformation: The Conservative Resurgence in the Southern Baptist Convention* (Nashville: Broadman and Holman Publishers, 2000), 14. By 1970, when he introduced this motion at the SBC, Turner was serving as a pastor in Los Angeles, California.

3. This controversy has generated a huge literature. Barry Hankins, *Uneasy in Babylon: Southern Baptist Conservatives and American Culture* (Tuscaloosa: University of Alabama Press, 2003), explains this phenomenon as a reaction to a changed American culture. Nancy Ammerman, *Baptist Battles: Social Change and Religious Conflict in the Southern Baptist Convention* (New Brunswick: Rutgers University Press, 1990), offers the most thorough account from a sociological perspective. Insider accounts from the moderate perspective include Bill J. Leonard, *God's Last and Only Hope: The Fragmentation of the Southern Baptist Convention* (Grand Rapids: William B. Erdmans Publishing Co., 1990), Joe Edward Barnhart, *The Southern Baptist Holy War* (Austin: Texas Monthly Press, 1986), Grady C. Cothen, *What Happened to the Southern Baptist Convention: A Memoir of the Controversy* (Macon: Smyth and Helwys Publishing, 1993), and Walter B. Shurden, ed., *The Struggle for the Soul of the SBC: Moderate Responses to the Fundamentalist Movement* (Macon: Mercer University Press, 1993). Accounts from the conservative or fundamentalist perspective include Sutton, *The Baptist Reformation*, and a six-volume series by James C. Helfy, *The Truth in Crisis* (Hannibal, MO: Hannibal Books, 1986, 1987, 1988, 1989, 1991, 2005).

4. These upheavals and their causes are ably detailed in Thomas Sugrue, *Sweet Land of Liberty: The Forgotten Struggle for Civil Rights in the North* (New York: Random House, 2008).

5. *Christian Century* (*CC*), April 24, 1968, 518–20.

6. *BR*, April 4, 1968.

7. *BR*, October 26, 1967.

8. *BR*, April 4, 1968.

9. *BR*, April 25, 1968.

10. *BR*, October 26, 1967.

11. *BR*, April 4, 1968.

12. *BR*, April 11, 1968.

13. *BR*, May 2, 1968.

14. *BR*, May 16, 1968.

15. *BR*, April 18, 1968.

16. *BR*, May 30, 1968.

17. H. Franklin Paschall and Porter Routh to Heads of SBC Agencies, State Secretaries, State Editors, May 13, 1968, in W. C. Fields Papers (WCFP), Box 85,

Folder 25, Southern Baptist Historical Library and Archives (SBHLA), Nashville, TN.

18. Mark Newman, *Getting Right with God: Southern Baptists and Desegregation, 1945–1995* (Tuscaloosa: University of Alabama Press, 2001), 146.

19. *Western Recorder,* May 30, 1968.

20. *Newsweek*, June 3, 1968, 55–56.

21. *BR*, May 30, 1968.

22. *BR*, May 30, 1968.

23. Survey results in WCFP, Box 85, Folder 25.

24. Baptist Press Release, June 4, 1968. "We Hold These Truths Material" in Race Relations and Southern Baptists Collection, Box 2, Folder 3, SBHLA.

25. *BR*, June 13, 1968.

26. *Annual*, Southern Baptist Convention, 1968, 63. Other details of the debate are described in *Biblical Recorder*, June 15, 1968.

27. *BR*, June 13, 1968.

28. For more about Criswell and his defense of segregation see Curtis W. Freeman, "'Never Had I Been So Blind': W. A. Criswell's 'Change' on Racial Segregation," *Journal of Southern Religion* 10 (2007), http://jsr.fsu.edu/Volume10/Freeman.pdf (accessed January 12, 2012).

29. Freeman offers further insights to the choice of Criswell as Convention president in this particular election cycle. Convention leaders regarded him as a stabilizing force that would comfort conservatives after the passage of the controversial and progressive "Statement on the Crisis." Freeman also shows that, in light of the statement and in response to the suggestion of SBC officials, Criswell offered rather public pronouncements about the "open-door" policy of his church; these statements and this policy represented rather sharp departures from his previous positions.

30. *Biblical Recorder*, June 15, 1968.

31. *Home Missions Magazine*, July 1968.

32. *BR*, June 13, 1968.

33. *BR*, November 14 1968.

34. *BR*, August 15, 1968.

35. *Newsweek*, June 3, 1968, 55–56.

36. Carl L. Morris To Whom it May Concern, January 7, 1969, Executive Committee Records, Box 21, Folder 23, SBHLA.

37. M. E. Carpenter to Dr. Jas. L. Sullivan, August 7, 1968, in Southern Baptist Convention, Sunday School Board Executive Office, James Lenox Sullivan Papers, Box 35, Folder 33, SBHLA.

38. Ethan Moore to Dr. Arthur B. Rutledge, July 22, 1968, in Southern Baptist Convention, Home Mission Board, Executive Office Files (HMBEOF), Box 26, Folder 8, SBHLA.

39. Mrs. Jeff Upton to Dr. Arthur B. Rutledge, August 5, 1968, in HMBEOF, Box 26, Folder 8.

40. *BR*, June 19, July 10, 1969.

41. *Newsweek*, May 5, 1969. See also *Christianity Today*, July 4, 1969, 33, 34.

42. *BR*, May 22, 1969.

43. *BR*, July 17, 1969.

44. *BR*, July 12, 1969.

45. *BR*, July 10, 1969.

46. *BR*, July 24, 1969.

47. Odle's statements in Sutton, *The Baptist Reformation*, 13.

48. In Sutton, *The Baptist Reformation*, 14.

49. Ammerman, *Baptist Battles*, 68.

50. R. Milton Winter, "Division and Reunion in the Presbyterian Church, U.S.:
A Mississippi Retrospective," *Journal of Presbyterian History* 78, no. 1 (Spring
2000): 67–86. Current PCA congregations in Mississippi taken from http://
www.pcahistory.org/churches/mississippi.html (accessed February 25, 2012).

51. The PCA's three most significant histories written by insiders in the tradi-
tion include Morton H. Smith, *How Is the God Become Dim: The Decline of the
Presbyterian Church, U.S., as Reflected in Its Assembly Actions* (Jackson, MS:
Steering Committee for a Continuing Presbyterian Church, Faithful to the
Scriptures and the Reformed Faith, 1973); Frank Joseph Smith, *The History of the
Presbyterian Church in America: The Continuing Church Movement* (Manassas,
VA: Reformation Educational Foundation, 1985); and John Edwards Richards,
The Historical Birth of the Presbyterian Church in America (Liberty Hill, SC: The
Liberty Press, 1986).

52. The actions of the 1964 General Assembly are described in *Presbyterian Outlook*
(*PO*), August 10, 1964, 29. The policy on open worship was clarified in a pastoral letter, a draft of which was published in the *PO*, February 10, 1964; another
draft appears in Division of Christian Relations of the Presbyterian Church, US
(DCRPCUS), Box 2, Folder 1964 (collection unprocessed), Presbyterian Historical Society (PHS), Philadelphia, PA.

53. *PO*, January 6, 1964, 1; May 18, 1964, 20, 2.

54. *PO*, May 11, 1964, 19, 11, 5.

55. *PO*, September 7, 1964, 9, 4.

56. *Minutes* of the Session, May 24, 1964, Alta Woods Presbyterian Church, Presbyterian Church in America Historical Center (PCAHC), St. Louis, MO.

57. Quotations excerpted from the following letters, all to Dr. Malcolm P. Calhoun:
Mrs. Katherine Kraft, July 29, 1965; E. C. Neely, III, August 2, 1965; Mrs. Alfred
Russell, May 10, 1965; Allie J. Ross, July 30, 1965; Mark Calhoun, July 28, 1965;
Mrs. John Bradley, July 31, 1965; Hubbard L. King, August 6, 1965; Mrs. M. F.
McCulloch, August 1, 1965; Mrs. L. B. Geddil, May 30, 1965; all in DCRPCUS,
Box 3, Folder Unidentified.

58. Winter, "Division and Reunion in the Presbyterian Church, U.S.," 73.

59. *PJ*, June 19, 1968, 7.

60. Winter, "Division and Reunion in the Presbyterian Church, U.S.," 73.

61. Winter, "Division and Reunion in the Presbyterian Church, U.S.," 75.

62. *PJ*, June 3, 1964, 14.

63. *PJ*, September, 1964, 3.

64. W. F. Mansell, "The Problems and Issues that Divide Us," in William Arnett Gamble Papers (WAGP), unprocessed collection, PCAHC.

65. Unidentified pamphlet, WAGP.

66. The *Holmes v. Alexander* Supreme Court ruling of 1969 invalidated Mississippi's "freedom of choice" plans and ordered immediate desegregation of thirty-three school districts.

67. William McAtee, *Transformed: A White Mississippi Pastor 's Journey into Civil Rights and Beyond* (Jackson: University Press of Mississippi, 2011); Winter, "Division and Reunion in the Presbyterian Church, U.S.," 74.

68. Bishop Edward Julian Pendergrass Papers, Box 1, Folder 4, J. B. Cain Archive of Mississippi Methodist (JBCAMM), Millsaps College, Jackson, MS.

69. Winter, "Division and Reunion in the Presbyterian Church, U.S.," 83, n.32.

70. Pamphlet for Southside Academy, Bertil Ivar Anderson Papers, Box 535, Folder 33, PCAHC.

71. Frank J. Smith, *The History of the Presbyterian Church in America*, 64.

72. Winter, "Division and Reunion in the Presbyterian Church, U.S.," 78.

73. For Johnston-Taylor correspondence, see Sovereignty Commission Files (SCF), 2-44-1-96-1-1-1 through 2-44-1-98-1-1-1, and 99-62-0-45-1-1-1, Mississippi Department of Archives and History, Jackson, MS, http://mdah.state.ms.us/arrec/digital_archives/sovcom/ (accessed February 27, 2012). For more on Taylor's role in the creation of the PCA, see Frank J. Smith, *The History of the Presbyterian Church in America*.

74. "Succession of Moderators in the Presbyterian Church in America," PCAHC, http://www.pcahistory.org/pca/moderators/pcamoderators.html (accessed February 18, 2012).

75. Morton H. Smith, *How Is the Gold Become Dim*," 173, 153.

76. Frank J. Smith, *The History of the Presbyterian Church in America*, 88.

77. Winter, "Division and Reunion in the Presbyterian Church, U.S.," 70. Horace L. Villee to Rev. Malcolm P. Calhoun, May 26, 1959, in DCRPCUS, Box 2, Folder unidentified.

78. Al Freundt, Jr., *The Citizen*, October 1962. Like Taylor, Freundt also collaborated with Erle Johnston in an effort to present the NCC as a subversive organization. See SCF, 99-62-0-45-1-1-1 (accessed February 27, 2012).

79. *Southern Presbyterian Journal* (*SPJ*), July 14, 1954.

80. Miller and the First Presbyterian Congregation were especially adamant in opposing a 1957 resolution from the Division of Christian Relations; see *SPJ*, June 19, 1957, and *JDN*, June 6, 1957. Also see "Presbyterian Laymen for Sound Doctrine and Responsible Leadership," 9, in DCRPCUS, Box 2 Folder 2.

81. See Peter Slade, *Open Friendship in a Closed Society: Mission Mississippi and a Theology of Friendship* (New York: Oxford University Press, 1989).

82. Carter Dalton Lyon, "Lifting the Color Bar from the House of God: The 1963–1964 Church Visit Campaign to Challenge Segregated Sanctuaries in Jackson, Mississippi," (Ph.D. diss., University of Mississippi, 2010).

83. Winter, "Division and Reunion in the Presbyterian Church, U.S.," 83, n.32.

84. "A Brief History of the First Presbyterian Church, Jackson, Mississippi," First Presbyterian Church, Jackson, MS, http://www.fpcjackson.org/general/history/index%20fpc%20history.htm (accessed January 12, 2012). For more on the role of Donald Patterson and First Presbyterian Church, Jackson, in the creation of the PCA, see Frank J. Smith, *The History of the Presbyterian Church in America.*

85. "A Message to All Churches of Jesus Christ throughout the World from the General Assembly of the National Presbyterian Church" in Historic Documents in American Presbyterianism, PCAHC, http://www.pcahistory.org/documents/message.pdf (accessed February 13, 2012).

86. See James Oscar Farmer, *The Metaphysical Confederacy: James Henley Thornwell and the Synthesis of Southern Values* (Macon: Mercer University Press, 1985).

87. The connection between these nineteenth-century arguments over slavery and the formation of the PCA becomes especially clear in Richards, *The Historical Birth of the Presbyterian Church in America.*

88. James Earl Price to Mrs. Debra McIntosh, August 20, 1999, in James Earl Price Collection, Box 1, Folder 2, McCain Library and Archives, The University of Southern Mississippi (MLAUSM), Hattiesburg, MS.

89. *JDN,* June 14, 1964.

90. *Information Bulletin,* May 1964. Francis B. Stevens, "Splinter Groups Develop in Mississippi," in *Letters and Documents, Social Struggles—1960s,* a bound collection of materials in JBCAMM.

91. A few other congregations had previously separated. See Stevens, "Splinter Groups Develop in Mississippi," and M. D. Tollison to Bishop Marvin Franklin, September 8, 1961, in Bishops' Office Papers, Box 1, Folder 19, JBCAMM. While Galloway's membership had been somewhere around 4,000 in the early 1960s, Reverend W. J. Cunningham, who assumed the pastorate of the church in 1963, estimates that it had fallen to somewhere around 2,500 by 1966. Even this figure does not accurately depict the effect that racial turmoil had on the church, as it represents the number of names on the roll, and Cunningham asserts that active membership was considerably less than the 2,500 figure. See W. J. Cunningham, *Agony at Galloway: One Church's Struggle with Social Change* (Jackson: University Press of Mississippi, 1980), 66–67. Three years after they formed, AIM reported twenty churches and a total membership of about 2,000; see Ray Branch, "Born of Conviction: Racial Conflict and Change in Mississippi Methodism, 1945–1983," (Ph.D. diss., Mississippi State University, 1984), 260.

92. "Resolution on Racial Integration," in James Earl Price Collection, Box 1, Folder 10, JBCAMM.

93. Randy Sparks, *Religion in Mississippi* (Jackson: University Press of Mississippi, 2001), 245–46. See also Galloway's website, where its section on the church's

history estimates that the opening of the doors caused a third of the members to leave, "History of Galloway," *Galloway United Methodist Church*, http://www.gallowayumc.org/index.php?option=com_content&view=article&id=61&Itemid=138 (accessed March 15, 2012).

94. The actual vote in the annual conference meetings was fairly complex. The North Mississippi Conference approved union with the EUB by a very narrow margin (150–145), but rejected elimination of the Central Jurisdiction decisively. Satterfield circulated a letter among Mississippi Methodists asking them to defeat both proposals, and the Mississippi Conference rejected both measures overwhelmingly. See Branch, "Born of Conviction," 236–38.

95. *Mississippi Methodist Advocate* (*MMA*), November 25, 1967.

96. *MMA*, November 25, 1967.

97. Accounts of this General Conference appear in *Newsweek,* May 6, 1968, and *CC,* May 15, 22, 1968.

98. *Newsweek,* May 6, 1968; *CC,* May 15, 22, 1968.

99. Branch, "Born of Conviction," 256.

100. *MMA,* March 17, 1971.

101. *MMA,* May 26, 1971.

102. *MMA,* April 21, 1971.

103. *MMA,* April 21, 1971.

104. *MMA,* April 21, 1971.

105. *MMA,* June 16, 1971.

106. *MMA,* June 16, 1971.

107. *MMA,* June 16, 1971. See also "A Resolution from the Upper Mississippi Conference, Official Response to the North Mississippi Conference on Merger," in John D. Humphrey Papers, Folder 2, JBCAMM.

108. Peter C. Murray, *Methodists and the Crucible of Race, 1930–1975* (Columbia: University of Missouri Press, 2004).

109. Membership totals for Mississippi Conference, United Methodist Church, antecedents 1965–1975. Data compiled for author by Debra McIntsoh from statistical tables in Journals of Upper and North MS Conferences, MS Conference Southeastern Jurisdiction, MS Conference Central Jurisdiction, in possession of author.

110. James Earl Price, "My Experiences During the Crisis," 17, 19, in James Earl Price Collection, Box 1, Folder 2.

111. Price, "My Experiences," 12, 16.

112. Price, "My Experiences," 7.

113. Email, name witheld to author, November 30, 2011.

CONCLUSION

1. Forman included the Catholic Church and the institutions of the Jewish faith as well. The manifesto may be read here: http://www.nybooks.com/articles/archives/1969/jul/10/black-manifesto/?pagination=false, but it was published in many places at the time.

2. For a set of well-developed arguments against the notion of southern exceptionalism, see Matthew D. Lassiter and Joseph Crespino, eds., *The Myth of Southern Exceptionalism* (New York: Oxford University Press, 2010).

3. Statement made by John Baker, associate director of the Baptist Joint Committee on Public Affairs, in *Jackson Daily News* (*JDN*), November 15, 1978, quoted in Randy J. Sparks, *Religion in Mississippi* (Jackson: University Press of Mississippi, 2001), 257.

4. Sparks, *Religion in Mississippi*, 253.

5. "Mississippi 2010 State Membership Report," *Association of Religion Data Archives* (*ARDA*), http://www.thearda.com/rcms2010/r/s/28/rcms2010_28_state_name_2010.asp.

6. Statistics compiled from "Partnering Churches of the Cooperative Baptist Fellowship of Mississippi," *Cooperative Baptist Fellowship of Mississippi*, http://www.cooperative-baptist-fellowship-ms.com/ and "Congregations, Theology Schools, and Organizations," *Alliance of Baptists*, http://www.allianceofbaptists.org/connect/congregations (accessed March 13, 2012). Kentucky, by contrast, claims nearly twice the number of such moderate congregations, thirty-eight, though its total Baptist population is only slightly larger than Mississippi's at about 1,000,000 "Kentucky 2010 State Membership Report," ARDA.

7. "Presbytery of Mississippi Congregations," *Presbytery of Mississippi*, http://www.presbyteryofms.org/ and "PCA Congregations in Mississippi," *Presbyterian Church in America Historical Center,* http://www.pcahistory.org/churches/mississippi.html.

8. The United Methodist Church claimed 181,795 members in 2010, a number slightly less than the numbers of white Methodists alone in Mississippi in 1954, while Mississippi's population is 50 percent greater than it was in 1954. "About Us," *The Mississippi Conference of the United Methodist Church* (*MCUMC*), http://www.mississippi-umc.org/pages/detail/715 (accessed May 12, 2012).

9. "Pastor's Welcome," *First Presbyterian Church, Jackson, MS*, http://www.fpcjackson.org/staff/welcome.htm (accessed April 15, 2012).

10. Jena McGregor, "Southern Baptist Convention elects Fred Luter as First Black President: What This Leadership Moment Means," *The Washington Post*, June 18, 2012, http://www.washingtonpost.com/blogs/post-leadership/post/southern-baptist-convention-elects-fred-luter-as-first-black-president-what-this-leadership-moment-means/2012/06/19/gJQA3xqXoV_blog.html (accessed June 25, 2012).

11. LaReeca Ruker, "Interview with Fred Luter: First African American President of the Southern Baptist Convention," November 5, 2012, *Mississippi Style*, http://blogs.clarionledger.com/msstyle/2012/11/05/interview-with-fred-luter-first-african-american-president-of-the-southern-baptist-convention/ (accessed November 25, 2012).

12. "Greetings," Mission to North America, Presbyterian Church in America, http://pcamna.org/africanamerican/index.php (accessed June 25, 2012).

13. See a description of one such incident in Black Mountain, NC, in Sonja Scherr, "Church Denomination Roots out Racism," *Southern Poverty Law Center*, http://www.splcenter.org/get-informed/intelligence-report/browse-all-issues/2010/summer/rooting-out-racism (accessed March 9, 2012).

14. "Welcome," *Redeemer Presbyterian Church*, www.redeemerjackson.com; *Reformed University Fellowship, Jackson State University*, http://www.jsuruf.com/home-page (accessed March 9, 2012).

15. See Peter Slade, *Open Friendship in a Closed Society: Mission Mississippi and a Theology of Friendship* (New York: Oxford University Press, 1989). See also the website for Mission Mississippi: www.missionmississippi.com.

16. "Breaking News: Bishop James E. Swanson Sr. Assigned Resident Bishop of MS AC," *MCUMC*, http://mississippi-umc.org/news/detail/2969 (accessed July 24, 2012).

INDEX

Note: Italicized page numbers indicate illustrations.

Carolyn Renée Dupont is Assistant Professor of History at Eastern Kentucky University in Richmond, Kentucky.